VIKING ART

THE NORDIC SERIES

Volume 6

VIKING ART

BY

DAVID M. WILSON

AND

OLE KLINDT-JENSEN

University of Minnesota Press . Minneapolis

FIRST PUBLISHED IN 1966
SECOND EDITION 1980

Published by the University of Minnesota Press,
2037 University Avenue Southeast,
Minneapolis, Minnesota 55414

Library of Congress Cataloging in Publication Data

Klindt-Jensen, Ole.
  Viking art.

  Translation of Vikingetidens kunst by Ole
Klindt-Jensen and David M. Wilson.
  Bibliography: p.
  Includes index.
  1. Art, Viking. 2. Art—Scandinavia. 3. Art,
Medieval—Scandinavia. I. Wilson, David McKenzie,
joint author. II. Title.
N7003.K563 1980   709'.48   79–26806

ISBN 0–8166–0974–8
ISBN 0–8166–0977–2 pbk.

THE NORDIC SERIES

In carrying out general plans for this series, the University of Minnesot
Press is advised on various aspects by the following scholars:

Thomas Bredsdorff
University of Copenhagen

Juha Yrjänä Pentikäinen
University of Helsinki

Sten Carlsson
University of Uppsala

George Schoolfield
Yale University

Rolf Fjelde
Pratt Institute and Julliard School

Ingrid Semmingsen
University of Oslo

Nils Hasselmo
University of Minnesota

Birgitta Steene
University of Washington

Einar Haugen
Harvard University

Sigurdur Thorarinsson
University of Iceland

Steven Koblik
Pomona College

Richard F. Tomasson
University of New Mexico

Stewart Oakley
University of East Anglia

PRINTED IN GREAT BRITAIN

PREFACE

The authors of this book wish to acknowledge with gratitude the help and co-operation of their friends and colleagues in many museums in Great Britain, Scandinavia, Germany, Russia, the Republic of Ireland and elsewhere, who have received them with kindness and answered tiresome and complicated letters with such patience. We wish to thank particularly the following scholars who have put their knowledge at our disposal: Professor Holger Arbman, Mr Richard Bailey, Mr R. H. M. Dolley and Mr Liam de Paor. We must thank Mr L. Larsen, who took most of the photographs, Mrs Eva Wilson, who drew many of the line illustrations, Mrs M. Hyslop, who read the book in proof, Miss J. Davis, who compiled the index, and our publishers for their patience through many a long battle.

We must thank the trustees of the Leverhulme foundation for a grant which enabled the English member of the team to spend some considerable time in Scandinavia and the trustees of the British Museum for giving him leave to do so. We are further indebted to the Ny Carlsberg fund which made a considerable grant towards the cost of photography and the University of Århus and the Carlsberg fund for the generous support they gave to the Danish member of the team.

OLE KLINDT-JENSEN
Århus, March 1963

DAVID M. WILSON
London, March 1963

ACKNOWLEDGMENTS

The copyright of the following photographs is acknowledged with thanks: Professor H. Arbman, pls. XXXI *d* and XXXIII *b*; A.T.A., Stockholm, pls. II *b*, V *c*, LXI, LXXI, LXXII; Bayerisches Nationalmuseum, Munich, pl. LIV; Mr K. Berg, Oslo, pls. XL and XLI; Mr A. Binns, Hull, pl. XXXIX *b*; Bodleian Library, Oxford, pl. LXIV *c*; British Museum, pls. XXX *e*, XXXI *a*, XXXVIII *a*, XLV *f*, LIX *c*, LXVI *a*, LXVIII, LXVIII *e*, and LXXVIII *a* and *b*, Guildhall Museum, London, pl. LVIII *a*; Historisk Museum, Bergen, pl. XXXII *f* and *g*; Irish Tourist Board, pl. LXXIV *b*; Sir Thomas Kendrick, Poole, pls. XXXVIII *b* and *c*, XXXIX *a* and *c*, XLII, XLIII *a*, LXV *d* and LXXIII *d*, LXXIX *a*; Lunds Universitets Historiska Museum, pls. IV *a* and XLIV *a*; Manx Museum, Douglas, pl. XLIII *b*; National Museum, Copenhagen, pls. XXXV, XLVIII, and XLIX; National Museum, Dublin, pls. LXIII *d*, LXVI *b*, LXVII, LXXV, LXXVI, LXXVII and LXXVIII *c*; National Museum, Helsinki, pl. XXXII *e*; National Museum, Reykjavik, pl. LX; State Archaeological Service, Oslo, pls. LXIX and LXX; Szcecin Museum, pls. LV and LVI and Universitetets Oldsaksamling, Oslo, pls. IX, X *a*, XIII, XV *b* and *c*, XVIII, XIX *a*, XXX *a*, *c*, *d*, LVII. Pls. XLIV *b*, XLV *a*, and LXV *b* and *c* are copyright of D. M. Wilson and the rest of the plates are the joint copyright of the authors.

The copyright of the following figures is also acknowledged: Professor Arbman, fig. 44; British Museum, figs. 45 and 64; Professor S. Lindqvist, fig. 42; the late Dr S. Müller, fig. 39; Professor Ole Klindt-Jensen, figs. 5, 8 *a*, 9 and 10; the Norwegian Government, figs. 16–30; the late Dr B. Salin, figs. 3, 32–34 and 36–38; Statens Historiska Museum, Stockholm, figs. 12 and 58. All the other figures (except fig. 53) are the copyright of Mrs Eva Wilson.

CONTENTS

LINE ILLUSTRATIONS

IN THE TEXT

PLATES

13

PLATES

PLATES

INTRODUCTION

In this book we have attempted to outline the history of the art of the Vikings—a people who were considered by their contemporaries to be barbarians. Our history touches but one facet of a rich culture which affected the whole of north-western Europe and, whether the Vikings are interpreted as barbarians or civilizers, the art which they left behind them has an originality and a stature second to none in Europe of the period from 800–1100. A great historian has summarized the impression which Viking art leaves on the modern mind:

'Today, among so many reminders of those heroic ages, the museums of the north preserve in their glass cases surprising quantities of gold and silver: largely the proceeds of commerce, no doubt; but much of it also, as the German priest Adam of Bremen remarked, "fruits of brigandage". It is a striking fact that these precious metals stolen or received as tribute, sometimes in the form of coins, sometimes as jewellery of the western type, should usually have been refashioned into trinkets conforming to the taste of their new owners—evidence of a civilization singularly sure of itself.'[1]

We have taken these sentences of Marc Bloch as a key to our understanding of Viking art. The idea of a people 'sure of itself' is, we believe, the clue to Viking art.

Although there has been much discussion concerning the influences present in Viking art, there have been few attempts to record its content. Every single ornamental element of each style has been analysed and every nuance has been traced to a hypothetical source; but the traces are so tenuous and the resulting theories so varied that it is difficult to achieve any clear-cut picture of the main elements which made up the art. It is our belief that the main influence in Viking art was the Scandinavian artistic tradition. We do not deny that foreign influences are present in the art—at some periods they are very apparent—but we believe that a close and critical examination of the material which survives indicates that in every case these influences were not merely taken into the art of Scandinavia, but were quickly submerged in it by a people sure of their taste.

While this is the theme of the book, we hope that it does not obtrude too noticeably in what we trust is a reasonably sober and considered description and history of Viking art, for our main purpose has been to present the content of the art—our interpretation of that content is secondary to our main purpose and we have tried to avoid special pleading.

In this respect the joint authorship of this book has been of great advantage to the two individuals concerned, and the reason for this collaboration must be explained here, for it forms one of the main excuses for the presentation of this history. The nodal problem in past discussions of each phase of Viking art has been to decide the extent of insular and Continental influence in the stylistic development. In an attempt to achieve true scholarly balance students, British, Irish, German, and Scandinavian, have leant over backwards to avoid charges of chauvinism. We felt that the one way to achieve a proper

[1] Bloch (1961), 18.

balance was by a Scandinavian and a Briton pursuing a study of the subject together. We have written different parts of the book, but at all stages we have consulted each other and each has translated his co-author's work into his native language—a method of analysis as severe as any devised in a human study—we have agreed on most points and we have tried to make our argument coherent, but if there are occasional contradictions we would ask our critics to remember that this is a collaboration.

A recent summary of the changing ideas concerning Viking art has been presented by Dr Christiansson.[1] It is unnecessary to repeat his resumé in detail here, for his book is readily accessible, but certain facets of the history of thought on the subject are essential if we are to appreciate the niceties of Viking art. Since 1880, when Sophus Müller presented his classic introductory work on Scandinavian animal ornament,[2] many scholars have tried to explain the influences which made up the art of the Vikings, among them Salin, Shetelig, Brøndsted, Lindqvist, Åberg, Arbman, Kendrick, Arwidsson, Forssander, Holmqvist, and Bertil Almgren.[3] Not one of these scholars has devoted a book exclusively to a straight history of the art of the Viking period, all were interested in a particular aspect of Viking art and the picture that emerges from their studies is of three distinct schools of thought, which interpret Viking art as derivative from (a) Insular (b) Carolingian, or (c) Eastern sources. Few scholars have emphasized the indigenous qualities of Viking art, which the present authors believe to be inherent in the self-confident nature of the Viking society and which is made more likely by the lack of satisfactory parallels for the various Viking styles in western Europe and in the East. Professor Lindqvist was the first to stress this indigenous element in the art, in one of the very few contexts where a straight history of Viking art was required.[4] A recent masterly survey of the same subject by Professor Arbman, while not so explicit, implies a similar view.[5]

There is an extraordinary reluctance among archaeologists to recognize any original cultural traits in their own country and this is particularly true of the Viking period, for scholars are obsessed by the fact that the Viking merchants, pirates and adventurers, penetrated every corner of the known world and brought back with them goods, customs and souvenirs to their northern homelands. This dramatic side of Viking history has coloured all aspects of the study of Viking civilization and scholars have tended to use this colour in their study of the art. They have seen the art as a product of the Viking adventures abroad—its elements having been imported with the slaves and the wine which were brought back to Scandinavia by the pirates and the merchants. It is easy to forget that, during the Viking period, there was a continuity of culture in Scandinavia —the continuity of an agricultural society with its demand for the accepted and familiar. It is only in this context of a stable society that Viking art can be understood, for such foreign influences as were brought into the country by the returning Vikings were immediately adapted to a native idiom by craftsmen who rarely, if ever, moved out of

[1] (1959), 9–31. There is an extensive English summary. [2] Müller (1880).
[3] The major works of these authors are quoted in the bibliography.
[4] Lindqvist (1931). [5] Arbman (1961), 118 ff.

Scandinavia. These men travelled with their wares from the farm of one petty chieftain to the next, or worked at home producing objects for the middlemen; they knew the taste of their customers and adapted their art to it.

This stable aspect of Viking culture has been neglected by the historians of its art, because the first steps in the study of the subject were taken at a period of romanticism concerning the Viking adventures, and at a period when Darwinism was being applied to objects as well as organisms. Viking art-historical studies grew up in the atmosphere of the typological theories of Oscar Montelius, whose pupil, Bernhard Salin, touched on Viking art in his classic typological study of animal ornament, *Die altgermanische Thierornamentik*.[1] The methods used by Salin have been used by nearly all subsequent historians of Viking art. As Salin investigated all Europe in an attempt to explain the growth of animal ornament from the end of the Roman period to *c.* 800, so his successors (particularly Shetelig and Åberg) felt it incumbent on them to use similar methods to explain Viking art. They analysed it and then sought origins for its original components, but in so doing they occasionally lost sight of the main aim of their study—the understanding of the totality of Viking art. Although analysis and examination of the origin of individual features are imperative to the study of any art, it is the whole art that matters. Shetelig and his successors laid a groundwork by their analysis, on which all modern study must be based, but, if we examine the whole art in its native setting, we see that they appear to have underestimated the originality and continuity of Viking culture and of Viking art.

In this book we owe a great debt to our predecessors in the study—without their accurate and minute study we could not possibly attempt to summarize this facet of Viking civilization. At this distance of time, however, we can afford to stand back from the general struggle of ideas, which reached its climax in the late 1930s with the work of Arbman, Kendrick, Arwidsson, Forssander and Åberg, and attempt an estimate of the whole art in the light of their discussions.

Only one modern scholar has attempted to tackle Viking art in a way different from his predecessors. In his brilliant study of Viking art Bertil Almgren[2] has attempted to provide a different analytical approach to the art by the examination of the curves, conscious and unconscious, used by the Viking artist in constructing his pattern. The method is an interesting study of one of the possible traits of the mind which guide the hand of the artist, but the method cannot be applied to a general study of this sort, as it tends to be at once too particular and too subjective. Only one scholar[3] has tried to adopt Almgren's scheme to a study of Viking art, and then only as a supplementary method, but the results he produced were not conclusive.

The methods used in this book therefore, are the tried analytical and comparative methods of our predecessors; by the very nature of the material we are limited in the same way that they were limited, but we have one advantage that was not available to them—a knowledge of their carefully worked out facts and theories, and these we have

[1] Salin (1904).   [2] Almgren (1955).   [3] Christiansson (1959).

tried to sift and tailor to a picture that some will find far from original, but which we believe to fit the facts.

One of the primary purposes of this book has been to erect a chronological sequence for Viking art. This is no easy task, for one style does not die suddenly to be replaced on the next day by a completely different style—styles overlap and linger on, they run softly into each other and there is no one place where one can draw a line and label a style on one side 'Ringerike', and the style on the other 'Urnes'. Not only do styles overlap, they can also be contemporaneous (Borre and Jellinge for example). The distinction between motif and style is an important one in Viking art, for it accounts for many apparent anomalies—we may see, for example, on the same Gotlandic object, 'Style E' animals alongside 'gripping-beasts' (e.g. pl. xxv *e*). Nevertheless we believe that some sort of chronological picture can be constructed and our method in so doing must be exposed.

In our attempt to construct this chronology we have started from the known and moved to the unknown by way of the partially known. Our starting point has been the well-dated material, which comes under two heads: 'personal dating' and 'coin dating'. Under the former heading we include objects the manufacture of which is dated by an inscription referring to a known historical event or personage—e.g. the Jellinge stone (pl. xlviii) or the Cross of Cong (pl. lxxvi). Such objects are more common towards the end of our period and are practically unknown at its beginning.

Coins provide a second method of dating. When an object is deposited in a hoard of coins the date of deposition is indicated by the date of the latest coin found in the hoard; this forms a useful date for the object as the latest possible date at which it could be made. Coins can now be so accurately dated, that some of the results of this method are quite remarkable. Most of our dates after 925 are confirmed, or suggested, by coin evidence. This method only applies to objects found in hoards which contain a considerable body of coins. It is impossible to date a grave by this method when one or two coins are found amongst the other grave goods. Similarly it is obvious that certain objects were old when placed in the hoard; nevertheless, the provision of one date in the life of an object cuts down the margin of chronological error by half, while the occurrence of a number of hoards containing objects decorated in a similar style allows one to use simple statistical judgments of probability of date.

When all dating material of this sort has been sifted, we fall back on more subjective judgments, dating on political probability, for example. The early Manx crosses, and the early ninth century sculptures of east Yorkshire, have been dated in this book by the probable political situation pertaining in the British Isles at a given time. But in most cases such methods have been used in association with primary methods of dating —by coin hoard material, for example—or by rather more reliable secondary methods, such as the comparison of a Viking style with a style influencing it, or influenced by it, in a well-dated context outside Scandinavia, as, for example, with certain of the pre-Viking, Vendel styles.

The method of last resort, and the least reliable method from a chronological point of view, is typology; whereby a style is seen to develop or degenerate and a relative chronological framework is constructed to fit the process observed. The relative chronology of an object achieved by using this method is sometimes confirmed by its recurrent association with other objects, which have also been set in typological sequences. This is, however, a subjective method, and one which we have used with great caution when every other method has failed. These methods are the normal archaeological methods developed by the prehistorians.

The material available for this study is unrepresentative, for the art chronicled here is mainly applied art (usually animal ornament) and is of secondary importance to the object it decorated. The primary purpose of a brooch is as a dress or cloak fastener; the ornament of the mounts on the hilt of the sword is secondary to the purpose of that weapon. In a few cases we have examples of art in the primary sense—art for art's sake —but these are surprisingly few, an odd piece of sculpture and a number of objects which might be classified under the heading *ars sacra*. This book relates, then, the history of a number of styles of the decorative art of the Viking peoples. We can make few of the exclamatory judgments which historians of the arts of, for example, the Renaissance can make; we can only fulfil our function as archaeological attributionists and catalogue the features of the art we study. Lastly, we cannot discuss every ornamented object, or even every type of ornament, but we trust that every major problem is touched on or elucidated in the essay that follows: the material used is that which seems to us most important and, if we have used material familiar to the student, this is because it forms the key to the study.

The last fifteen years have seen a certain progress in the study of Viking Age art. No further survey of the subject has, however, appeared. While Peter Anker's important book[1] includes a general survey it is more concerned with the post-Viking period. The most significant discoveries in relation to Viking art were made in York: these have shifted the emphasis of the chapter on the Jellinge style[2], although the main arguments remain. The most important work in the whole of Viking Art has been done by Signe Fuglesang on the Ringerike style, her cyclostyled doctor's thesis[3] (hitherto available only to a few scholars) will shortly be published in emended form by Odense University Press. In this short appendix to the introduction we can, therefore, merely draw attention to the chief contributions to the study since the book was written.

The work of Mogens Ørsnes[4] was published at the same time as this volume, and we had no contact with him at the time of writing. It is mainly concerned with the pre-Viking Age and is useful in pin-pointing regional differences between the various styles. It retains a belief in the Hiberno-Saxon school as an influence in style D and E and includes a long discussion on style F (basically an expression of the Anglo-Carolingian

---

[1] (1970).   [2] See papers in Laing (1978).
[3] Nordhagen (1974).   [4] (1966).

style, p. 43 ff.), which was so labelled by Ramskou in a paper published while this book was in press[1]. Ørsnes's arguments, however, have little effect on the arguments in the first three chapters of this book, which we still hold to.

There has been no major progress in the discussion of Early Viking styles, but the Borre style has received a certain amount of attention. We have realised[2] that the style is much commoner in the British Isles than we had appreciated fifteen years ago and two, as yet unpublished, openwork pewter brooches from the York excavations ornamented with the well-known Borre animal point this moral even more clearly. Jansson[3], in an important paper on the chronology of both the Borre and Jellinge styles as they appear on oval brooches, has criticised a rather muddled discussion by Capelle[4] of the same subject. Whilst Jansson's discussion of the styles is detailed the direction of his arguments does not seem to us to contradict our general chronological conclusions.

New finds in York[5] have high-lighted certain problems of the Jellinge style. The basic chronological position remains roughly as it was, but it is now clear that there was a metropolitan Jellinge style in York in the late ninth and early tenth century. This presence demonstrates that the Middleton stones (pl. xxxix *b*)[6] are a degeneration or an expression of local incompetence rather than an early phase of the Jellinge style. The Middleton stones should be of a later date than we thought (p. 104), but it is most likely that they belong to the period before 954, when the Viking Kingdom of York collapsed. Of incidental interest is the presence in York of an unfinished stone, one of the first indications of a sculptor's workshop in England, although Bailey's recognition of the use of templates on Viking Age sculpture over a wide area of northern Yorkshire and southern Durham also illuminates our knowledge of the art[7]. Bailey in the same paper emphasises the comparative rarity of the Scandinavian animal styles in the north of England, a fact which was not clearly expressed by us.

The presence of the Mammen style in Britain is a matter of some controversy. It is clearly present in the Isle of Man, is possibly known in Ireland, and is found occasionally in England (pl. xlv *f*). Fuglesang[8] has attempted to transfer the Skaill hoard (p. 115 ff) to the Mammen style. While we cannot accept such a re-identification, the attempt does underlie the difficulties of division between Jellinge and Mammen. We were probably a little glib in our interpretation of this style. There can be no doubt that it exists, but in its earlier phases the overlap with the Jellinge style should have been given greater emphasis. The chronological position of the style we believe to have remained unaltered although it is interesting that both Moltke[9] and Fuglesang[10] still prefer the early dating, of the Jellinge stone[11] to the 960s.

Fuglesang[12] has however, helped to distinguish the Mammen and Ringerike styles by a

---

[1] (1963)—published in 1965.   [2] Wilson (1976).   [3] (1969).   [4] (1968).

[5] Cf. Lang (1968), 145 ff. for references.

[6] We are promised a book on the Middleton Stones by R. Bailey in the course of next year.

[7] In Lang (1978), 179 ff.   [8] In Lang (1978), 207.   [9] (1976).   [10] In Lang (1978), 207.

[11] There has been a major re-examination of the Jellinge monuments in *Medieval Scandinavia*, vii (1974), 156–234, and viii (1975), 1–26.   [12] *Loc cit.* and Nordhagen (1974).

brilliant piece of visual recognition. She has pointed out that the scrolls of the two styles differ: the Mammen scroll 'extending over the entire surface and filling it by wavering, crossing and turning. The composition lacks symmetry or axiality, yet the diagonal tripartite knots lend it some unruly balance.' Every one of the few tendrils is of the same width and hence has the same compositional value as the stems which spring from the central spiral at the bottom of the design.

By comparison the Ringerike scrolls, typified by the Vang stone (pl. LVII), 'has clearly defined stems which form the backbone of the composition based on axiality. The multitude of tendril offshoots is concentrated in the intertwined clusters. Each tendril is slim and short, clearly differentiated from the stems. The tendril groups are placed asymmetrically in relation to the stems'. This axiality or symmetry is an extremely good test for the recognition of the Ringerike. The dating of the style remains unchanged. Fuglesang's forthcoming book, *The Ringerike Style* is eagerly awaited.

Work on the Urnes style has been little affected by recent work although it has been discussed by Anker[1], Blindheim[2], and Holmqvist[3]. A great deal of work on Irish aspects of this style has been published by Henry[4], but her definitions are often unclear and dated. With respect to the Urnes style we should point out a mistake on p. 153. The crucifix from Gåtebo, Öland, does not come from a hoard.

[1] (1970).   [2] (1965).   [3] (1963).   [4] (1967).

PART I

BY
OLE KLINDT-JENSEN

CHAPTER I

SCANDINAVIAN ART
BEFORE THE VIKINGS

Viking art cannot be understood without a proper appreciation of its roots in the earlier art of Scandinavia. Such an appreciation is not easy to achieve as the styles of the pre-Viking era were not mutually exclusive; they frequently overlapped and are even found together embellishing different panels of the same object. This chapter attempts to order these styles within a general Scandinavian context.

In the study of both pre-Viking and Viking art it is important that the mind should not be fettered by geographical preconceptions. The distribution of the various styles was not necessarily limited by the boundaries of ancient or modern national or physical regions. A constant cultural contact, for example, persisted over a long period, with varying degrees of intensity, from the Trondheim district of Norway, across the mountainous Scandinavian backbone, to the Gulf of Bothnia and Finland. Similarly, at certain stages of the pre-Viking age, Norway, north Sjælland and south-east Scandinavia were mutually connected by trade. The comparative ease of sea transport, as against overland travel, was a constant factor in Scandinavia before relatively modern times, and was the reason for the prominence of the Baltic islands as cultural centres during the first millennium of our era. Gotland lay, spider-like, at the centre of the Baltic sea-routes, and its web linked it with the only slightly less important islands of Öland and Bornholm. However great the political and geographical differences between the various Scandinavian districts, their common relationship and tradition played a decisive role in the development of the art.

Much of the art chronicled in this book is decorative art. It is based on an animal ornament which emerged during the fourth century AD to become a vital element in Scandinavian art. When it first appeared in northern Europe it naturally contained many foreign elements, but, by the beginning of the Viking Age, such elements had become submerged and indigenous traits were completely dominant.

Although the major part of the surviving art is based on animal motifs, a considerable body of naturalistic art remains, which can be traced into the Viking Age alongside the more abstract art. While the decorative art of Scandinavia repeatedly shows a tendency to extreme stylization, resulting sometimes in an almost abstract play of lines, naturalistic art always retained its contact with reality. Plant ornament, on the other hand—so popular in the rest of Europe—was of little interest to the Scandinavian artist. When leaf motifs do occur, they are clearly alien to the indigenous art, and it is not until the Mammen style appears in the late tenth century that foliage is used in successful combination with animal motifs.

Throughout this early period, if we are to judge from the surviving material, naturalistic art leads a very shadowy existence. Only in certain corpuses of material, such as the Gotlandic picture stones and certain objects in the Oseberg find, is naturalism of any great importance. Otherwise it is found in an almost casual fashion, as a lightly engraved decoration on the back of certain brooches (where it would not normally be seen) (fig. 1), on the underside of the plank of a ship (fig. 2), or on the base and lid of a box (pl. xix *b*). The assured quality of such casually drawn scenes is without exception remarkable—the rarity of such ornament was obviously not due to any lack of artistic ability. In applied art naturalism was rarely used: decorative, less naturalistic, art took its place. Naturalistic art, however, always influenced applied art and we shall demonstrate the ornamental craftsman's interest in certain naturalistic motifs—it is noticeable, for example, how the form of the horse, with its sub-triangular body and curved neck, lent itself to stylization in decorative art.

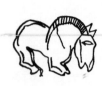

FIG. I. Animal scratched on the back of a square-headed brooch from Nordheim, Hedrum, Vestfold, Norway. *Universitetets Old-saksamling, Oslo.*

The importance of the indigenous artistic elements and the creative ability of the individual artist must not be underestimated in an examination of the sources of inspiration of Scandinavian art. This is particularly so when we consider the products of the outstanding artists of the Viking period. Their art became the model on which the simpler, more

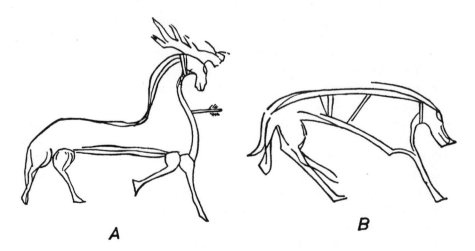

FIG. 2. Naturalistic animals scratched on the underside of a plank from the Oseberg ship. *Viking ships Museum, Oslo*

popular art of the period was based. The stylistic influences of the major artists represented at Oseberg, for example, with their originality and sense of experiment, help us to understand, in some measure, the central elements present in the creation of the style.

The history of stylistic development in Scandinavia is based on an increasing interest in animal ornament, which becomes apparent for the first time in the late Roman Iron Age, when animals appear as decorative features on various objects (fig. 3). Running deer, or horses, form a frieze round the rims of the silver beakers from Sjælland (pl. 1a). These were undoubtedly executed, together with a series of related objects, under the influence of Romano-Celtic art—a fact adequately demonstrated by the technique used (repoussé work) and by the form of the running animals.[1] Human masks (fig. 3e), which are so popular an element of Scandinavian art at this early period, demonstrate an initial element of one aspect of Migration period art.

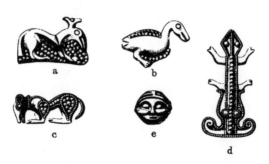

FIG. 3. Animal motifs from the late Roman Iron Age in Scandinavia: (a and b) applied to a disc from Thorsbjerg, Schleswig; (c–e) from gold collar from Olleberg, Karleby, Västergötland, Sweden. Scale ¼

The preoccupation of the artist with animal motifs at this early period, and his lack of interest in foliate designs, is demonstrated in a number of ways. The discovery of a number of leaves made of gold foil at Brangstrup, Fyn, Denmark, demonstrates this point admirably (pl. 1 b, c). Most of the leaves are obviously imported from the Danubian region, but one of them is distinctive. On this leaf each frond terminates in animal heads of a typical Scandinavian form—a detail which must have given sense and interest to a motif which was otherwise meaningless to the Scandinavian people of the period.

Despite their obvious origin in provincial Roman ornament, such motifs were used and transformed into a peculiarly Scandinavian design. The two large discs from Thorsbjerg in the south of Jutland clearly demonstrate this fact. Their origin is clearly recognizable in a provincial Roman milieu, but each disc has indigenous elements in its ornament. One is decorated with a frieze of repoussé deer in style closely related to the Sjælland beakers (pl. 1 a). On the other disc, small sheet metal animals (figs. 3a and b) have been added secondarily to a panel originally decorated in a straightforward Roman style. These applied animals are clearly not of classical inspiration. As their reflection can be seen in Scandinavian ornament of the succeeding period (pl. II a) there can be little doubt that these secondary motifs, together with the Brangstrup leaf, were made by a Scandinavian craftsman experimenting with a new style. On the other hand it is difficult to decide whether the other disc, the deer frieze on the Sjælland beakers, and

[1] Klindt-Jensen (1952), 195 and Werner (1941).

certain other objects decorated in the same technique, were made by indigenous or immigrant craftsmen. It is clear, however, that the high standard of craftsmanship of the Thorsbjerg disc and the Sjælland beakers could be achieved by Scandinavian artists and that objects of this type, executed with great technical competence, were widely distributed throughout Scandinavia.

The secondarily applied creatures on the second Thorsbjerg disc—a fish, a quadruped seen in profile, a duck or a goose (figs. 3a and b)—are fairly naturalistic. It seems as though the Scandinavian artist wished to explain some of the original classical motifs of this disc—motifs which must have seemed strange to him—and to achieve this he attached a number of more familiar figures of his own. In doing so he demonstrated his non-acceptance of foreign art. One feature—the mask—was a motif common to Scandinavian and classical art, but in Scandinavia it was given a stiffer, more formalized character (e.g. fig. 3e).

Certain provincial Roman features were adopted by the Scandinavian artist and quickly and thoroughly transformed into a northern idiom. Thus chip-carved ornament (of the sort seen in pl. 11 a) was adapted from provincial Roman sources; it became popular and was used, for example, to accentuate animal ornament. The ornamental effect of the glittering surface, with its varied light and shade, was heightened by the use of openwork and strong relief.[1]

Chip-carving came to be used in Scandinavia on elegant square-headed brooches (pl. 11 a) which were ornamented with geometrical and animal patterns executed in this technique. The bodies of the animals of these brooches were stylized and often contorted to be fitted into the available space. The rows of bird's heads with curved beaks, which are so prominent a feature of this art, had some of their roots in Eastern European art. A delightful aspect of the same style, in a different technique, can be seen on the Swedish gold collars (figs. 3c–e).

This first animal style of the Migration period, which Salin identified and labelled as 'Style I',[2] flourished in Scandinavia in the latter part of the fifth and throughout most of the sixth century. It is found all over northern Europe: it was popular in England and in Poland and Hungary, where it was presumably inspired from Scandinavia. Style I, at its most elegant, is seen on large brooches like the nielloed, silver-gilt example from Gummersmark, which is covered with chip-carved, geometric, zoomorphic and human ornament (pl. 11 a).

Another style gradually made itself felt in eastern Scandinavia towards the end of the sixth century—Salin's Style II. This was based on the tendency of the northern artist to adapt animal motifs into plaits, scrolls and knots—motifs which, in the main, spread from the eastern Mediterranean. Geometric patterns were given animal characteristics, but did not take the form of organic animals (pl. 11 b). They retain their abstract, firm character, but are treated in a number of ways. The interlaced element of the style probably came to Scandinavia from southern Europe.

[1] Forssander (1937), 78 and Voss (1954), 171.
[2] (1904). *Cf.* Arbman (1945), Chadwick (1958), Bakka (1958).

The wide diffusion of Style II throughout western and central Europe and Scandinavia demonstrates the universal quality of an art which over-rode national boundaries and penetrated the remotest areas. Technical peculiarities (the use of niello, for example), together with distinctive ornamental motifs, make it possible to compare almost identical swords with provenances as far apart as Imola (north Italy), Herbrechtingen (south Germany) and Endrebacke (Gotland).[1] Rich east Scandinavian cemeteries, like the Swedish grave-fields of Valsgärde and Vendel in Uppland, are closely related in style and material to the royal burial at Sutton Hoo in Suffolk (dated by coins to c. AD 655.[2] In the ship burials at all these sites are ornamented Scandinavian weapons demonstrating a universal taste.

The people of eastern Scandinavia also maintained contacts with the peoples of eastern Hungary, while the Langobardic culture, which can be traced in Pannonia and later in northern Italy, exhibits undoubted Scandinavian traits. Thuringen clearly acted as a link between the northern and southern cultures.[3]

The wide distribution of Style II must always be borne in mind, for, although the style develops independently in the different areas, its common origin is responsible for the final form of the ornament and the similarity of the products of the style throughout Europe. Although, therefore, it may be tempting to emphasize points of resemblance in objects from two different areas, such comparisons are of little value in any attempt to correlate two groups of art. In order to establish such a correlation it is necessary to distinguish an aggregate of distinctive features common to both groups, features which could only have been created in the area of one of the groups. It is clearly not sufficient to show that certain forms of composition are common to two areas, when they may have had a common source.

In Scandinavia itself, local developments complicate the interpretation of Style II. In Norway, for instance, Style II rarely occurs; here the motifs of Style I were broken up into their component parts, these were then re-assembled in an haphazard fashion to give the ornamented surface a restless, almost untidy, appearance.

Style II flourished in eastern Scandinavia, particularly in Uppland and on Gotland, and also became popular in southern Scandinavia. Despite the obvious similarities of the Scandinavian Style II with, for example, the ribbon-like animals found in Anglo-Saxon and south German contexts, its development in the North was distinctive. This development is exemplified by a number of exquisite objects from the famous Swedish cemeteries of Vendel and Valsgärde in Uppland (pl. III c), the material from which abounds in interest.

The Vendel gravefield was discovered in 1881, and at least fourteen men's graves, dating from the seventh to the tenth century, were excavated there before the turn of the century. The burial rite is significant: the dead warrior lay in the stern of his ship with his shield, sword, spear and (in at least four cases) helmet. Horses were found in the

[1] Werner (1950), 45 and (1958), 29.
[2] Bruce-Mitford (1949), passim.
[3] Bóna (1956) and Werner (1962).

grave with bridle and harness mounts; glass vessels, drinking cups and a number of tools were also found in the ship, together with dogs, cattle, sheep and pigs.[1]

The remarkable Valsgärde cemetery was discovered in 1928 by Sune Lindqvist, and he has excavated it with the aid of his assistants, among whom were Greta Arwidsson and Pär Olsén, who have published some of the material and discussed the styles which decorate the grave goods.[2] They have labelled these styles A to E. Style A is a link between Salin's styles I and II, B is identical with style II. Styles C, D and E are Scandinavian styles typified in pls. III c, IV a and VII.

The cemetery, which was for some five hundred years the burial ground of a chieftain's family, is situated on a ridge above the River Fyris. Among other interments, fourteen ship burials were found, they are largely contemporary with those from Vendel, save only that the latest grave dates from c. 1100. The richest graves belong to the earliest periods of the cemetery's history and contain lavishly decorated objects—swords, for example, with scabbards embellished with delicate animal ornament, and helmets decorated with figural scenes.

The objects recovered from graves XI and XII at Vendel and graves 5, 7 and 8 at Valsgärde are decorated with a simple variant of Style II—a variant which the Uppsala school of archaeologists have christened Style B (pl. II b). Two of the graves also contain objects decorated in the more elaborate Style C—a style characterized by a large animal caught up in thin interlacing ribbons, which sometimes take the form of snakes (pl. III c).

In grave 8 at Valsgärde were found objects of impressed metal decorated in a style transitional between Style I and Style II—this has been labelled Style A.

Style B is characterized by animals with ribbon-shaped bodies which interlace gracefully together in an undulating manner (pl. II b). The head of each animal looks backward and has a pointed chin and a rather large eye, while the line indicating the eye socket terminates in a triangular lappet. The mouth either takes the form of a closed beak or is open to display long pointed teeth. The ribbon-like body is made up of two lines which run parallel to each other (save for an occasional thickening in the region of the front hip, which is pear-shaped). The feet are sub-triangular and slightly curved and are sometimes feathered, to give the effect of claws; they have a spiraliform toe at the back.

Style C (pl. III c) clearly developed out of this ornamental repertoire; but new motifs appear, which have close parallels in insular art and which probably indicate influences and contacts with western Europe.[3] The new motifs, together with the permanent combination of certain features, and the production of animals of a distinct character of their own demonstrate that this is a new style. We shall show that Style C only appears in certain specific areas and that in other regions the transition between Styles B, C and D is fluid.

[1] Stolpe and Arne (1927).
[2] Arwidsson (1942 a and b), (1954) and Olsén (1945).
[3] Ibid., 92.

Style C (pl. III *c*), as we have stated, is characterized by an animal with a large sub-triangular body. In eastern Scandinavia the contours of the body are more heavily accentuated than the surrounding interlace. The heads of Style C animals, unlike those of Style B, are not usually backward turned. Snakes with heads in profile occur occasionally, and this combination of snake and animal is of some importance as it occurs repeatedly in Scandinavian art of the later periods.

The mouths of Style C animals either take the form of a beak (as in Style B) or are more naturalistic, being open and of bell-like form. An oblique line occasionally occurs in front of the mouth, which sometimes has a pointed chin. The eye socket sometimes terminates in a lappet.

The contour of the horse-like body of the animal is emphasized (sometimes with a double contour) so that it stands out clearly against the confusion of tight ribbon interlace which surrounds it (pl. III *c*). The strong neck is arched and joins the back either in a gentle curve or at an angle, as though the head were lifted in sudden movement. The body is rounded and the clearly-drawn hips are almost pear-shaped; the hind leg is clearly delineated, but only the lower part of the foreleg can be seen below the contour of the body.

The animal is represented in many positions—with outstretched legs (as though at full gallop), standing, or lying down. The motif has its origin in such contemporary naturalistic representations of horses[1] as the carefully executed bronze horse from Veggerslev, Jutland (pl. III *b*) or in the animals carved on certain Gotlandic memorial stones, to which we shall return.

The Veggerslev horse is of remarkably high quality; it is naturalistic in character and stance, while the head, with its slightly pointed chin, large round eye and strongly emphasized contour, is reminiscent of Style II. The ear protrudes slightly, rather like the lappet of the Style B animal. The contour of the body is accentuated, the back-hip is outside the contour of the body and the upper portion of the foreleg is contained within the chest. The tail passes obliquely behind the rear leg. Semi-naturalistic horses of this type have been taken into the decorative art and almost obscured by interlace; but, as we have seen, certain characteristic features of the legs and heads clearly indicate their stylistic affinities.

In eastern Scandinavia the main motif is, as we have shown, emphasized by means of a heavy contour: in western Scandinavia, however, there is less contrast between the interlacing ribbons and the main contours—in this area, indeed, the whole composition is quieter and more symmetrical.[2] Certain smaller objects, which are most conveniently included under the heading of Salin's all-embracing Style II, show a clear relationship between Styles B and D. An impression of the development of Style C in the south-western region is given by such well-designed objects as the sword from Kyndby, Sjælland, Denmark.[3]

[1] Olsén (1945), 79, has developed this theme in greater detail.
[2] Cf. Ørsnes-Christensen (1955), 122.
[3] Ibid., figs. 18–34.

While Style C appears to have been less distinctive in southern Scandinavia, Styles D and B are found together in this area and the gradual transition between the two is clearly seen. Professor Arwidsson quite naturally took south Scandinavia as the cradle of Style D.[1]

Animals of this style (e.g. fig. 4) are characterized by their ribbon-like bodies, consisting of three or more parallel lines, which may enclose transverse hatching, small circles or lozenges. Two legs usually emerge in a more or less inorganic manner from the body, to develop, occasionally, in a startling fashion. The form of the head varies, but it is usually of the same width as the body and lacks the pointed lower jaw so typical of Style B. The eye is often almond-shaped, while the mouth sometimes has horse-like characteristics, with distinctive front teeth—but there are so many variations in form that generalization is impossible. Spirals occur frequently in the design, but the most characteristic feature of the style is the symmetrical nature of the composition—the gracefully curved animals often flowing into a figure-of-eight design. The pattern frequently consists of pairs of symmetrically opposed ribbon-like animals. This form of ornament can clearly be derived from older, intricate interlace patterns; but, even when the head or limb of an animal appear to break the flow of the Style D pattern, the general impression always reveals the regular semi-geometrical character of the design.

Style D is distributed fairly widely throughout Scandinavia and is seen at its best, and in its most intricate form, on a series of rectangular brooches of which the Skabersjö brooch (pl. IV a) is the most remarkable example. The style also occurs on many other types of object, of which the plate from Böda, Öland (fig. 4) may be taken as an example. It is a well-known type[2] and is of remarkably high quality. It is silver-gilt and is inlaid with niello and decorated with two slim ribbon-like animals. The body of each animal has a carved zigzag midrib, while the legs, which emerge from pear-shaped hips, have delicately formed feet. The pair of opposed interlacing animals form a well thought-out and very effective composition.

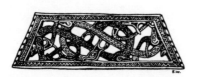

FIG. 4. Sword guard from Böda, Öland, Sweden. Scale ⅓. *Statens Historiska Museum, Stockholm.*

Style D had a long life in Scandinavia. In south Scandinavia it is found in association with Style B, while in the rich Uppland graves it occurs with Style C (in grave 6 at Valsgärde, for example) and Style E (in grave VII at Vendel, for example)—the latter style extending, as we shall show, into the early Viking period.

Although Style D was particularly suited for the portrayal of snakes, it exhibits many interesting variations, which illustrate the craftsman's tendency to experiment with new designs. On the Danish island of Bornholm, for example, naturalistic motifs are of fairly frequent occurrence;[3] a beautifully executed figure of a bird from Kobbeå,

---

[1] Arwidsson (1942a), 31. [2] Ibid., 24.
[3] These will be dealt with by O. Klindt-Jensen in a forthcoming study.

Bornholm, for instance, grips a snake in its beak and claw (pl. iv *b*). The bird's body is elegantly compact, the wings are emphasized by a double contour and the tail-feathers are delicately portrayed. It has a large, round eye. Despite a certain amount of stylization in the ornament of the body and the position of the wing, the design has naturalistic overtones.

Related to this object, but more stylized in ornament, is a mount from grave 47 at Lousgård on Bornholm (pl. iv *d*). It is made of gilt bronze and is partly inlaid with garnets (some of which are now lost). The object, which is executed in openwork, is made up of two opposed, identical, bird-like figures. It is carefully and imaginatively composed. Each bird grips a ribbon-shaped animal, which in turn clings, by means of its long claws, to the lower jaw of the bird. The hips of the ribbon-like animals are ornamented with double interlocking spirals. The hind-legs bend below the body and the head consists of two small circles, one at the eye and the other at the snout. The body and hind-leg are billeted.

The smooth curve of the inner contour of each bird is broken below the eye by two curves which meet in a point. Each head is crowned by a three-element crest, the tail is claw-shaped and the hip and spur of the leg terminate in animal heads.

On both the Lousgård 47 and Kobbeå objects a bird is clearly seen gripping another creature, with which it is inextricably involved. The same gripping motif can be seen on the brooch illustrated in pl. iv *c*, which was also found in the Lousgård cemetery (grave 12) and takes the form of a quadruped seen from above; its ornament exhibits a mixture of naturalistic and stylized features. The snakes coiled round each leg are substantial, lively creatures and the manner in which those at the forelegs are held foreshadows the gripping-beasts, which became so popular at a later date. The main animal of this brooch has two round eyes and an elongated snout, its legs emerge from almost pear-shaped hips (square-cut at the base) and the body is panelled and filled with transverse lines, which are perhaps meant to represent ribs. The hips and the central panel between the shoulders were originally inlaid with garnets, while a trefoil appears in a field at the base of the spine. The animal has an interesting parallel at a later date on the Oseberg cart (pl. x *a*).

Among the other objects found in the same grave as this important brooch were two small oval brooches.[1] These objects must be dated to the pre-Viking period—to a phase of the eighth century before the larger oval brooches had become popular.

The Lousgård cemetery is remarkable for its richness. It apparently represents the cemetery of one or two prominent families and was in use for a number of generations; its history extends into the Viking Age, when the material is somewhat poorer than it was in the Vendel period. Other contemporary cemeteries in Bornholm, for example that from the neighbouring village of Bækkegård, have produced material of a much humbler quality. We see here two different milieu. Lousgård was obviously the cemetery of wealthy people who could afford to pay for the services of competent craftsmen, while the people who were buried at Bækkegård were less wealthy and were buried

[1] Arwidsson (1942*a*), pls. 85 and 87.

with more ordinary products. The finds from Lousgård would seem to indicate that an independent and imaginative group of craftsmen were working in Bornholm—a group with contacts with other regions, and particularly with south Scandinavia; it would seem that this group of craftsmen ultimately influenced other, less original, metal-workers. The quadruped seen from above which, combined with ribbon-shaped animals of Style D, was the most important motif of this group, occurred in earlier contexts in Scandinavia (fig. 3 *d*).[1] It is fairly common, in a semi-naturalistic form, in Bornholm and is occasionally found elsewhere in Scandinavia[2]—particularly on a series of small oval brooches. It is impossible to say whether this motif originated in south Scandinavia, but it is noteworthy that the typical gripping feature is found in association with the quadruped seen from above and the bird seen in profile. The scene probably had a specific meaning and was not merely an abstract interplay of motifs.

The snake itself is also found on the early, rather slight, oval brooches. Occasionally a spread-eagled animal, like that from grave 12 at Lousgård (pl. IV *c*), occurs; but in such a case it is usually made up of two slender animals, one on each side of the brooch, which together form a quadruped with a common head.[3]

The brooch from grave 3 at Lousgård, illustrated in fig. 5, is of particular interest. In the centre of this brooch is a man with raised hands, flanked by semi-ribbon-shaped animals, the forelegs of which have distinctive, elongated claws. The animals have hips which are accentuated by circles. The hind-leg is similar to that of the animals gripped by the bird in the Lousgård openwork ornament (pl. IV *d*). As on the early oval brooches, the heads join to give the illusion of a single animal, while two tongue-like coils issue from the mouth. A billeted line serves to draw attention to the finely-drawn human figure in the centre.

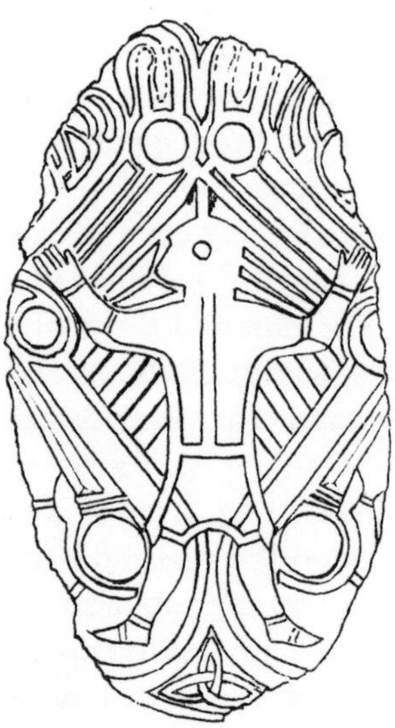

The man is fully-dressed; he wears knee-length trousers, shoes and a waist-length shirt which appears to be gathered in front. The full-length sleeves are hatched transversely at the elbows. His body is seen from the front, but the head is seen in profile with his long hair falling to his left forearm. The man dominates the design and partly obscures the two lateral animals, the outline of which can be clearly seen within the contour of his body. Both the flanking animals and the man are drawn with a double contour (save that the forearm, the head and the lower leg have a single contour). As on the brooch from grave 12 there is a trefoil pattern in a triangular field at the base of the brooch.

FIG. 5. Ornament of an oval brooch from grave 3 at Lousgård, Bornholm, Denmark. *National Museum, Copenhagen.*

---

[1] Salin (1904), figs. 499*d* and 502*c*; Arwidsson (1942, *a*), fig. 45.
[2] Vedel (1886), 165; (1897), 84.　　　　　[3] Petersen (1955), pls. 3 and 4.

The motif of a man between two animals is seen on a number of related objects from Bornholm, but few of them are so finely executed as the Lousgård design. The motif obviously harks back to a popular and widely-distributed earlier motif, which can be seen, for example, on the dies from Torslunda (pl. III *a*) and on a Norwegian button-on-bow brooch.[1] The ornament has a very definite contact with Christian art of southern Europe. The design, which was at one time known as 'the Daniel in the Lion's den motif', occurs on a series of buckles from the Merovingian area and consisted of a man, with his arms raised in a classical attitude of prayer, flanked by two animals, which stand either on their fore-feet or on their hind-legs. The striking parallels between the French and Scandinavian versions of this motif indicate the southern origin of the design.[2]

Human masks are also popular in the Vendel styles. They sometimes occur by themselves, as on the semicircular mounts from Valsgärde grave 6 (fig. 6), or else in combination with interlace patterns, with beards intricately plaited into ribbons and large staring eyes, as on the sword pommel from Pappilanmäki, Eura, Satakunda, Finland.[3]

The most sophisticated style of this immediately pre-Viking period, Style E, comprises the greater part of Salin's Style III. It appears to have had its origin on Gotland, an island which, throughout the Migration period, provided an art of rich originality. Style E, however, became very popular throughout Scandinavia and its strange, coiled animals, with their abstract interplay of lines, became a

FIG. 6. Human mask from a mount from Valsgärde, Grave 6. *Gustavianum, Uppsala.*

familiar feature of pre-Viking and early Viking art (fig. 7). In this style basic animal forms were used in a new and lively fashion; the form of the creature was distorted and it was embellished with fan-like, foliate offshoots emerging from coils—the whole composition being completely divorced from naturalism. It is a highly stylized, completely Scandinavian, art, in which symmetrical and asymmetrical compositions go hand-in-hand with graceful coils and swelling ribbons.

The typical animal head is dominated by a large pear-shaped eye, while the mouth is seen in profile (fig. 7). The hips take the form of an open, usually heart-shaped, piercing of the body. This 'opening' forms a frame and a medium for the interlaced coils, from which are produced foliate offshoots. The feet and toes are often elegantly extended, while the bodies are slender—expanding and contracting in even curves. Two animals are frequently interlaced together or set in apposition to each other. The best motifs of this style reveal a sensitive eye for asymmetrical composition and provide an elegant abstract style of decoration, built up out of skilful fantasy. It is a style which lasts well on into the Viking period and has an enormous influence on later Viking art, particularly in Gotland.

[1] Holmqvist (1955), pl. xxxii, 79; Salin (1904), fig. 494, cf. fig. 394.
[2] Ibid., fig. 301.   [3] Olsén (1945), fig. 327.

Before turning to a consideration of the naturalistic art in the immediately pre-Viking Age, we must consider shortly some of the foreign ornamental elements of this pre-Viking art. In the main the Scandinavian style which succeeded Style II (B) followed the indigenous tradition of the North, but certain elements of eighth century Continental art can be clearly seen among the detail of the ornament.

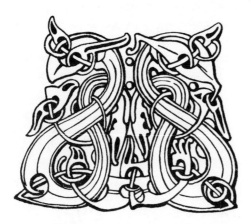

FIG. 7. Style E ornament on a disc-on-bow brooch from Othemars, Othem, Gotland, Sweden. *Statens Historiska Museum, Stockholm.*

In the eighth century, the British Isles was the most important artistic centre of north-west Europe and influenced the art of the Continent considerably. On the Continent the variant of Salin's Style II, which had been such an important element in seventh century art, had largely disappeared and was being replaced by a new art related to that of the British Isles. Decoration in metal, stone and manuscripts, witnesses to influences from a more sophisticated art. There are naturally certain differences between Anglo-Carolingian and insular art, just as there are regional differences between the art of the Hiberno-Saxon area (Ireland, Scotland and Northumbria) and southern England. But the different styles were closely related and there was a continuous contact between them. Certain motifs distinguish the different areas: plant ornament, for example, is rare in eighth century Irish art, although it is quite commonly seen in northern English contexts.[1] On the other hand, traditional Celtic designs—the spiral whirl and basket-work filling (fig. 12),[2] for example—occur not only in the Hiberno-Saxon area throughout Britain, as in the Book of Cerne.[3] In recent years the wide recognition of the Books of Durrow and Lindisfarne as Northumbrian products emphasizes the fact that the Hiberno-Saxon area formed a unified cultural region, so that it is often impossible to distinguish between Irish and English artistic products. The problem that faces us in this context is whether the undoubted insular elements in eighth century Scandinavian art came directly from the British Isles or indirectly through Anglo-Carolingian art.

Anglo-Saxon art on the Continent reflects the work of the insular Christian mission which was active on the Continent in the eighth century. Starting from Friesland, British missionaries moved up the Rhine into Thuringen, Bavaria and the Salzburg area. Throughout western and southern Germany they established a series of monasteries—like the great monastery at Fulda—which often included on their strength Anglo-Saxon, or Anglo-Saxon trained, monks and artists.

[1] Brøndsted (1924), 16; MacDermott (1955), 97; Haseloff (1951), 50.
[2] Wilson (1960a), pl. 58. [3] Zimmermann (1918), pl. 295, a.

Anglo-Saxon influence is particularly strong in the southern part of the region, and from this area comes one of the most important surviving Anglo-Carolingian objects—the great chalice, preserved at Kremsmünster, which bears the name of the Bavarian Duke Tassilo, who was deposed by Charlemagne in 788.[1] The inscription dates the chalice to between 777 and 788, for in the former year the Duke founded the two monasteries of Mattsee and Kremsmünster, in an area where the mixture of indigenous and Anglo-Saxon art prevailed. The chalice was undoubtedly given to Kremsmünster by the founder.

The chalice, by virtue of its incontrovertible date, is of primary importance in the study of the art which embellishes it. The animal ornament of the chalice is not only found in ecclesiastical contexts, as in the sculptures of the church of St Johann at Münster,[2] but is also seen on secular objects, some of which found their way to Scandinavia—as, for example, a cup found at Fejø in Denmark[3] and a strap-mount found in the ancient Swedish town of Birka.[4] The period when this style was flourishing on the Continent coincides with the appearance of an Anglo-Carolingian mission to the south of Denmark, which even ventured into Scandinavia itself.[5]

The ornament of the Tassilo chalice, which has been fully discussed by Haseloff,[6] is in all respects, save for a group of Evangelist figures, characteristic of Anglo-Carolingian art and it is practicable, therefore, to use it as a basis for a description of this style.

Within a geometrical framework, made up of conjoined sections of circular and straight-sided figures, are various motifs—particularly a series of animals, which

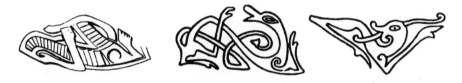

FIG. 8. Animals from (*a*) the Gudhjem brooch (fig. 9), (*b*) the Tassilo Chalice, (*c*) the Kells Crozier.

typically (fig. 8*b*) have splayed back legs, but are otherwise seen in profile. Their feet rise towards their backward-turned heads, while the rear hips are usually pear-shaped or occasionally, as with almost all the forelegs, have a small incised spiral hook. Simple, stylized plant motifs with straight stems and curved or trefoil leaves are also found on the object, as well as interlaced ribbon ornament which contains an occasional trefoil feature. The chalice is of heavily gilt copper: it is executed in deep chip-carving and is inlaid in places with glass.

The slightly clumsy animal of the chalice has its ancestry in insular ornament. The relationship between back leg and head occurs, for example, more than a hundred years

[1] Haseloff (1951).
[2] Werner (1959), pl. 26.
[3] Wilson (1960*d*).
[4] Haseloff (1951), pl. 15, 3.
[5] Ibid., 74; Arbman (1956), 110.
[6] Haseloff (1951).

earlier, in the great Anglo-Saxon chieftain's grave at Sutton Hoo.[1] The plant ornament also occurs in insular contexts[2] as does the method of dividing up the surface,[3] which is also known on the Continent,[4] and the clearly drawn (but rather thin) ribbon interlace.[5] Although many of these motifs ultimately emanate from Mediterranean art it seems reasonable, in view of their very definite insular affinities, to place them in some sort of relationship to the British Isles. It is impossible to say, however, whether the craftsman who made the Tassilo chalice was an Anglo-Saxon working on the Continent, or a continental craftsman trained in an Anglo-Saxon school. In view of the large number of deviations from pure Anglo-Saxon art in the Anglo-Carolingian school, the latter hypothesis seems most reasonable.

Anglo-Carolingian art is no more than a significant episode in the history of western and central European art. Insular art, on the other hand, continued in a set and defined sequence. In the Hiberno-Saxon area were produced, alongside such great artistic achievements as the Book of Kells, works of less brilliant quality, such as the MacRegol Gospels, which, like Kells, is dated *c.* 800 (on the basis of an inscription). In the Hiberno-Saxon area the elegantly interlaced animal motifs were developed further and continued to influence continental art. Long after the Tassilo chalice was made such objects as the Kell's Crozier[6] (fig. 8c) and the Trewhiddle mounts (fig. 46)[7] witness to a more developed form of the style in ninth-century Britain. One characteristic insular feature—basket-work hatching—never became popular on the Continent.[8]

In this light we must examine the origin of the 'insular' influences in Scandinavian art: did they come directly from the British Isles, from the Continent, or from both areas? To answer this question we must examine some of the Scandinavian material which betrays foreign influence.

One of the commonest Scandinavian antiquities is the oval brooch (sometimes known as the tortoise brooch). It is an indigenous form which developed from a small, undecorated dress fastener into a large and elaborate ornament, embellished with zoomorphic decoration. Brooches of this type occur frequently in the form of animals seen from above—the animal being sometimes constructed from two slender animals, joined at head and hips. Significant variations occur and new details are added as the style matures. Two oval brooches from the Gudhjem area of Bornholm, for example, bear a distinctive ornament (fig. 9) dominated by a pair of animals placed on each long side of the brooch. The ribbon-shaped bodies of the animals do not meet, but form part of a geometrical framework which is completed by ribbons. The mid-rib is decorated by a ring-chain and interlace pattern. The hips and eyes of the two lateral animals are emphasized by free-standing rosettes—like the rivet heads at the joints of the framework on other objects—while the feet take the form of knots.

[1] Haseloff (1951), 21.   [2] Ibid., 49.
[3] Forssander (1943), 228; Haseloff (1951), 58.   [4] Arwidsson (1942a), 36.
[5] Haseloff (1951), 56.   [6] MacDermott (1955).
[7] Wilson and Blunt (1961); cf. the interesting find from Källby: Wilson (1955).
[8] Arwidsson (1942a), 36, mentions some rather remote parallels.

In the semicircular fields at either end of the brooch, and in the adjacent fields, are crouching animals. Each animal has a raised foreleg and a hind-leg which touches the backward-looking head. The body is arched, the hind hip is pear-shaped and the front hip is spiraliform. The creature occurs, as we have seen, in insular (fig. 46) and Anglo-Carolingian art (fig. 8 *b*) and it is difficult to imagine how these motifs—the framework, the rosettes and the animals—could be found together if there were no inspiration from

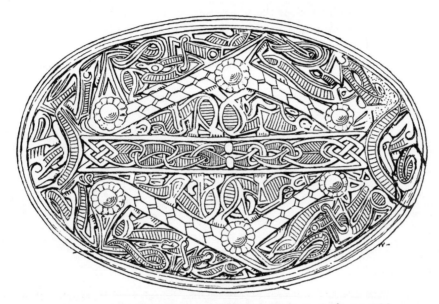

FIG. 9. Brooch from Gudhjem, Bornholm, Denmark. Scale: ⅓. *National Museum, Copenhagen*

one of these sources. The animals in the triangular fields next to the midrib are of Scandinavian form, but certain details betray foreign influences: the head has a pointed beak-like mouth (reminiscent of some sort of griffin or other fabulous beast) and the tail curves between the legs, as on the Tassilo chalice. The feet touch the frame, but, as the brooch must be dated almost at the beginning of the Viking Age, this feature may be influenced from the gripping-beast style and is not necessarily an early expression of the motif.

The area for decoration is divided up, on a number of oval brooches, by intersecting lines. The same division of the field can be seen on other objects, as, for example, on the strap mount from Stora Ihre, Gotland,[1] which is divided by a framework with holes for boss-headed rivets at the intersection of the lines. On this object the triangular corner fields contain chip-carved, stylized, foliate motifs, not unlike those on the Tassilo chalice: the remaining fields of the mount are decorated in typical Style III ornament.

[1] Arbman (1937), pl. 34, centre left.

41

The most sensitive barometer of decorative taste in the immediately pre-Viking Age is the series of flat, rectangular brooches. The development of this late Roman Iron Age form, and of the motifs which adorn the series, is so similar in south Scandinavia and Norway that it is difficult to decide whether certain brooches found in Norway were, as has been suggested, imported from south Scandinavia, or whether they were made by Norwegian craftsmen. The motif most commonly found on these brooches is the carefully drawn ribbon-like animal of Style D, which, sometimes with geometrical overtones, curves gracefully over the whole surface of the brooch.

On certain larger rectangular brooches the field is also divided by a framework with boss-headed rivets where the lines intersect. Some of these brooches, like that from Bækkegård, Bornholm (fig. 10), exhibit rather odd features. The edges of this brooch

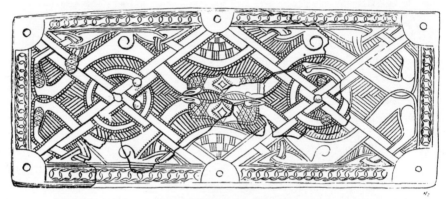

FIG. 10. Reconstructed ornament of a rectangular brooch from Bækkegård, Bornholm, Denmark. Scale ⅔. *National Museum, Copenhagen.*

are flanged, while the rivets, by which the catch-plate and pin were attached, interfere slightly with the ornament, although an attempt has been made to disguise this fact by further engraving; it is possible, therefore, that this object was not originally intended as a brooch—it may, for example, have been mounted on a box. The object is damaged and the boss-headed rivets are missing, but, as the decoration is symmetrical, it is not difficult to reconstruct the whole design.[1]

The surface of the brooch is divided up by quadripartite transverse bands, which form a central lozenge. Circles interlace with the dividing lines at the intersections and a pair of semicircles are added in the centre of each long side. The brooch originally depicted four slight animals with their heads towards the centre; the space between the animals and the dividing lines was filled with hatching and the whole is bordered by a developed ring-chain pattern.

The Bækkegård brooch is not of the highest quality—indeed few objects found in this cemetery are—but it forms an interesting starting point for a discussion of the style

[1] Arwidsson (1942a), 35; Forssander (1943), 226 ff. and Arbman (1956), 100 ff. are among those who have discussed this object.

it exhibits. The composition is carefully worked out; indeed the actual animal ornament appears to be secondary to the framework—the foreleg, for example, becoming part of the dividing framework.

The division of the surface of a rectangular field in this manner is a typical feature of both insular and Anglo-Carolingian ornament,[1] while the border motif is a simplified version of an insular ring-chain pattern already known in Scandinavia.[2] The lightly engraved linear ornament together with the slight body of the metal of the Bækkegård brooch are reminiscent of a group of smallish oval brooches, some of which are found on Bornholm. They bear a debased basket-work hatching and the field is divided by semicircles.[3] Although these objects are undoubtedly indigenous, certain ornamental details may have a foreign origin. Similarly, a small cylindrical metal box from the cemetery at Nørre Sandegård, not far from Bækkegård, has Anglo-Saxon parallels and is decorated with hatching like that found on the Bækkegård brooch.[4]

The animals of the Bækkegård brooch are related to, but quite distinct from, those found on certain oval brooches. The closest parallel is provided by the brooch illustrated in fig. 9, for here are creatures with double-looped legs—a detail so odd that it must be derived from a common source. The form of the animal, like the framework,

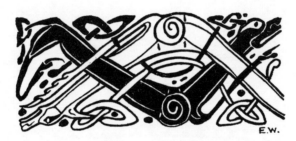

FIG. 11. Detail of fol. 1r. of the MacRegol Gospels.
Bodleian Library, Oxford.

has purely insular prototypes; similar animals occur, for example, in the MacRegol Gospels (fig. 11) and it is further noteworthy that there are triquetra motifs in the MacRegol animal frieze in approximately the same position as those on the Bækkegård brooch. Although the broken hatching of the brooch can be paralleled in Scandinavia,[5] more numerous and satisfactory parallels occur in insular contexts (fig. 12). Hatching of this form occurs, at a much earlier date, on the sixth century Torslunda dies, but merely as a method of representing clothing (pl. III *a*), and not, as in Celtic contexts, as a frame to emphasize the figures.

The fragmentary and much worn rectangular brooch from Råbylille, Møen (pl. v *a*) is unique. The surface is divided, by a number of overlapping circles, into a series of

[1] Cf. Forssander (1943), 228.
[2] It is more clearly to be seen on the Svejstrup example, Arbman (1937), pl. 44.
[3] This material will be published in a monograph by Ole Klindt-Jensen.
[4] Becker (1953), 146.　　　　　　　　　[5] Arbman (1937), fig. 26, centre.

concave-sided squares filled with animal ornament, similar to that found in Anglo-Carolingian contexts (fig. 13). The animal head is in the centre of the field and there is a leg in each corner, the hips form an open spiral and the curved body fits into the remaining space.

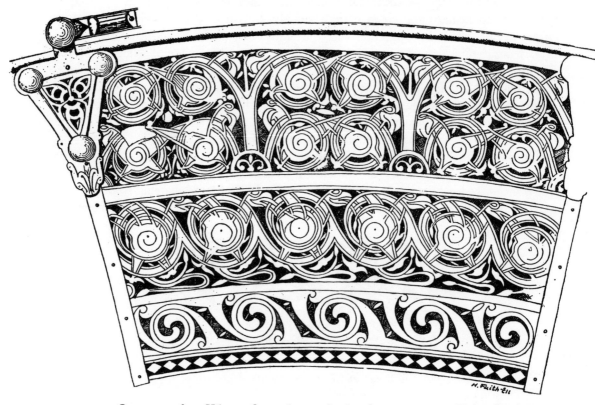

FIG. 12. Ornament of an Hiberno-Saxon bronze bucket from grave 507, Birka, Sweden. *Statens Historiska Museum, Stockholm.*

The largest and most elegant rectangular brooch comes from Skabersjö in the Swedish province of Skåne (pl. IV a). Its perfect, symmetrical design has caused it to be compared to the illuminations of the Lindisfarne Gospels.[1] The ornament is executed in sharply faceted chip-carving which varies in depth. Professor Arbman has argued that, both in technical detail and in design, the Skabersjö brooch is reminiscent of insular art; he has further suggested[2] that the design is based on that of an insular book cover and has drawn attention to the unusual panels of interlace in the border and the cruciform basis of the design (fig. 14). Despite the fact that most of its ornament consists of Style D animals and that in the centre of the cross is a naturalistic bird, there is an obvious Christian prototype behind the Skabersjö brooch.

[1] Forssander (1943), 188 f.   [2] Arbman (1956), 93; cf. Arwidsson (1942 a), 35.

A certain amount of Christian symbolism is seen elsewhere in this art. A cruciform mount need not necessarily have a Christian derivation. The shape may merely be functional or ornamental—it is a convenient form, for example, for a strap-distributor. There can, however, be little doubt of the origin in a Christian context of the design of the mount from grave 13 at Valsgärde, illustrated in pl. v*b*. The cross, with its curved arms and terminals, is of a form well known in Christian art.[1] The carved animals in the arms are reminiscent of forms found on the Tassilo chalice (fig. 8*b*).

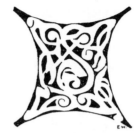

FIG. 13. Animal ornament from a brooch from Råbylille, Møen, Denmark. Pl. v *a*. Scale: ¼. *National Museum, Copenhagen.*

Indications such as those quoted above show that there was a considerable western European influence in the eighth century art of Scandinavia. Certain motifs, such as basket-work hatching, were almost certainly introduced into Scandinavia directly from the British Isles, while other motifs—the animal on the mount from grave 13 at Valsgärde, for example—seem to indicate influence from the Anglo-Carolingian areas of the Continent. On balance it would seem that in the immediately pre-Viking period, Anglo-Carolingian elements were more influential than insular elements in Scandinavian art, although the latter were certainly present. One point emerges from this discussion: namely the fact that, where foreign motifs do occur in Scandinavian ornament, they were quickly adapted to fit the indigenous Scandinavian art.

We have traced here the parallel development of naturalistic and decorative art and have attempted to show how naturalism introduced new motifs into the different styles. Thus the chief motif of Style C—the horse—and one of the motifs connected with Style D—the animal seen from above gripping snakes— are derived from naturalistic art and are at odds with the abstract tendencies which otherwise dominate the early decorative art of Scandinavia.

At the same time, however, it is clear that naturalistic art was not untouched by the development of the various styles of decorative art, the result of this influence can be observed in certain details and simplifications. This can best be seen on the Swedish helmets of the Vendel period and on the picture stones of Gotland.

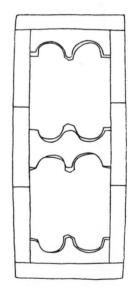

FIG. 14. The division the field on the Skabersjö brooch (see pl. IV *a*). Scale: ½.

As early as the sixth century a number of richly decorated metal helmets are found in Swedish graves. They are decorated with bronze panels pressed out on a die and, in one instance (from Torslunda, on the island of Öland), a group of dies have themselves been recovered (pl. III *a*). The carefully composed and balanced scene of a man between

[1] Haseloff (1951), pl. 11, 6.

two bears, which can be seen on one of the Torslunda dies, is not unlike that which occurs on the Bornholm object illustrated in fig. 5. This motif has a long history—its prototypes being found far back in Celtic, Roman and Germanic art. The scene has dramatic tension; the man sticks one bear with his sword and defends himself against the other with a dagger. The skin of the bear and the man's hair are clearly shown, the man's clothes are, as we have noted above, represented in a basket-work pattern. A possibly significant feature, in relationship to motifs like that illustrated in pl. VIII and to the gripping-beast motif of the early Viking Age, is the manner in which the paws of each bear grasp the man.

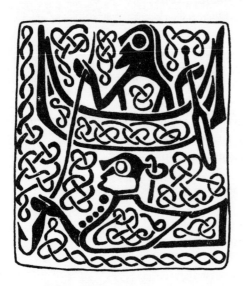

FIG. 15. Ornament of a mount from Solberga, Östergötland, Sweden. Scale: ⅓. *Statens Historiska Museum, Stockholm.*

The mount from Solberga in central Sweden (fig. 15) bears a more stylized ornament; closely packed interlace frames the scene of a man fishing from a boat. A mermaid-like creature grips the hook below the boat. Both the figures and the boat are drawn with a single, sharp line (only the upper half of the man is shown) and the two heads are stylized—a feature demonstrated by the line running from the nose to the dominant eye. A certain amount of naturalism—hands, oar and fishing hook—is, however, present. This object was found in association with a number of mounts decorated with Style II animals (in this case presumably an Östergötland variant of Style C).[1]

Other slightly stylized representations of animals—horses, deer and swine—also occur in this period[2] and demonstrate the artist's appreciation of the decorative potential of such motifs.

The picture stones of Gotland reveal a most fascinating art. Although geometric designs were a considerable element in their ornamental repertoire from an early date, naturalism dominates their art.

Sune Lindqvist has listed two-hundred and fifty stones,[3] many in excellent condition, and this must be but a small fraction of their original number. Traces of colour found on the stones indicate that they were originally painted. This fact (as Lindqvist has shown) hinders any final interpretation of their ornament; for, not only are the colours now missing, but, apart from the clearly carved major scenes, much of the surface of many of the stones is covered by fine, scratched lines. It is consequently difficult to tell

[1] Olsén (1945), 109, figs. 87–97 and 339. [2] Ibid., 109, fig. 98.
[3] Lindqvist (1941) and (1955).

what was the final design, which were the rejected sketches, and which scenes were emphasized or obscured by paint, for there can be a number of possible interpretations of some of the more complicated—or more badly preserved—scenes.[1]

Some of the stones can be roughly dated by means of motifs which fall within a well-dated decorative series, but the patterns on others are of the sort which have a fairly long life. The earliest group (probably to be dated to between the fifth and seventh centuries) comprises stones with almost straight sides, which expand slightly towards the convex top. They are decorated chiefly with geometrical patterns, some of which—the whirl pattern, for example—indicate a relationship to Celtic art. Other motifs—ships, riders, warriors, horses, fabulous beasts etc.—also occur and are scattered over the whole surface without forming any recognizable scene (pl. v c). The general effect is elegant and restrained.

A later series of Gotlandic picture stones take the form of large mushroom-shaped slabs; the scenes are placed horizontally across the field of decoration, while interlaced ribbons, of a type encountered on pre-Viking and Viking metalwork, frame the stone and divide the scenes (pl. xxvi). The stones clearly tell of dramatic happenings. Particularly common are scenes of a ship sailing across stylized waves, of a battle, or of a warrior returning home on his horse to be greeted by a woman holding a drinking horn. The actual heroic stories behind these scenes can be imagined, but the identity of the actors is lost forever.

Although certain details may have been introduced from foreign sources, this is an indigenous art. The stones reflect the art of the helmets and the Solberga plate: it is an art executed on a grander scale, but it is the same art, and one which bears witness to the fertile imagination of the artist and to the wealth of material which was at his disposal in the immediately pre-Viking era. These stones bring us into the Viking period itself and will be discussed more fully in the following chapter.

We have shown in this introductory chapter the rise of the naturalistic and decorative art which forms the background to Viking art. We have demonstrated the strong tradition of its animal ornament and its continual contact with other, related regions. We have seen the indigenous style of Scandinavia grow stronger until, towards the end of the eighth century, we stand on the threshold of a new period—the Viking Age. The art styles of the earlier periods—Styles C, D and E—were the ones out of which Viking art grew.

[1] Cf. Hauck (1957), 354; Arrhenius and Holmqvist (1960), 173.

CHAPTER II

THE EARLIEST VIKING STYLES

The surviving art of the early Viking Age exhibits a brilliancy, originality and competence, hard to equal in contemporary Europe and, while it is impossible to speak with any accuracy of the chronology of the period through lack of pieces documented by history or numismatics, one may, by using the methods of the prehistoric archaeologist, set this rich material in a tentative evolutionary sequence within the first half of the ninth century. The conclusions reached by such methods are based on commonly associated typological traits, which can be related to material—both earlier and later—which has been dated by various means.

The kaleidoscopic quality of this art, which might almost be interpreted as the development of a single style in the course of a generation, is demonstrated by the greatest of all Viking Age discoveries—the Oseberg ship burial. Finds of smaller objects, however, like the gilt-bronze mounts from Broa on the Swedish island of Gotland, demonstrate beyond question the high quality and varied character of the art of this period.

No Scandinavian archaeological find can rival in scope and opulence the Oseberg find. Among the furnishings of this Norwegian royal burial were found a group of wooden carvings—on the prow of the ship itself, on a cart, on a number of sledges and on other objects and utensils—which are of the highest quality. The motifs are varied. Distinctive and wholly original works of art occur alongside objects decorated with bizarre imagination; not every piece is completely successful, but each one witnesses to the catholic and sometimes eccentric taste of the owner.

Unfortunately this grave, like so many other large mounds of this period, was plundered in antiquity. A few small finds, however, indicate that metal objects of the same high quality as the wooden sculpture, were also buried with the ship.

The Oseberg grave, which was found and carefully excavated in 1904, was situated on the west coast of the Oslo Fjord, near the modern town of Tönsberg. A mound, twenty feet (6½ m.) high and about a hundred-and-thirty feet (about 40 m.) long, covered a ship, in the centre of which was a wooden chamber containing the funerary accoutrements of a high-born lady, who has (not unjustifiably) been identified as a queen. She was accompanied in the grave by another woman. Each body lay on a bed, furnished with eiderdowns, quilts and pillows; the chamber was surrounded by tapestries, and contained chests filled with various objects, an ornamental bucket and two looms.

In and around the prow of the ship were found the skeletons of fourteen horses, three dogs and an ox which, possibly with the slave-woman in the chamber, were obviously sacrificed for the funeral. In the stern of the boat stood a four-wheeled cart, four sledges (three of them beautifully carved), three beds, two tents, plates for tablet weaving, a small chair and various shipboard items, such as a baler, an anchor and a gangplank.

These items, which are now in the Viking Ships Museum at Oslo, are an object of pilgrimage to student and tourist alike. To the student they are probably best known from the masterly publication of the find by Haakon Shetelig, one of the excavators of the ship. The third volume of his book, with its detailed treatment of the art of the Oseberg masters, forms the basis of all subsequent studies of Viking art.[1] Shetelig gave personality to the individual Oseberg craftsmen and, in our treatment of the art of this find, the present authors owe a great debt to Shetelig's insight into its artistic intricacies. It should be said, however, that in this book we cannot accept some of the arguments—particularly with regard to chronology—put forward by Shetelig forty years ago.

The most remarkable object found in the grave was, of course, the ship, with its matchless carvings on the prow and stern-post. The boat itself is a well-found, if rather clumsy, craft: somewhat low and beamy in its lines, it is a monument to the undoubted superiority of the Viking ship-builder. Clinker-built of oak, it is some sixty-six feet (21·44 m.) long and, although equipped with mast and sail, has rowlocks for thirty oarsmen. It was presumably the private boat of a wealthy family—used in the fiords and in coastwise traffic—and its extravagant carvings express the owner's passion for ornament. There can have been few boats like this.

The posts at stem and stern curve gracefully above the body of the ship, the prow terminating in a spiral snake (reconstructed in pl. VI). Above the water-line each face of the flat-sided, curved posts is carved with a frieze of contorted and interlaced animal patterns. The animals are reserved against a sunken background and their bodies are articulated by the use of criss-crossed lines, zigzags, etc., as surface decoration (pl. VII). The body of each animal approximates to the form of a figure-of-eight, from which emerge the head and limbs, as well as certain semi-foliate offshoots. Superficially the animals seem to be identical, but only the general composition is standardized. No two animals are the same, each one differs in its intricacy.

The head of each animal is seen in profile, it has a large eye, a pigtail, an open mouth and a long neck. As the body swells it opens into two heart-shaped holes which produce offshoots from the internal angle. The limbs are bent and have no organic meaning—they are more like accidental appendages—and tend to clasp the frame which encloses the ornament. The animals fit perfectly into the long, narrow field. But they are more than just clever decoration; they make a strong visual impact, for the contours of the animals and the decoration of their bodies give character to the flat relief as they stand out against the deeply-carved background. The sculptor obviously had a strong sense of plastic effect, but his work was based on Style E, which was, as far as it survives, very much a two-dimensional style. Within the discipline of the basic design the sculptor of

[1] Shetelig (1920), iii.

49

the ship achieved a three-dimensional freedom of a kind that we have not encountered previously in Scandinavian art.

The artist of the prow and stern-post was also responsible for the ornament of the cross-pieces inside the prow. Here the motifs used by the sculptor differ strangely. The two animals at the bottom-right and the bottom-left of the so-called *tingl* (pl. VIII) and the two animals on the lowest cross-piece have the same sort of body as that which occurs on the stem and stern-posts, but the head is seen *en face*. The upper three animals on the *tingl* are classic gripping-beasts with round heads, small mouths, gross noses, popping eyes, pigtails and beards—one animal apparently has a pair of horns (unless they too can be interpreted as pigtails). This type of animal is more realistic than the rather abstract figures of the stem and stern-posts: their limbs are spindly, while the thighs and biceps are accentuated by almost pear-shaped panels, filled with the same varying types of cross-hatching and pelleting that occur on the prow and stern-posts. They grip each other with their hands and feet, forming motifs which are known, for obvious reasons, as gripping-beasts. These creatures normally have a slim waist, a head *en face* and limbs which grip the nearest frame, body or leg. These strange animals belong to an entirely different menagerie to those on the two main posts of the ship. Similar ornament is found inside the top of the stem. The sides of the stem at this place are decorated with ornament of the kind found in the long friezes of the stem (fig. 16), but inside the prow there are three anthropomorphic creatures with gripping tendencies. Two of these creatures have beards, while the lower one has a pigtail; they look like thoughtful, elderly men and have a slightly comic aspect.

It is clear that the same artist was responsible for these two entirely different motifs. It is, however, impossible to say whether this sculptor was the first man to develop the gripping-beast. He seems to have been more accustomed to the early, flat style and later came under the influence of the new, more plastic motifs.

Scholars have canvassed the influence of foreign prototypes on the carving of the rhythmic chain of flat, interlaced animals on the stem and stern-posts of the ship. Many students, especially Forssander, have compared the ornament of the prow and the stern-post with Hiberno-Saxon motifs.[1] It seems more likely, however, that similarities between the two schools of ornament are the result of a parallel artistic development, of the sort which might be expected when we consider the common origin of the two interlace patterns.[2] There is nothing of the ship artist's fertile eclecticism in the surviving foreign work. There is, however, an indigenous tradition of animal ornament in Scandinavia itself and this forms a natural source for the animals of the frieze. Although the Oseberg artist may have used the general outline of insular ornament as the basis of his designs, it was not essential for him to have done so in order to create these carvings, for all the elements could have been derived from the native art of Scandinavia.

We must now turn our attention to two other pieces of work which Shetelig—we believe mistakenly—attributed to the same artist. Firstly, let us consider the two bed-posts, the terminal of one of which is shown in fig. 17a. It takes the form of a gaping

---

[1] Forssander (1943), 229. [2] Lindqvist (1948), 19.

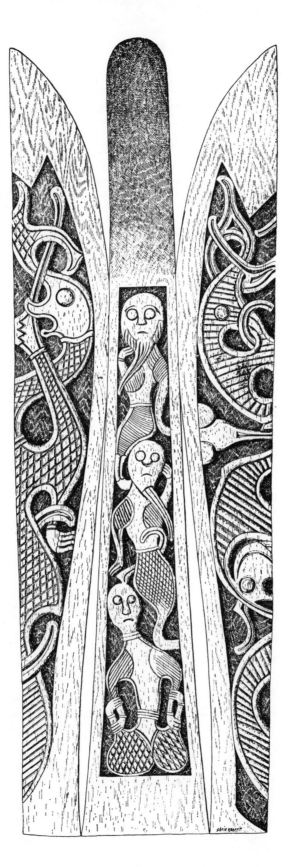

FIG. 16. Detail of
the prow of the
Oseberg ship.
*Viking Ships Mus-
eum, Oslo.*

animal-head and bears, within a triangular field, bordered by a zig zag band, the rather stylized representation of a bird. It is an elegant creature, executed in slight relief, with a fine, long neck, a small head, an imposingly curved beak and a large, round eye. The

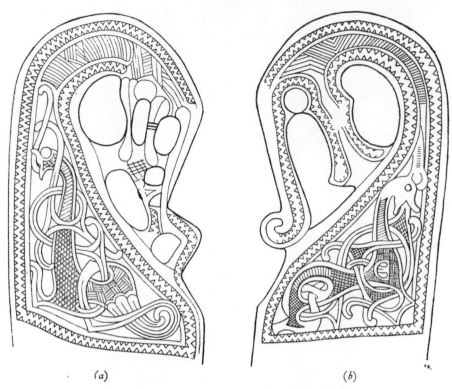

(a)   (b)

FIG. 17. The tops of two bed-posts from Oseberg. *Viking Ships Museum, Oslo.*

neck and part of the body are panelled with cross-hatching of the type seen on the prow. The wing and tail are curved in graceful loops. The creature exhibits features of Style E, although its sub-triangular shape is more reminiscent of Style C. A quadruped treated in an exactly similar fashion occurs on another bed-post (fig. 17*b*).

The bed-posts demonstrate the sure hand of a first-class sculptor and it is rather surprising that Shetelig considered that the same man carved the cart. If Shetelig is right, then this artist not only changed his style, he also changed his technique.

The separate, curved body of the oaken cart (pl. IX *a*) rests on two curved pieces of wood which terminate in semi-naturalistic human masks.[1] The four heavy wheels and the front portion of the shaft are plain, and the rear of the shaft and the front of the under-carriage are carved, partly in openwork. The richest decoration, however, occurs on the body of the cart. The planks which form the back, front and sides of this vehicle are covered with square-cut figures in relief. The greater part of this ornament

[1] Shetelig (1920), fig. 30.

is narrative, and consequently differs from the purely ornamental, stylized art so far encountered at Oseberg. It is a strange art, but it is possible to demonstrate, as Lindqvist has done,[1] the prototypes and later developments of the art.

The larger portion of the long sides of the cart are decorated with archaic animal ornament (fig. 18), immediately reminiscent in style and lay-out of the ribbon-shaped

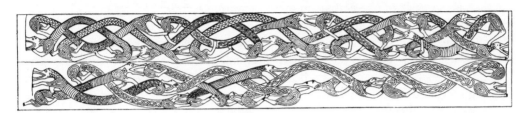

FIG. 18. Left long side of the Oseberg cart. *Viking Ships Museum, Oslo.*

animals of Style D (cf. fig. 4). Non-zoomorphic interlace of similar form fills the bodies of many of the animals of the cart, a feature which may also be derived from Style D. Distinct features, however, differentiate these motifs from Style D. The animals clasp each other in the typical gripping-beast manner, and, as with gripping-beasts, often have pear-shaped thighs. The heads, with their long jaws, are reasonably naturalistic and, although they are mostly seen in profile, a few appear as cat-like masks. Even the inserted scene (pl. x *b*) which portrays a woman, a man carrying a sword, a rider and a dog, has certain details characteristic of the gripping-beast motif.

The scenes on the boards at the back and front (pl. x *a*) of the cart are no less strange. The same snake-like creatures occur round the curved edge of the front board (save that the central animal has an openwork body of the form found on the ship). They form a frame for a group of scenes, one of which portrays a man grappling with a number of snakes and a single quadruped which are attacking him. Another scene shows a man fighting a quadruped, while the rest of the space is filled with fighting birds, animals and snakes. This is not a rational composition. The pictures are ordered in a naïve fashion, the story was obviously well known—possibly the story of Gunnar in the serpent pit—and it is remarkable that an artist, trained in a severe style, should thus break away from his traditional chains.

The ornament of the back board is even more casually laid out with snakes and animals, some with heads set in profile, some with cat-like masks. The snakes and animals grip each other, as though they were fighting.

Even though there are elements of Style D in the ribbon-shaped animals of the cart and even though the human figures have earlier prototypes in Scandinavia,[2] there are many surprising new features here. One of these new features is the cat-like mask which is reasonably naturalistic. Although these cats have certain features in common with the gripping-beasts, they are quite distinct from them.

[1] Lindqvist (1948), 21 ff.   [2] Mackeprang (1952), pl. 5, 14.

An animal like the biting quadruped in the Gunnar scene, is found, for example, on the brooch from Lousgård, grave 12, discussed above (pl. IV c). It is, therefore, of interest that the ornament of this brooch represents an animal (seen from above) fighting serpents. This creature has many features in common with the gripping-beasts of the *tingl* (pl. VIII).

Shetelig placed these three groups of carving—ship, bed-posts and waggon—together as the work of one craftsman in his definitive account of Oseberg. There seems little evidence to support such a suggestion. It is impossible to compare such widely differing objects of such widely differing quality and, when in this book we refer to the 'ship's master', we refer only to the man who made the ship and not to a person whom Shetelig imagined to have made a whole group of objects. It is occasionally possible at Oseberg to recognize different works of art by the same hand, but we do not believe this to be so in this case.

An artistic personality related to that of the ship's master, but not nearly so fascinating, is revealed in two works which clearly belong to the same group—a post in the form of an animal-head (pl. XI) and the draw-bar of Gustafson's sledge (fig. 19) (the latter so named after the director of the Oseberg excavations).

These works are remarkable for their extreme elegance, precise carving and well-conceived composition. The vigour and variety of the artist of the ship is, however, clearly missing from these pieces. The 'Academician', as Shetelig christened this craftsman, worked with a carefully thought-out, thin, rather flat motif. It is tempting to compare the craftsmanship of these objects, perhaps the most sophisticated in the find, with the work of the finest jewellers of the period, for the sculptor has produced an art as refined as theirs—an art which is at the same time free from any monumental sense, and executed in a manner equally suited to objects of any size.

Three symmetrically placed bird-like figures are set in the triangular, central field of the sledge-pole (fig. 19). They are plaited and their bodies are pierced in the manner characteristic of Style E and of the animals of the stem and stern of the ship. It is also interesting to compare them with the animal on the head of the bed-post illustrated in fig. 17*b*. There are certain similarities (particularly in the form of the heads), but the Academician, despite his attention to detail, his tendency to abstraction and the skill with which he fits the animal into the available field, produced a sterile ornament. The artist of the bed-post, however, produced a proud, bold bird, which dominates the field. Silver nails embellish the carving—a feature encountered frequently at Oseberg.

The same sure craftsman's hand fashioned a post in the form of an animal-head (pl. XI) with a well-designed, plastic, predatory mask. Its open mouth has great, bared teeth: it has a squarish snout and large eyes. The head and neck are covered, like a grotesque carved tattoo, with bird-like figures. They are the most fantastically elaborate birds imaginable (fig. 20)—a sinuous whirl of coils, each logically composed in the minutest detail. We can only marvel at the manner in which the artist has adapted the pattern to the curves of the head. The restraint of the smooth, curved neck and the simple geometrical ornament of the bottom of the post, contrast with the restless pattern of the head and accentuate the skill of the artist. This is the Academician's masterpiece.

A completely sophisticated craftsman, he worked exclusively with Style E motifs, but his mastery of naturalistic form is clearly demonstrated by the curves and outline of the animal-head.

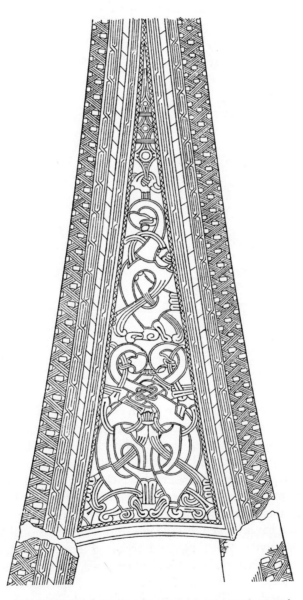

FIG. 19. Detail of the ornament of the Academician's sledge-pole from Oseberg. *Viking Ships Museum*, Oslo.

The two animal-head posts pictured in pl. XII and fig. 21 are more plastic in ornament. Despite various major ornamental differences, Shetelig identified these objects as the work of one artist—again we feel that, although this may be the case, it cannot be proved as the differences are too great. One of the posts, which is rather coarsely carved,

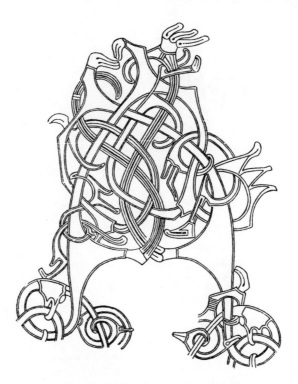

FIG. 20. Detail of the 'Academician's' animal-head post from Oseberg. *Viking Ships Museum, Oslo.*

bears on the head and on most of the neck the same motif as the Academician's post. The composition of the head itself is based on a series of strong curves and, above the heavy eyebrows, is a gripping-beast (presumably the figure of a man) clasping its own feet.[1] He has a long moustache and strange horn-like features on his forehead.

The animal-head post, the ornament of which is illustrated in fig. 21, is a more successful piece of wood-carving. The animal-head itself is ably formed, with a richly carved snout, open mouth and strong teeth. Above the staring eyes and on the crown of the head the artist has achieved, by the use of three-dimensional gripping-beasts, an illusion of seething activity. Writhing and interlacing together, each animal clings to its neighbour and tries to reach the frame of linked ovals, which can most clearly be seen on the neck (pl. XIII a). The slightly clumsy animals, despite their delicately decorated bodies, are semi-naturalistic. The triangular heads, with their great popping eyes and

[1] Shetelig (1920), fig. 67, *b.*

long ears, are seen from above. The limbs are thick-set and as firm as their grip. As on the previous post, a single animal is placed on the side of the large animal-head itself. At the bottom of the post are a series of simple quatrefoils.

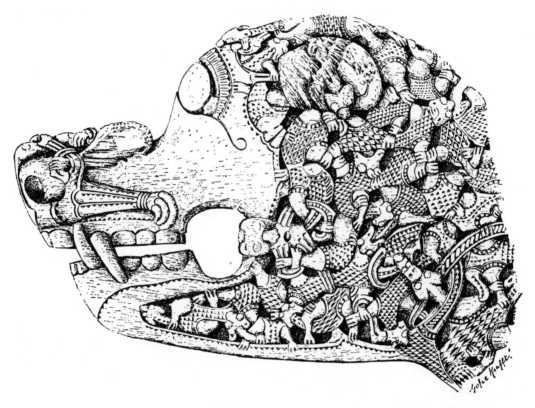

FIG. 21. Detail of the 'Carolingian' animal-head from Oseberg. *Viking Ships Museum, Oslo.*

The division of the surface into fields, which we have seen in Continental and insular contexts, is also found at Oseberg. A typical example of this occurs on the body of the sledge which bears Shetelig's name (pl. IX *b* and fig. 22). The presence of naturalistic, predatory animal-heads on the corner posts of this sledge is worthy of further investigation; as is the fact that the sledge reveals traces of paint, a new ornamental technique in this context.

The strong even curves of each animal-head portray a rapacious animal—probably a lion. The head is almost round, with a short, whiskered, pug-like snout, large flat eyes and upstanding ears. The mouth is slightly open and reveals great, canine teeth. Despite the naturalistic aspect of these heads, which would seem to indicate that the artist was familiar with this kind of animal, Shetelig[1] supposed them to be direct copies of classical

[1] (1920), 201.

lion motifs. These animals need not necessarily be lions, any feline creature would fill the bill—a cat or a lynx, for example, which would have been perfectly familiar to northern artists.

The carvings of the sides and ends of this sledge are executed on three planes—one above the other. The carving of the lowermost plane consists of vaguely discernible

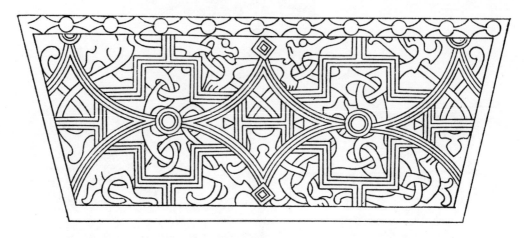

FIG. 22. Back board of Shetelig's sledge from Oseberg. *Viking Ships Museum, Oslo.*

Style E animals. The head, which has a prominent eye and curved snout, is seen in profile; it has a pigtail. The curved body, which is rather indistinct, is pierced and interlaced with limbs and ribbons. Above this is a framework of lozenges or equal-armed crosses, over which is laid a framework of conjoined, concave-sided, or plain, lozenges. Ring-and-dot motifs at the points of intersection clearly imitate silver rivets.

The effect of all this ornament is heightened by the application of paint. The background is painted black and painted lines emphasize the contours or backbone of the coiled animals. The borders of one side are decorated with dots, while the uppermost framework is embellished with contour lines which flank a line of dots. Finally the small, circular, rhomboidal and semicircular fields are prettified with black paint.

The division of the carved framework of this sledge and the similar division of the field on a number of metal objects of a rather early date (figs. 9 and 10), demonstrates the inherent probability of Shetelig's thesis that this sledge was the earliest object in the Oseberg grave. Similar divisions can be seen on a number of other objects—but in these cases the framework neither dominates the field nor encloses ornament of an especially early style. This early dating is not contradicted by the form of the three-dimensional animal-heads of the corner-posts.

A similar framework is used with great skill on the runners of another sledge—sledge 4. Here can be seen animal motifs intricately involved in rows of circles (pl. XVI *a*), although here the framework is in the same plane as the animals. The creatures of sledge

4 are closely related to Style E animals; they have the same heart-shaped openings in their bodies, the same wing-like features springing from the body and a lappet. The largest animal of this series (fig. 23) has a large, sub-triangular body with an inner contour line, features which are reminiscent of Style C; the hip, however, is accentuated by a double contour, in the manner of the gripping-beast (fig. 16). The animal has an

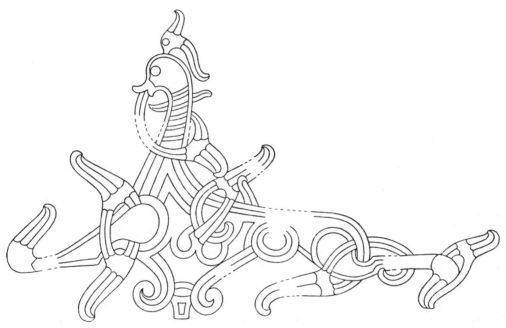

FIG. 23. Animal from the runner of the fourth sledge at Oseberg (see pl. XVI *a*). *Viking Ships Museum, Oslo.*

almost monumental quality and flaunts its idiosyncratic mixture of various styles. It has a long, elegant neck, lifted boldly above the body, and its simple head is reminiscent of the heads of the animals on the bed posts (fig. 17). On the other hand we have in this animal something which foreshadows such well-known motifs as the animal of the famous Jellinge stone (pl. XLIX).

A characteristic trick of the artist of the fourth sledge was the way in which he fitted each animal into the field available, shaping the animal in relationship to it. At the same time he was not too rigorously regimented by the shape of the field, for the form of the animals often influenced the form of the framework: the circles of this framework, for example, are not purely geometrical constructions, they have been embellished with curlicues and protuberances. The line of the belly of the large beast is broken and bifurcated to form elegant spirals which flank a small, central billet. It is clear that the semi-geometrical framework has been largely responsible for the form of the animal; the curved lines of the true animal have been subordinated to the necessity of filling the empty space. In the small, circular fields, which flank the large animal, are a series of smaller, related creatures with strangely coiled bodies.

Similar creatures occur on the hindmost panel of the sledge and on the frame built round it; here again the animals interlace with the circles and ovals which divide the field (pl. xv c). The same ornament is to be seen—but not in openwork—on the front of the sledge. The fourth sledge, in fact, exhibits some of the most elegant carving found in the Oseberg grave—well balanced, easily understood and beautifully designed, it is a most accomplished piece of work. Stylistically it is most closely connected with Style E, for it has the foliate offshoots, the double contour and the pigtails so typical of that style; at the same time such features as the clearly defined hip relate it to other styles.

Ornamental silver rivets embellish the sledge. Strangely enough the rivets do not occur in the expected place—where the circles meet and join—a feature which might indicate that they were added by a later craftsman.

One motif, which occurs in a number of places on this sledge—for example on the strut of the runner (pl. xv b)—and which is very popular throughout the Viking period, is the human mask which we have noted occasionally in earlier Scandinavian ornament. On this sledge the masks are of high quality; they have large staring eyes and a moustache which is plaited through each cheek.

In fine, although the sculptor of the fourth sledge stands by himself amongst the Oseberg masters, his style is most closely related to the sculptor of the ship. His ornament is largely the ornament of Style E, but certain traits of the gripping-beast motif can be discerned in his treatment of the heads and the hips.

Another craftsman, and one with a distinctive personality and a sense for plasticity, has been labelled by Shetelig 'the Baroque Master'. Two animal-head posts, together with two sledge poles and a smaller fragment, can be assigned to the hand of this exceptional artist. The decorative area was usually divided by oval panelling, but the ornament is not always contained by its clean lines. The artist varied his animal motifs and modified them to give the illusion of geometrical figures: his rather mischievous designs are not always easy to understand but were always most carefully planned.

The remarkable animal-head posts show his style at its best. They are of the same size and form (pl. xiv) and were apparently made as a pair. Each has a long, almost dog-like, head and both the head and long neck are covered with ornament. The mouth is open, showing strong, canine teeth; the eyes stand out and are embellished with silver plates. The ornament covers all the available surfaces and is further richly embellished with silver nails.

The ornament writhes over the neck in strong relief against a background of oval fields. Above the snout is a fabulous beast with two pairs of wings, a bird's tail, long neck and full-face head with two long ears or horns. The other creatures vary enormously. Both birds and quadrupeds are represented, they are interlaced together, distorted into strange forms, and sometimes lack body or limbs: twisting themselves in the deeper parts of the carving, their necks cross and their heads—in profile or *en face*—

bend forward to bite each other. These creatures have a dual origin in the gripping-beast motif and in Style E: the feet are derived from the latter style, while the bodies (which are rather amorphous) appear to be executed in the manner of the gripping-beasts. The lozenge-shaped billet which fills certain empty spaces on this object is a new element in Viking art and one which, as we shall show, has some significance in relationship to the later Borre style. The ornament is embellished, in a most accomplished manner, by varying types of cross-hatching, beading, engraving, etc.

The most important element in the art of the baroque master is his use of plasticity. In no earlier style is the same skilful and deep relief achieved; the heads of the animals form firm, accentuated focal points, while the bodies seem to sink and writhe in the shadows.

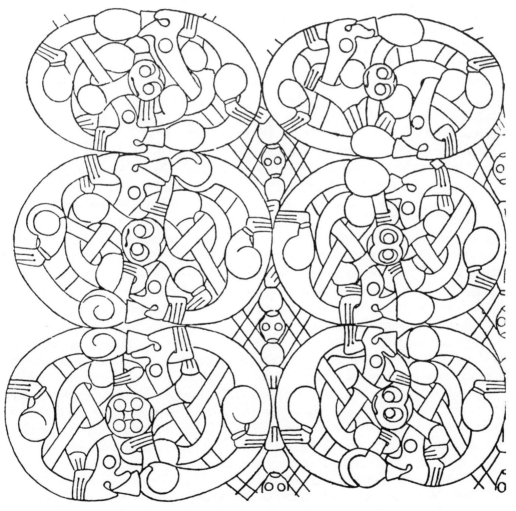

FIG. 24. Ornament of the 2nd baroque animal-head post from Oseberg. *Viking Ships Museum, Oslo.*

The same generalization is true of the other animal-head post which is covered with ribbon-like animals. The series of oval frames on the neck (fig. 24) are so deeply carved that the animals sometimes appear in the round and the light, shining through the openings, gives a fantastic, flickering quality to the ornament. Some of the limbs and bodies spring from strange, raised heads, with large staring eyes, in the centre of the oval fields. Each oval consists of two animals, skilfully articulated with each other and interspaced with masks and odd limbs.

The composition is fertile almost beyond imagination, for the artist has disregarded the conventional animal patterns to achieve his effect. The staring heads (in the centre of the oval fields) have two bodies, each with one front leg and one elongated, straight hind-leg. Further they have two lappets which, turning downwards, interlace with those of the animals forming the oval to become the deepest element of the interlace. The animals which form the oval frames are ribbon-shaped and their heads are seen in profile; the foreleg has a clearly defined hip and the foot, with its long toes, touches the outermost contour of the body. The rear foot grips the neck of the animal opposite and the rear hip is spiraliform.

Two other pieces of the same high quality, probably made by the same artist, were found in the grave, these are two brilliantly carved sledge-poles. On these objects a more complete balance between the general design and the ornamental detail is achieved.

It is perhaps characteristic of the Baroque Master's genius that he changed the normal form of the sledge-pole to give it a fine curve, while the Academician retained the usual straight form. He lengthened the lower, forked portion of the pole and decorated its curved sides with carving, in which the motif and the framework interlock in emphatic relief.

The animals move freely within and across a series of conjoined ovals (fig. 25), which form a frame for the ornament, accentuating, rather than confining, the liveliness of the creatures. The ovals are an integral part of the pattern, the contours split and form unusual interlaced designs and the animals are fantastically distorted. It is extraordinary that such a complicated mass of animals and ovals should form a strongly effective unity and achieve such a tightly balanced harmony.

On one of the poles—the damaged one (fig. 26)—two significant types of animal stand out. One of these (fig. 26, *right*) has an almost ribbon-shaped body and a strange, elongated head set in profile, a large eye, a plaited pigtail and accentuated legs and tail. It has spiral hips and the leg, tail and offshoots are twisted into three-dimensional knots. The animal itself, with its double contour, is derived from Style E; but the finely patterned treatment of the surface is a characterictic feature of Oseberg decoration. Many of these animals become involved in each other, their necks cross and—a typical trait of this sculptor—one creature frequently bites another at the neck.

The second type of animal (fig. 26, *left*) is a tailed quadruped with a mask-like face and a pigtail: its limbs become involved in an intricate plaitwork of limbs and in a less well-defined type of offshoot. These animals also hark back to Style E, but the carving

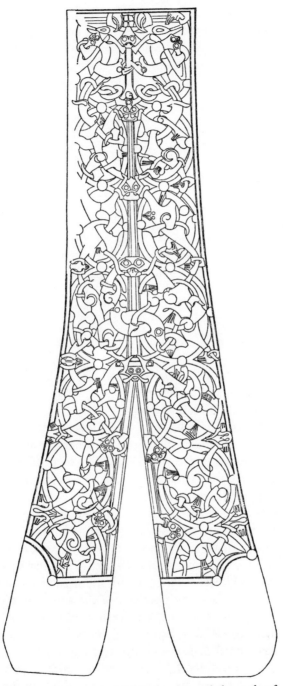

FIG. 25. Ornament of the fragmentary sledge pole of
the 'baroque master' from Oseberg. *Viking Ships
Museum, Oslo.*

is tighter—almost knotted—the animal is seen *en face* and the figure is accentuated by finely carved relief. The long toes touch the contours and, if they are not true gripping-beasts, there is a strong element of this design in their make-up. A characteristic feature of both animals is the double contour—a feature also encountered in the later Mammen style (pl. XLIX).

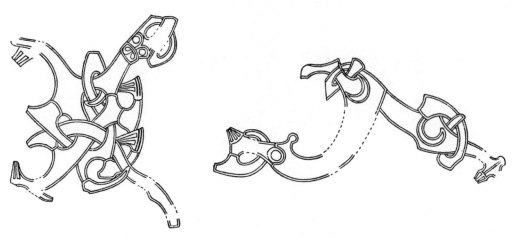

FIG. 26. Two animals from the fragmentary sledge-pole from Oseberg. *Viking Ships Museum, Oslo.*

The overall effect given by this pole is one of linear mobility—the ever-changing form and position of the animal bodies being disciplined by the clear rhythm of the ovals, which are at once a division and a link.

The other sledge-pole—the complete one—is no less outstanding in quality (pl. XV *a*). The fork-like portion is decorated with animal ornament, which springs from a complicated pattern of interwoven and contorted animals to produce two double rows of ovals, filled with complemented animal ornament, one on each member of the fork.

The rhythm of the pattern is more noticeable on this pole than on the damaged one. The animals in each row are different, if only slightly so, but they interlock bravely with each other. Each oval in the uppermost row (innermost in fig. 27) contains a single animal. This creature has a strong diagonal axis; the head, neck and back-leg pass across the field to link up with a similar axis in the diagonally opposed oval. This continuous pattern of parallel, diagonal lines, combined with the regularly placed oval fields, gives a surprising discipline to the fantastic plasticity of the animal design.

There are two main types of animal, one with a head in profile (fig. 28), sharply defined limbs and foliate-formed feet, lappet and epaulette. The other, in the uppermost row, is similar, but has a head *en face* and one gripping foot. The limbs and necks of both animals are long and carefully delineated and the bodies are without emphasis.

The carving at the point where the two members of the fork join is subordinated to the overall composition. Portions of animals, masks, heads in profile, loops and broad ribbons, cover the field. The terminal mask has small teeth and large, pear-shaped,

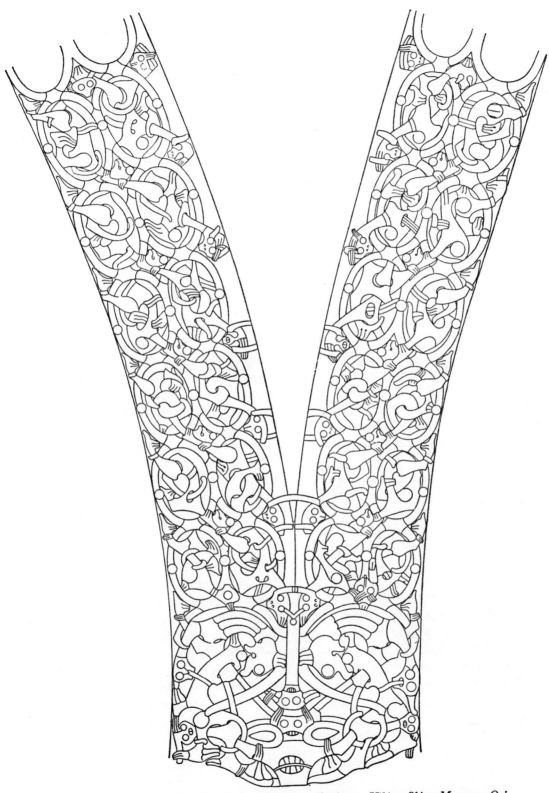

FIG. 27. Ornament of the complete sledge-pole from Oseberg. *Viking Ships Museum, Oslo.*

double-contoured eyes. From the eye-brows spring two curved animal bodies which terminate in animal-heads, seen in profile with large eyes, beak-like snout, lappet and curved mouth.

A detailed examination would suggest that one master produced these two animal-head posts and the sledge-poles. He demonstrates to us the artist's skill in using old

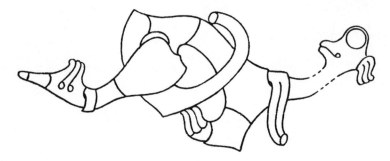

FIG. 28. Animal from the complete sledge-pole from Oseberg.
Viking Ships Museum, Oslo.

motifs, inventing new ones and combining them together. The artist was familiar with the gripping-beast motif, but he used its elements sparingly: the compact, rounded body, the sense of plasticity and the gripping paw of this creature was skilfully grafted on to an animal of Style E. The animals bite each other, their necks cross and the whole composition is made more compact. The artist used masks and even fashioned knot patterns, but his special trick was the division and sub-division of an area into small lozenges.

This was no narrowly limited artist, he drew on many motifs and, in fact, developed a new style: his work demonstrates the potential achievement of any Viking artist. In his products we may catch a glimpse of the artist's genius in adapting many combinations of motif and composition into a form which would influence the next generation of sculptors. We also gain an impression of the achievement of an original and capable indigenous artist; for, even in applied art, style is influenced by the personality of the artist. A style is not created simply by combining two stylistic elements on the same object, it is born out of the creative perception of the artist. An artist like the Baroque Master had a range which extended over the theoretical boundaries of what is labelled 'style'. This is confusing to scholars for typological dating falls down and Lindqvist[1] argues that the Baroque Master is contemporary with the Ship Master, while Shetelig[2] argues that he is the leader of a group of later sculptors.

Shetelig christened one of these later artists, 'the Careful Eclectic'. This man's work can clearly be seen on two objects—on the undercarriage and runners of Shetelig's sledge and on the body of Gustafson's sledge. His style is clearly related to that of both the Ship Master and the Baroque Master, but he never achieved the quality and origin-

[1] (1948), 16.   [2] Shetelig (1920), 151.

ality of these artists; he borrowed motifs and his slightly ham-fisted manner is evident in a number of places. The triangular fields at the point where the struts emerge from the runners of Shetelig's sledge (fig. 29) contain strange anthropomorphic figures. The double-contoured limbs are separated from the body in a manner which has been encountered elsewhere in Oseberg and which is reminiscent of the gripping-beast motif.

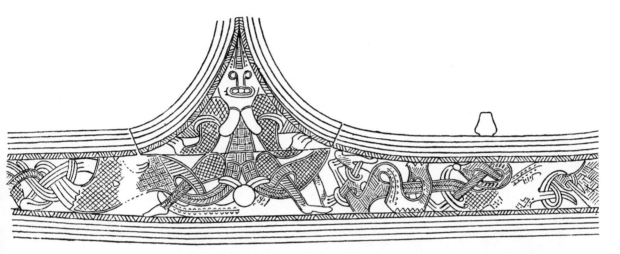

FIG. 29. Part of the runner of the sledge of the 'eclectic master' at Oseberg (Shetelig's sledge). *Viking Ships Museum, Oslo.*

They have a pigtail and their forked beards curl round their outstretched arms; the legs are splayed, as though to indicate a sitting position. The figures are involved in Style E coils which emerge from the body and interlace with it. The whole motif is a mixture of naturalism (cf. the feet) and bizarre impressionism. The rest of the field is filled, in an apparently casual manner, by loops and a number of undoubted, if rather odd, animal motifs. The bodies of the animals are hatched with various patterns—basket-work, criss-cross lines, etc.—of a type encountered on the Bækkegård plate (fig. 10) and the Torslunda dies (pl. III *a*). The human figure and the separate mask, which occur on the sledge, are found elsewhere in the Oseberg series and are clearly traditional motifs which have been only slightly modified in this context.

The animal-head posts at the four corners of the other sledge (pl. XVI *b and c*) are the most accomplished pieces of ornament in the whole group. Animal ornament, mostly in the form of Style E birds, enlivens the dog-like mask of each post and the neck is covered with animal patterns interlaced in ovals.

The 'Baroque Impressionist', who made the body of the fourth sledge (pl. XV *b*), is undoubtedly a more interesting artist. The decoration of this object (fig. 30), which is carved in deep relief, is elegant and varied. A criss-cross lattice-work divides each side, to form a framework through which another pattern twists. This underlying pattern is only superficially zoomorphic and, although it has elements of Style E, the ornament itself consists of dismembered animal bodies and not of whole creatures. It seems to be made up of figure-of-eight-like creatures set in irregular coils, with a limb or a head casually inserted for effect. It is clear that the artist envisaged the whole design without reference to the organic meaning of the motifs he was using. There is a mercurial restlessness about the sure composition of these panels and the flowing curves of the design

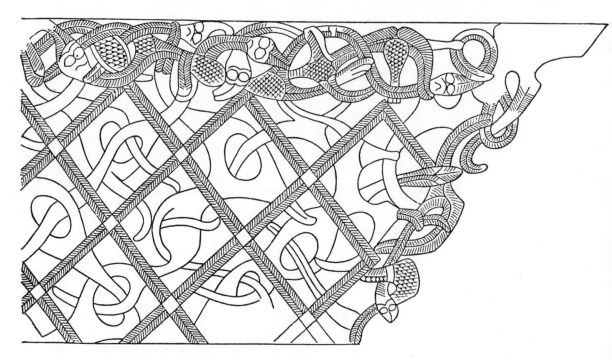

FIG. 30. Ornament of the 'baroque impressionist's' sledge from Oseberg. *Viking Ships Museum, Oslo.*

are accentuated by the simple dividing framework. We have seen that, in most cases, heads and limbs have no true relationship to any complete animal. On the only occasion on which a fully articulated animal was attempted, it became completely grotesque and one can only interpret it as the product of a craftsman who wished to poke fun at his colleagues' pedantry.

The corner posts terminate in animal-heads (pl. XVI *b-c*), and are carved in the same manner as the rest of the sledge. Each neck is covered with tightly packed oval frames inset with heads and limbs which seldom have organic sense. The semi-zoomorphic motifs curl in and out of the oval medallions in a fashion far from naturalistic and are embellished with strange spirals and knots. The terminal animal heads are of rather exaggerated form, having strong canine teeth and great staring eyes; an almost complete animal figure, like others elsewhere on the post, is carved on the snout. This animal is the artist's most completely developed motif and is clearly borrowed from the parallel ornament on the post illustrated in pl. XII.

If it were not for the brilliant technical ability of this artist, which is especially apparent when his work is seen from some distance, it would be easy to be irritated by his devil-may-care attitude—but the fact that his style is original makes one, perhaps, a little more charitable.

Before discussing the wood sculpture of Oseberg as a whole, we must turn our attention to certain animal heads carved from flat planks of wood. The terminals of tent-posts and bed-posts are executed in this technique, but they are, despite their different effect, executed in the same spirit as the plastic animal heads. They are clearly of the same genus.

The flat animal-headed bed-posts from Oseberg (pl. XVII) indicate this relationship clearly. They have the same, almost round head with large eye, the same half-open mouth, strong canine teeth and long tongue; a pigtail issues from the crown of the head and the ears lie alongside it. The head is bent (on the tent-posts it is straight). The upper jaw is remarkably long. The pigtail forms a loop on the neck and the head and eye are accentuated by a double contour.

Such heads as these enable us to understand some of the stylistic features of the Gokstad find. Only a few decorated pieces were found in the boat burial at Gokstad, not far from Oseberg, in Norway; among these were tent-poles and bed-posts with animal-heads carved at the terminals of flat planks.

The Gokstad heads (pl. XVIII) are similar to those from Oseberg, but it is noticeable that the pointed ears are much larger and stick straight up from the crown of the head. The eyebrow, which like other parts of the object is painted, forms an impressive curve and the upper jaw is disproportionally long. Each jaw has great canine teeth which would not have engaged if the mouth were closed. A particularly important trait is the form of the snout with its clearly defined lip-lappet curving above the nostrils, for this is the first occurrence of this feature; it is not found at Oseberg. The lip-lappet is a clear indication of a late date for the Gokstad sculptures and must be seen as a precursor of the lip-lappet so common in the later Jellinge style.

At the same time the scratched scene on an oval lid from Gokstad,[1] which shows a running horse and dog, portrayed with elegant economy of line (pl. XIX b), demonstrates the unbroken indigenous artistic tradition, for this naturalistic scene is closely related to the figures which inspired Style C.

If we look at the assembled corpus of Oseberg sculpture we receive, first and foremost, an impression of a group of most competent craftsmen who appear to be creating a new art; as they experiment with their art they influence each other. It is clear that they form a group of strongly individual personalities, working with different stylistic elements at roughly the same time. It is possible that at Oseberg we have the products of a single generation of artists. The earliest object in the find is undoubtedly the body of Shetelig's sledge (which shows clear traces of the Scandinavian style of framework, influenced ultimately from Anglo-Continental sources, and containing Style E animals) but it would be difficult to arrange the other objects in a chronological sequence.

[1] Hinsch (1958), suggested that it was from a game basket.

Generally speaking, the artists were but little influenced by outside ideas (one of the few examples of foreign influence is the sub-division of the field of ornament by a framework). The artist's work is the product of his own taste; the common forms of Styles C, D and E are combined and given a new form. Thus, the large animal with triangular body of Style C develops the openwork characteristics and leaf-like offshoots of Style E. Gripping-beasts were produced by experiment and developed in the round.

One cannot, therefore, with any degree of confidence, arrange the different Oseberg objects in direct relationship to each other; they simply bear witness to a strange and yet rich period of artistic activity in the first half of the ninth century. It is noteworthy that certain objects (e.g. the ship), which one would like to attribute to an older phase, show little signs of wear, while others (like the Academician's animal-head post) are much worn. This is, however, hardly a valid basis for judgment; some objects need not have been used very often, while others may have been in daily use. The Master of the ship, particularly, was very receptive to, and knowledgeable about, the art of the period, for he used traditional animal forms alongside the new-fangled gripping-beast motif. This particular artist used a considerable amount of the Oseberg artistic repertoire; in his work we may see the smooth transitions between the various styles and the co-existence of stylistic features which, if we were to judge them in vacuo, would have to be placed in a chronological progression. We do not know the age of this artist, we will never be able to say whether he was a young innovator or a tradition-bound, but brilliant, survivor of an older group of artists. The methods of prehistoric archaeology cannot set in chronological progression the products of a single man.

A similar interpretation of stylistic development must be applied to a Swedish find of metal objects from Broa on the island of Gotland.[1] In richness of detail and in competence of production the objects in this find are no less impressive, in their smaller scale, than the products of the Oseberg sculptors. They form the mounts of a bridle and were found together with a bit, a sword hilt, the small amber bridge of a stringed instrument and several other objects. The artist of these bronze pieces, like the Oseberg artists, used many varied motifs alongside each other, but his ornament was always disciplined by a geometrical framework which was used both to divide the composition and to clarify the motifs. The animal ornament is either contained within a single field or passes from one field to another, sometimes it appears as though the animals are seen through window-like openings in the surface of the metal. This is a particularly Gotlandic refinement, which is only occasionally encountered elsewhere.

The Broa master frequently introduced animal masks in low relief into his ornamental scheme. It has been suggested[2] that these masks portray lions, whether this is so or not is a matter of personal judgment—they could just as easily be cats or lynxes—but some are surely human masks. These heads do not lend themselves to art-historical analysis, for definite stylistic features, which might tell of their artistic affinities, are missing, and we cannot be sure whether they have foreign prototypes.

[1] Salin (1922).　　　　[2] Salin (1922), 194.

Three different types of animal motif can be seen on the Broa mounts. The first type consists of a broken, flat, double-contoured animal, which is closely related to Style E; (fig. 34) the animal is occasionally given elements of naturalism. Secondly we have animals with curved plastic bodies and heads; despite the fact that they belong to the same art phase, these creatures often lack the typical double contour (fig. 36). The third group consists of gripping-beasts of the usual, chunky form (pl. XXII e); they are executed in slight relief and occur, on a number of objects, alongside animals of the first group.

One of the typical motifs of the Broa artist is a balanced composition of large, backward-looking creatures. Each animal has a gracefully curved neck and softly rounded head set in profile; it has a large round eye and a characteristically rounded snout which terminates in a spiral (pl. XXI h). The small mouth is curved and the ear forms a knot with the neck. The artist was fond of using punched patterns—and he does it very skilfully. Among the punches he used were tools which produced semicircles, beaded lines and cross-hatched rhombic figures. The object richest in such punched decoration is the large mount illustrated in pl. XXI g.

The artist adopted a tendency of Style E by breaking the lines of the body of the animal, particularly at the hip, to produce tendril-like offshoots. He used this trick to its limit, tying the neck into a knot with the ear, or with a lappet, and developing the contour lines independently of any organic context. Great whirls of offshoots tend to break away from the bodies of the animals and, as the creatures are shaped in relation to the available field, strange geometrical shapes are created, which combine oddly with the limbs and heads. Only rarely, as in the upper part of the mount in pl. XXI d (fig. 33), does the animal disappear entirely.

His main interest was in composition. Using the framework skilfully, he placed rounded paws in small round openings, as though in windows (cf. pl. XXI c), or put a whole animal, or a strange foliate motif, under the arm of a plastic animal so that its general shape can just be discerned in three different places. The motifs on these objects fit together tightly so that at first glance they seem to be completely symmetrical; but, in fact, two apparently similar compositions are always different in detail (e.g. figs. 32 and 33).

The importance of the general composition in the determination of the form of the animal has already been noted, the motif is stretched or twisted to fit the general design. A remarkable example of this process can be seen on the two objects in the form of animal heads (pl. XXI a and b) which, although similar in general form, bear completely different patterns. Each object takes the form of a strongly delineated head and neck, with open mouth and large teeth, a lappet and a pear-shaped eye. Framed in the mouth of each animal is the contorted figure of a bird and each neck bears the representation of a quadruped. These secondary animals are treated in completely different ways; one (fig. 31) shows a remarkable combination

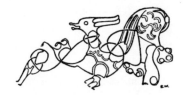

FIG. 31. Detail of mount illustrated in pl. XXI b. From Broa, Gotland. Scale ⅓.

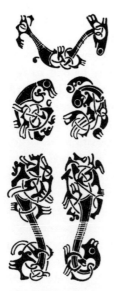

of naturalism and stylization (it is tempting to call it a lion but the mane-like feature may be interpreted as a lappet). The mouth gives an impression of a bird of prey, while the great claws are those of a predatory beast. The legs vary in length; the tail is long and terminates in a tight coil. The contour is, for the most part, clearly delineated, but in the centre of the neck and behind the hip is an openwork, heart-shaped field. An interlacing ribbon is produced from the former and terminates in an odd amorphous feature.

This is but one example of the Broa artist's skill in using the space at his disposal. Although the shape of the field apparently accounts for the uneven length of the limbs, there are enough empty spaces in the field to accentuate the animal's contour.

The style of this mount differs from that of its twin (pl. XXI *a*); only the bird in the mouth of the confining animal being similar on both objects. A pair of flat, double-contoured creatures face each other on the neck of the mount; their bodies are broken by heart-shaped openings at neck and belly and the heads have an almost timid expression on their faces. The legs have characteristically curved claws. The ornament gives an impression of chip-carving.

FIG. 32. Detail of mount illustrated in pl. XXI *c*. From Broa, Gotland. Scale ⅓.

Similar creatures occur on another pair of mounts, each of which is divided up into six oval fields (pl. XXI *c and d*). The oval acts as windows through which the animal ornament can be seen: some animals stretch from one field to the next, but others are contained within a single oval. At one end of each mount is a modelled mask, the forelegs of which are cut off by a semi-circular line to appear again in two irregularly shaped fields. The animals on each object are double-contoured and their bodies are frequently broken by whirling masses of ribbons which break away from heart-shaped openings. Beneath the mask on one of the mounts, in the fields divided by the legs of the plastic animal, is a quadruped; in similar fields on the other mount appear the disjointed elements of an animal's body.

The less corroded of the two mounts (pl. XXI *c* and fig. 32) has birds in the ovals below the terminating animal mask and, in the next two pairs of ovals, quadrupeds with elongated necks and backward turned heads. In the two ovals nearest the terminal of the more corroded example (pl. XXI *d* and fig. 33) is a dragon-esque creature, with tendril-like offshoots springing from openings in the body at the back and front of the animal.

Another pair of mounts (pl. XXI *e and f*) have animal heads in

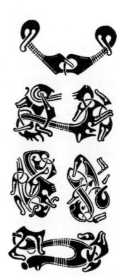

FIG. 33. Detail of mount illustrated in pl. XXI *d*. From Broa, Gotland. Scale ⅓.

relief at the terminals. These have been interpreted as lion heads,[1] but they are so schematically portrayed that it is impossible to define their species—it would, perhaps, be fairer to say that they represent men. A midrib, perhaps to be considered as a spine, divides the mount longitudinally and two legs with pear-shaped hips spring from it. On each side of the midrib are extended animal motifs divided up, in the Broa master's typical florid manner, by tendril-like offshoots. One of them has a fairly distinct head on a long neck, but the head of the other animal is not quite so clearly represented (fig. 34). Both come very near to being purely abstract ornament.

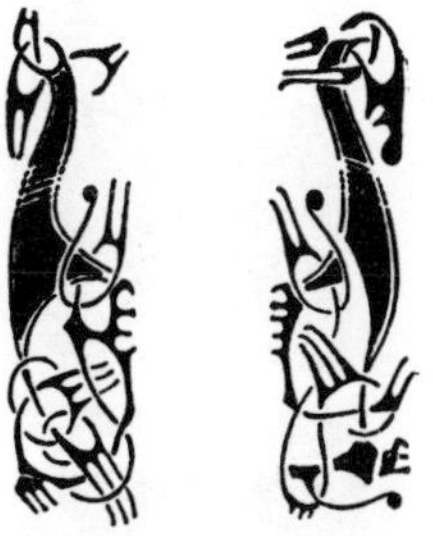

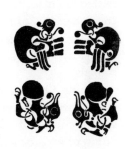

FIG. 34. Detail of mount illustrated in pl. XXI *e*, from Broa, Gotland. Scale ⅓.

One of the mounts stands alone (pl. XXI *g*): it is elegantly embellished with punched ornament and is crowned by an animal of elongated S-shape (fig. 35). This very stylized composition is cleverly designed in a semi-symmetrical manner. The slender, elegantly curved, body terminates in a small head with a tiny mouth, large eye and long lappet. The hips, like the body of the animal itself, are clearly delineated by a double-contour and the neck exhibits the typical Gotlandic knot of the period.

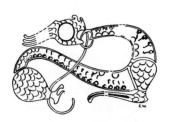

FIG. 35. Detail of mount illustrated in pl. XXI *g*. From Broa, Gotland. Scale ⅓.

The framework of two almost identical mounts (one of which is illustrated in pl. XXI *h*) is constructed of straight lines which define rectangular fields. In the two upper fields are large animal heads, the contours of which form the border of the mount, while the four lower fields (fig. 36) contain fairly naturalistic, small, stylized creatures—two quadrupeds and two birds—all executed in considerably rounded relief.

The elegant ornament of the four fields in a trapeze-shaped mount (pl. XXII *a*) is of an entirely different nature; it is related to that of the mount illustrated in pl. XXI *h*, save that the stylization is a little more developed and that the offshoots are nearer to Style E. The birds in the two upper fields (fig. 37) give liveliness to the ornament. The leg appears a little to one side in a flurry of ribbons and offshoots and the hips are spiral hooks. The fan-like feature of the animal to the right presumably represents the tail of the birds—in its centre a curved line terminates in a spiral. There are backward-looking quadrupeds in the two lower fields.

The motifs on the mount illustrated in pl. XXII *b* are distinctive. The bodies of the animals, which appear in pairs in two diagonally opposed fields on this object, have degenerated into a meaningless interlace pattern below two large opposed animal

FIG. 36. Detail of mount illustrated in pl. XXI *h*. From Broa, Gotland. Scale ⅓. *N.B. The figures have been inverted in relation to pl.* XXI, *in order that the birds may more clearly be seen.*

[1] Salin (1922), 194.

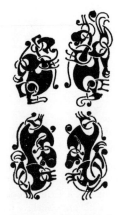

FIG. 37. Detail of mount illustrated in pl. XXII *a*. From Broa, Gotland. Scale ⅓.

heads. The two other fields contain semi-naturalistic quadrupeds with circular heads, large eyes and spiraliform upper lips. The body in each case turns into interlaced openwork ribbons in two places and an elaborate lappet can be seen behind the neck.

Another abstract motif is provided by a pair of animals on the mount illustrated in pl. XXII *c* and fig. 38. The surface is divided by a cross and the animals curve under the two short arms, to produce an almost symmetrical pattern. The motifs have little organic structure; they have been distorted and subdivided by the artist and forced into the available space, to produce a remarkable, lyre-shaped composition.

Three rectangular mounts (pl. XXII *e-f*) are each divided by means of a cross springing from a central circular field. In each circular field is a chunky gripping-beast, whilst the remaining fields are filled with various types of animal ornament.

A fourth object (pl. XXII *g*) has the same general design as these three mounts, but the central field is slightly larger and encloses a semi-naturalistic gripping-beast, which is closely related to the animals in the surrounding fields. It is remarkable, however, that the heads of these animals are portrayed in profile—a feature rarely encountered among gripping-beasts. Each animal grips the borders and the two animals in the lower fields grip their lappets. Vaguely related to this group is a small mount ornamented with true gripping-beast decoration (pl. XXII *h*).

The Broa mounts display a varied stylistic treatment but their rhythmic qualities and related peculiarities show that they were all made by one man. The imagination and creative genius of this artist is demonstrated by his use of animal heads in low relief, semi-naturalistic creatures and gripping-beasts, as well as by his skilful use of his own brand of Style E animals.

Taking Oseberg and Broa as signposts to our study of early Viking art, and ignoring their local peculiarities, we are presented with a corpus of material of extraordinary richness, and with a group of objects which tell of the aims, talent and skill of a number of individual artists. In looking at them we gain a remarkable impression of the mind of the artists of the period: we see how they used the many stylistic influences to their own taste—forming, in the process, new styles and adjusting old styles to their own fashion. When all is said and done, a brilliant artist adapts a style to his own idiom and we are fortunate in that we can see in these two finds the products of a number of clearly identified artists of brilliance. There is an extraordinary vigour in early Viking art, more than might have been anticipated if we had had

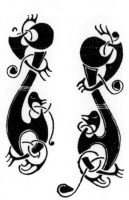

FIG. 38. Detail of mount illustrated in pl. XXII *c*. From Broa, Gotland. Scale ⅓.

to base our judgments on the type of object normally found in Viking graves, which is usually bound by heavy conventionality and shows no great variation of style.

There were so many motifs which were available for the Viking artists to adapt to their own taste and to the bounds of the composition, that it is often difficult for an art-historian to assign an object to a particular style—a difficulty encountered in our discussion of the art of the previous period.

It is noteworthy that the gripping-beasts are almost naturalistic, if rather clumsy, creatures by comparison with the contemporary animals influenced from Style E. The gripping-beast represents a new motif which has no apparent connection with its predecessors, and which was developed because it did not need the space demanded by the contemporary, abstract, tendril-like animals with pierced neck and head in profile. The distinct differences between the two animals has caused scholars to look outside Scandinavia for the origins of the gripping-beast. Sophus Müller put forward the theory that these creatures were copied by Scandinavian craftsmen from Carolingian lions. Unfortunately it is impossible to find their prototypes in Carolingian contexts and in desperation other scholars have searched, without great success, for insular parallels. Animals of a distinct gripping-beast type occur on the Anglo-Carolingian Lindau book-cover,[1] which is otherwise mainly decorated with zoomorphic ornament of the type found on the Tassilo Chalice, and it seems most reasonable to interpret the ornament of these round fields, as did Brøndsted,[2] as evidence of Scandinavian influence on Continental art; for this is the only major occurrence of the true gripping-beast motif outside Scandinavia.

The most remarkable similarity between the gripping-beast motif and certain facets of contemporary Continental and insular art is the physical contact between the animal and its surroundings. Just as the Scandinavian creatures cling either to the border, or to each other, so, in Christian art, birds, animals and even human figures, clutch vine-scrolls with their claws and hands.[3] It is clear, however, that, even if the Scandinavian artists did copy such details, they did not take over the whole motif.

The gripping-beast, in fact, does not depend on foreign prototypes, for all its details can be traced back to older Scandinavian art, in which animals with head *en face* and large round eyes, are clearly delineated with hips and feet which grip other animals. The Lousgård brooch (pl. IV c), for example, exhibits all these features. Motifs like that portrayed on this brooch (which is repeated on the Oseberg cart (pl. X a)) show an actual scene in which there is a definite physical contact between two animals, of a sort encountered in early Scandinavian narrative art (e.g. on the Torslunda dies (pl. III a) where men and beasts appear to be fighting).

As well as the gripping-beast material from Broa and Oseberg there is a considerable body of Scandinavian objects, ornamented in a naturalistic fashion, which are convenient to use as a starting point in any discussion of the gripping-beast motif. The significance of these pieces in relation to the relief ornament of Oseberg is underlined by the ornament of a number of brooches which are executed in high relief. The limbs of

[1] Brøndsted (1924), fig. 129. [2] (1924), 157. [3] Cf. Kendrick (1938a), pls. 47, 1 and 70, 2.

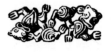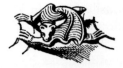

FIG. 39. Ornament from a strap-end and an oval brooch from Sjælland, Denmark, *National Museum, Copenhagen.*

the creatures on these objects are so portrayed that they appear to lift the animal away from the background (fig. 39).

The pair of oval brooches from Lisbjerg, Jutland (pl. XXIV a), which are sub-divided by a geometrical framework, are ornamented by splendid gripping-beasts These creatures are vigorous, carefully executed and beautifully fitted into the fields provided. The feet grip legs, necks and border, but in the main they are not connected with their surroundings. Some of the animals have elegantly curved lappets which terminate in a spiral. The head, which is seen *en face*, is practically cat-shaped, with triangular ears, a lined forehead, round eyes and a small face with a short snout. The two parts of the body are broad with a narrow waist, clearly defined hips, short legs and long, curved claws. Animals like these, executed in the round, are paralleled by a group of amber and jet carvings from various sites in Scandinavia (cf. pl. XX *a and b*).

The framework which contains the animals on the oval brooches is, as we have seen above, a well-known feature of the Anglo-Carolingian and insular ornament. The bosses and interlace patterns, although they may have had ultimate insular prototypes, are indigenous, while the isolated biting animal heads are Scandinavian and will be seen again in the later Borre style.

It would be surprising if the Scandinavian artist had not wanted to experiment with the gripping-beast. By using details of the ornament, with little respect for its organic significance, he could achieve remarkable articulation of the rhythmic, plastic surface. This is particularly seen on certain Norwegian oval brooches, which Jan Petersen called the Berdal type,[1] where the bossed surface is divided into two groups of three circles, reminiscent of the oval brooches seen in fig. 5.

The gripping-beast was also a popular motif on the large equal-armed brooches and on the fragment of one of these, illustrated in pl. XX *d*, we can see an odd attempt to make the gripping-beast motif symmetrical.

Animals with Style E features occur alongside gripping-beasts on the disc-on-bow and drum-shaped brooches of the island of Gotland. The circular tops of many drum-shaped brooches (pl. XX *c*) are decorated with groups of intertwining gripping-beasts, while the sides are panelled with classic Style E animals and gripping-beasts. Thus two-dimensional animals, with elegantly curved bodies, leaf-like offshoots and carefully turned heads, fitting beautifully into the confining fields, are found on the same brooch as lively, three-dimensional, no less well designed, gripping-beasts, set against an undecorated smooth background and contained by the arm of a cross. The cross, which can be dimly discerned on the face of this brooch and similar objects, is presumably derived from Anglo-Carolingian prototypes.[2] The cross is picked out with small, punched circles, which contrast with the hatched bodies of the gripping-beasts with

[1] (1928), 18 and fig. 15.   [2] See above p. 45.

their carefully drawn heads and long curved lappets. The artist was clearly interested in articulating the ornament by varying the texture of the surface.

Disc-on-bow brooches like the example from Gumbalde, Stånga (pl. xxv e) are decorated in a similar manner. The bow of this brooch is divided into three rectangular fields, two of which contain extremely elegant, highly articulated, Style E animals. The fields flank a central panel containing three normal gripping-beasts, which, although well designed, are already somewhat unnaturalistic. The head is seen *en face* and is loosely joined to the body by means of a thin, ribbon-like neck—the waist of the animal is also very slight. The feet indiscriminately grip the frame or the nearest animal giving an impression of clumsiness to the whole design.

On another disc-on-bow brooch, from Broa, Gotland (pl. xxv *a* and *b*), the back of the rectangular head plate is engraved with a pair of semi-naturalistic animals which have a number of interesting stylistic features. Each animal has a long broad lappet and the position of the hind-legs can be compared to that of many gripping-beasts. The feet occasionally touch the bordering line, or another limb, in a fashion encountered in certain gripping-beast patterns. These two backward-looking animals form a practically symmetrical composition. Similar creatures, executed in the same technique, occur on the back of the central disc. Here a bird and three quadrupeds exhibit certain naturalistic features alongside a mixture of Style E coils and more realistic shapes. The front leg emerges from the plaited pattern in the neck—an odd feature which can be seen on several of the animals on the Broa mounts (pl. xxi *c*). The bird and one of the quadrupeds are related to the ornament of another Gotlandic object, the sword from Ristimäki (fig. 40), which is discussed below.

It may be useful at this point to summarize the characteristics of the gripping-beast motif. The motif is basically three-dimensional and the animals themselves are usually built up in an articulated fashion with clearly delineated limbs springing from a body with fairly slim neck and waist. The abstract interplay of contours and openwork, which threatened to dissolve Style E animals into nothing, rarely occurs in the gripping-beast motif and, when it is seen, it always results from an external influence. This motif preserved its distinctive form in the later Borre and Jellinge styles; on one Jellinge style object, indeed, the motif occurs in the round (pl. xxxvi *b*).

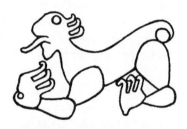

FIG. 40. Animal ornament from the hilt of a sword from Ristimäki, St Karins, Finland. *National Museum, Helsinki.*

On certain oval brooches, like that from Ytterdal, Norway, is a bird-motif which is closely related to the series we have just discussed. The openwork upper plate of this brooch is decorated with two addorsed birds (pl. xxiii *e*), the backward-turned heads of which are seen in profile. The birds' claws grip the frame in a manner which may be compared to that of the gripping-beasts in the lower panels. The symmetrical composition of this brooch is reminiscent of other Scandinavian objects as, for instance, the key from Berg, Norway, decorated with two rather more natural-istic birds.[1]

Certain naturalistic details, as for example the gold filigree bust of a man on the button of the Broa brooch (pl. xxv c), are reminiscent of the techniques of earlier orna-ment.[2]

The gradual stylization of naturalistic motifs is occasionally seen in this phase of the art and it is even possible to trace this process through a series of objects which have minor differences in ornamental detail. In this context it is interesting to examine a series of animals, like that portrayed on the Kaupang brooch shown in pl. xxiii d, which are closely related to some found at Oseberg (pl. xvii) and have bodies, the contours of which are broken by knitted and plaited ornament. Another horse, an elegant creature with traces of earlier stylistic features which came from Birka (pl. xxiii b), is rather more naturalistic and more surely characterized. It is a highly competent piece of work, delineating an obviously powerful animal. Carefully drawn, naturalistic horses are also found in stone (pl. xxvi) and they also occur, as on the small equestrian figure from Birka (pl. xxiv f), *en miniature*.

A number of other small figures, such as the full-length representations of women (pl. xxiv c–e), dressed in a long dress and shawl and with their hair arranged in a knot at the neck, are related to the Birka equestrian figure. The female figure from Klinta (pl. xxiv c), however, has her hair simply brushed back and carries a beaker, or drinking-horn, in a manner similar to that found on many carved stones from Gotland. The small figures from the side of the head of the well-known disc-on-bow brooch from Nygårds, Vesterhejde, Gotland (pl. xxiv g), are more stylized but clearly reminiscent of this group. The head has a single round eye and a protruding tongue; the hair is gripped by an arm. The ribbon-shaped body with its spiraliform hip and raised leg foreshadow Jellinge style motifs (cf. pl. xxxvii b).

The finest examples of the naturalistic representation of an animal occur on two Gotlandic objects of the highest quality—the well-known openwork roundel from Othem and the Stora Ihre sword pommel. The roundel from Othem (pl. xxiii c) dis-plays three birds, each set in a pair of circles. The birds stand on the border of the mount and point a parallel to the more extreme ornament of the type found on the object shown in pl. xxiii c. Ornament of this type occurs on a number of other Gotlandic pieces, such as the Broa mounts (pl. xxi b) and the sword pommel from grave 174 at Stora Ihre (pl. xxiii a). On this sword pommel the bodies of the two animals on either side of the central ornamental element are broken, as though overlaid by circles or other geometrical figures. These quadrupeds exhibit a remarkable mixture of naturalism and fantasy: they have birds' heads and their tails curve between their legs to terminate in curved claws, the front hips are embellished with a spiral and there is a small point behind the head.

In the centre of the pommel the illusion of a creature seen through windows is most completely worked out (fig. 41). The three openings—two round and one heart-shaped

[1] Almgren (1955), pl. 18, *a*.　　　　[2] Salin (1904), 13, 212 *et passim*.

—reveal a quadruped with a bird's head. The neck and hips are pierced and produce florid tendrils of typical Style E form.

The trick of circles and 'openings' is undoubtedly of Gotlandic origin, although found universally in Scandinavia. The Othem plate represents an indigenous Nordic form, despite the parallels—which we believe to be of doubtful value—in contemporary Continental ornament produced by Arbman.[1]

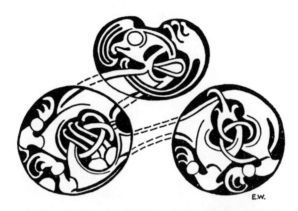

FIG. 41. Animal on the pommel of a sword from Stora Ihre, Gotland, Sweden. See pl. XXIII *a*. Scale ⅔. *Statens Historiska Museum, Stockholm.*

A sword from Ristimäki, St Karins, Finland,[2] has a hilt divided up into fields which contain animal ornament, the whole aspect of the ornament indicates that this object is also a Gotlandic piece. The oval fields (which in many ways resemble the composition and form of the mount from Broa illustrated in pl. XXI *c*) mostly contain bird motifs with intertwined wings, but quadrupeds—obviously lions (fig. 40)—also occur. These latter are naturalistic creatures with large claws, rather like the related animal illustrated in fig. 41. The tongue hangs out of the open mouth and the lappet takes the form of a mane with scrolled terminals.

The most impressive artistic products of Gotland are the carved stones which, as we have seen in the previous period, were most beautifully executed. At the beginning of the Viking period a group of stones was carved in a rather deeper relief than, but lacking the quality of, the earlier stones. A typical stone is that from Tjängvide (pl. XXVI); it is damaged, but it clearly had the familiar Gotlandic outline of curved top and indented neck, with decorated borders at the edge of the stone and a thick plaited pattern across the centre dividing the field of decoration into two. To the bottom-right is a strange design consisting of a figure-of-eight-like ribbon animal. The head and pigtail of this creature are seen in the upper loop, while the ainmal's body terminates in the lower loop in a leg or in another head. This carving is clearly not of the highest quality —as the central band of plaiting shows—but it has a Style D motif of a type similar to

___

[1] (1937), 121.   [2] Nordman (1931), fig. 19.

that on the Ardre VIII stone (fig. 42) (e.g. to the left and in the lowermost border). A ribbon-like animal fills the upper frieze, and is again exactly paralleled on the upper border of the Ardre VIII stone. The frieze takes the form of a broken regular interlace pattern, each element of which terminates in an animal-head, which bites the nearest ribbon so that only the upper jaw can be seen. As well as these three filling motifs, there is a simple ribbon motif, which has good parallels in metalwork.[1]

In the upper field of the Tjängvide stone is a semicircular figure which has been interpreted as a representation of Valhalla and is clearly paralleled on the Ardre stone (fig. 42). Below this motif, a man with a battle-axe faces a woman, while below them is a dog-like creature. The bottom right-hand corner is dominated by a rider on an eight-legged horse—the latter presumably representing Sleipnir. A woman, carrying what seems to be a drinking-horn in one hand and a key in the other, faces the horse. The rider holds the reins, carries a club or wreath (cf. the rider on the Ardre stone) and wears a sword. These representations can be compared with those illustrated in pl. XXIV: in both cases the woman's hair is knotted at the neck before falling down her back, and this is but one of a number of similarities. The rider could be Odin, but he could equally well be a dead warrior who, having been carried on his last journey by Sleipnir, is welcomed by a woman in Valhalla. In the semicircular field are two further figures, which perhaps represent fallen warriors, a spear and a bird-like creature.

The field at the bottom of the stone is filled by a splendid ship with a square sail; as at Oseberg (pl. VI) the stem and stern-posts are spiraliform. A group of armed men stand on the prow, their swords hanging from their belts. In the stern stands the helmsman with a long spear. Here, beautifully portrayed, is the chief tool of the Gotlandic Viking —a well-found ship.

The runic inscription records that the stone was raised by his brother to the memory of a man called Jurulv, who died while travelling.

The fine stone from Ardre is decorated with even more splendid scenes (fig. 42), although its composition is less disciplined and the juxtaposition of so many different scenes produces a rather untidy effect. This stone provides a fascinating corpus of myths and tales.

The division of the stone and of the two fields is exactly similar to that of the Tjängvide stone. At the top of the Ardre stone is a representation of Valhalla, similar to, but clearer than, that of the Tjängvide stone; it is represented as a semicircular building with three arched entrances and seven, slit-like openings. Sleipnir appears to be dancing —his eight legs interlacing in a rather alarming fashion. Above the rider is what appears to be a dead warrior: in front of this scene a group of people are engaged with a long, pole-like object. In the bottom panel is a Viking ship in full sail; it carries a large number of warriors and a look-out and a helmsman are clearly depicted. To the top right of the stone two men kneel with a sack-like object in what is possibly a house, while another figure stands outside. Below this scene two men, in knee-length tunics, lie side by side, head to toe, and are tied together by interlacing ribbons. A woman in a long dress stands

---

[1] Cf. the Skabersjö brooch, pl. IV a.

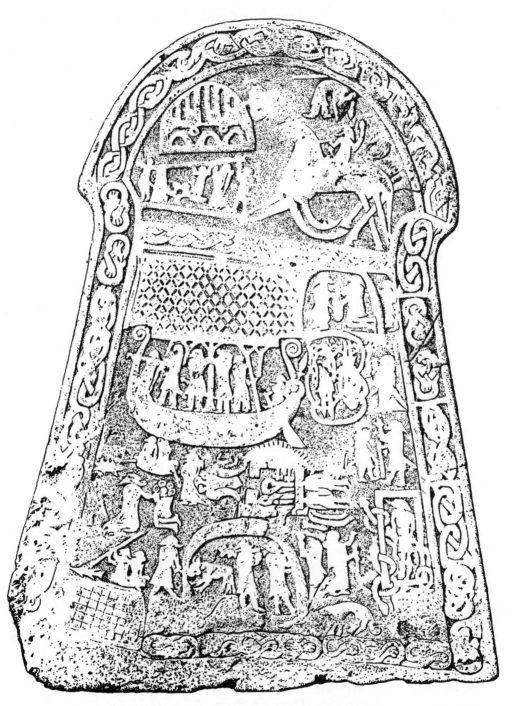

FIG. 42. Picture stone from Ardre, Gotland, Sweden.

next to them, carrying a sword at her side and another in her hand. Below them stand two warriors, wearing knee-length tunics and swords, one of whom has a raised hand. To the right a man lies within a rectangular frame, round which are coiled four snakes, to his left stands a woman holding a beaker, or horn, in each hand. The woman is clearly Sigyn, waiting to catch the snake's venom and thus help her imprisoned husband Loki. The quadruped below her and a figure of a woman, apparently holding a horn, immediately to her left, possibly relate to this scene.

In the centre of the large field is a scene from the story of Weyland the Smith. The smithy, with its curved roof terminating in animal heads, is in the centre; a pair of hammers and two pairs of tongues are within. To the left, a man, disguised as a bird and therefore presumably Weyland, flies away from the woman, presumably the daughter of King Niðað. To the right of the smithy are two headless bodies, King Niðað's sons. Below this scene is a group of objects which look like two boats and two oars.

To the left are two scenes of apparent mythological significance. One of them depicts two men—Thor and the giant—fishing from a boat with a bull's head as bait. Below this is a kneeling man in front of a creature with five heads. The other scene also portrays two men fishing from a boat, one of them spearing a fish; below this is a fishing net. At the base of the field, in the centre, is a representation of a stable in which are a cow and two men, one of the men carries a club over his shoulder. Just outside the stable is another man who appears to be untying the cow's halter.

These two stones illustrate excellently the ability and imagination of the Gotlandic sculptors and their preoccupation with mythology and heroic tales. Ships are rarely absent from the Gotlandic stones and their frequent occurrence and the splendour of their execution witness to the islanders preoccupation with ships and the sea. But pictures like these, which would be familiar to the contemporary spectator versed in heroic stories, were not only produced on Gotland and at the court of Oseberg. There is an interesting mention in the ancient Scandinavian shield verses, for example, of painted scenes on shields.[1]

In any judgment of Scandinavian narrative art a knowledge of the heroic canon of Scandinavian history and mythology is a necessary prerequisite. While the contemporary spectator would immediately recognize a scene as a conventional image of an event or an action in the life of a person who had just died, this image may well be impossible for us to interpret. Only certain well-known tales, like the gruesome story of Weyland, for example, are immediately recognizable to a modern audience. From Viking Age literature we know of the wall paintings at Harðarholt on Iceland, which depicted scenes of Thor's fishing trips, Loki's fight with Heimdall, Balder's pyre, etc. These paintings may well have been similar in style to the Oseberg tapestries, of which only fragments are preserved, or, like the fragment of tapestry from the rich grave from Rolvsöy, Östfold, Norway, which bore a picture of a boat and a group of people, in a style reminiscent of Gotlandic art. These tapestries, which are carefully woven in many

[1] Lindqvist (1941), 1, 105.

different coloured wools, are long and rather narrow (about 20–23 cm.) so that they could be hung as a frieze round the walls of a room.

One portion of the Oseberg tapestry—which shows a procession of people, some walking and some riding—has been reconstructed (pl. XIXa). The warriors wear wide, knee-length trousers and carry spears (more rarely a sword). The women wear full-length dresses with short train and shawl, of a style we have encountered before. The people are dominated by the high-stepping horses with their naturalistic high necks, flying manes and tails knotted like the hair of the women in pl. XXIV *d and e*. The carts in the picture have four wheels and seats and occasionally, a high superstructure. Another fragment[1] of these textiles shows a gallows-tree with people hanging from it, this scene may well refer to the god Odin, to whom were dedicated those who died by hanging.

Narrative art and decorative art are easily distinguished from each other. On the Gotland stones and the Oseberg cart they appear side by side, and it is characteristic that in both cases, as in earlier times, ribbon-shaped animal interlace frames the natural-istic scenes.

Viking art follows on in an unbroken tradition from earlier Scandinavian art, and is strengthened by the independence and creative powers of its practitioners. Foreign art may have influenced Viking art in this period, but such influences were soon adapted to a native idiom, they brought about no change of style, only a change in emphasis. Foreign influences are rarely identified in their original form in Viking art. Plant orna-ment, which is one of the few readily identifiable foreign motifs, was always alien to Scandinavian art. We have seen how the vine-leaf was transformed during the Roman Iron Age to suit Scandinavian tastes. During the early Viking period Scandinavian artists adapted plant motifs, as for instance on the trefoil brooches decorated with acanthus motifs in a Carolingian style. Trefoil brooches, apart from imported examples[2] are often quite simple objects, but as a class they stand alone. The plant motif only becomes significant much later in the Viking period when acanthus leaves are taken into the ornament of the Mammen style.

Scandinavian taste always gains the upper hand. The interesting mount from Stora Ryk, Färgelanda, Sweden (pl. XXV *d*) is apparently decorated in imitation of a foreign acanthus leaf, but closer examination reveals that the decoration is made up of small animal heads, not leaves. Animal art was the only art which really satisfied the Viking mind.

[1] Krafft (1956), 35.   [2] Arbman (1937), 147 ff.

PART 2

BY

DAVID M. WILSON

CHAPTER III

THE BORRE STYLE

It is with a sense of anticlimax that we turn from a discussion of the overwhelming richness of the Oseberg material to the consideration of the ornament appearing on a handful of tawdry trinkets, a few vulgarly ostentatious brooches and an occasional successful piece of jewellery, which is the content of the succeeding Borre style. Oseberg so completely overshadows, by its material and by the accident of its discovery, the art of the succeeding styles that it takes a great effort of imagination to evaluate correctly the later styles, which appear on such a paltry material. In this phase of art there are no grandiose carvings to demonstrate the full tortuousness of the Viking craftsman's imagination, here there is no sense of the artist's achievement in his native material—wood. All that remains are a few scraps of metal which are of specialist interest only. It is, however, a mistake—and one only too often made—to equate the apparent anticlimax, provided by the surviving art of the post-Oseberg period, with an actual, artistic anticlimax at this period of Viking history. Nothing could be further from the truth, for the century after Oseberg also produced its artists, some perhaps of no less stature than the Oseberg artists, but their activities can only faintly be discerned in objects which do not flaunt the quality either of their craftsmanship or their art.

It is difficult, therefore, to be balanced in any qualitative judgment of the Borre style and it is just as difficult to be balanced in any historical discussion of the style, for its chronology is hedged round by many other difficulties. Although it is possible for the first time in the study of Viking art to make firm chronological judgments, on the basis of absolute dates provided by objects found in coin-hoards, the situation is complicated by the fact that for the sixty-five years between c. 860, the date of the deposition of the Hon hoard, and c. 925, when the Vester Vedsted hoard was deposited, there is no fixed point in the art-historical chronology. The situation is further complicated by the lack of a satisfactory terminology for the succession of styles in the late ninth and tenth century and the fact that the two main styles of this period—Borre and Jellinge—have a considerable chronological overlap. All these difficulties must be kept in mind in the following discussion.

The Borre style takes its name from the objects (many of which are illustrated in pl. xxvii) found in the ship burial in a great barrow at Borre in Vestfold, Norway, a few miles north of Oseberg. This style is not the only successor to the art of Oseberg, for, perhaps at the same time, another style—the Jellinge style—was making itself felt in Scandinavia. We shall return to the Jellinge style in a later chapter, meanwhile the Borre style can be discussed separately as it is homogeneous and in many respects stands apart from the main-stream of later Viking Age ornament.

Although the metalwork of the Borre find is not perhaps the most exciting group of material decorated in the style which bears its name, it is the most typical. The most remarkable motif in the Borre repertoire, and one which is unique to the style, is a ribbon plait (pl. XXVII *h*). The plait consists of a symmetrical interlace pattern, each intersection of which is bound by a circle which surrounds a hollow-sided lozenge. The design is made up of a double ribbon and its cast contours are often nicked transversely. The pattern is often terminated by an animal mask, which is sometimes cast in quite high relief. This interlace pattern, usually known as a 'ring-chain' pattern, normally occurs on small harness mounts and similar objects of cast gilt-bronze and is remarkably uniform wherever it is found; whether at Borre itself, in the nearby ship burial at Gokstad (pl. XXX *b*), at the Swedish merchant centre of Birka[1] or in a Viking grave at Gnezdovo in Russia.[2] It also occurs as a filling motif on objects decorated with zoomorphic ornament.

Chief among these motifs is an articulated, ribbon-like quadruped with a head in the form of a mask. The motif occurs in a modified form at Borre (pl. XXVII *g*), but is more clearly seen on the remarkable, concave-sided brooch, probably from Sweden, illustrated in pl. XXVIII *a*, on one of the pendants from the Hon hoard (pl. XXIX *i*,) on the brooch from Aaserum, Vestfold, Norway (pl. XXVIII *b*) or on the two filigree brooches illustrated in pl. XXIX *k and l*. The mask is similar to that seen at the terminal of the Borre strap-ends, where it occurs in association with the interlace pattern, and consists of two eyes and the snout of an animal, with a formalized forehead and, occasionally, two prominent semicircular ears. The head is almost invariably of triangular form and sometimes has one or two lappets or pigtails. The band-like neck joins a broad, sub-triangular hip in one corner of the field. The body is formed of a broad band, which passes below the mask from a hip in one corner of the field to a hip in the other corner. The legs emerge from either side of each hip and the feet tend to grip the body of the animal or the border of the mount. Occasionally the animals are found on large objects, on oval brooches (pl. XVIII *c*) or saddle-mounts, for example, where they will occasionally interlace with, or grip, each other; usually, however, they appear as single, articulated animals.

The third main motif of the Borre style, rarely encountered outside the Borre find itself, consists of an animal seen from the side, it usually has a backward turned head and a lappet. The neck and body, although formalized, are of more-or-less naturalistic proportions, the hips form a spiral and the legs are usually bent forward. The feet are sometimes hook-like, sometimes have a formalized two- or three-element paw and sometimes grip the border of the field. It normally occurs as the only motif in a single field.

[1] Arbman (1940–43), pl. 88.　　　[2] Arne (1914), fig. 18.

Other motifs found in the Borre series—isolated masks, heads in profile, etc., are of minor importance.

An interesting, though not universal, technical feature of objects of cast metal decorated in the Borre style is, as we have seen, the series of transverse nicks on the interlacing bands (cf. pl. XXVII). These very probably reflect the imitation of a filigree technique, the nicks representing the divisions between each individual bead of filigree wire. If it is remembered that many of Borre objects are gilt, their resemblance to gold filigree is striking. It is interesting, therefore, that the richest surviving Borre style objects, the remarkable gold spur, strap-end and belt-slide found at Værne Kloster in Norway (pl. XXIX a–e), bear ornament executed in gold filigree wire and fine granulation. The objects are of exceptionally fine quality and the ornament is more elaborate than that normally found in the Borre style. On the spur the familiar ring-chain motif is given zoomorphic character by replacing the interlacing bands with animals, the bodies of which are formed of the hollow-sided square in the centre of the ring (the heads of the animals are in profile and are related to those of the Jellinge style). A rather more evolved pattern gives a similar character to the strap-end (pl. XXIX e); the animal heads are seen in profile and have a lappet which interlaces with the creature's neck or body. The belt-slide (pl. XXIX d) and the centre of the spur (pl. XXIX a) are decorated with typical Borre masks. Objects of filigree, decorated in the Borre style, are quite rare, but a number of pieces in the Hon and Vester Vedsted (pl. XXIX l) hoards, a very carefully executed mount from the Lackalänge grave-find (pl. XXIX j) and one or two similar objects, witness to the Borre artist's skill in this medium. It is possible that the nicks, which obviously reflect filigree techniques, indicate the original medium of the style—in which case most of the surviving objects must be seen as cheaper, less elaborate productions.

The Scandinavian origin of one of the motifs of the Borre style is clearly evident. The animal with gripping feet is obviously derived from the gripping-beast motif, seen in its most elaborate form at Oseberg. On certain oval brooches (e.g. pl. XXIV b) it is difficult to tell whether a Borre, or an earlier gripping-beast, motif is represented. This derivation can also be seen in the detail of the ornament; the Borre lappet, for example, must be based on the similar feature common in the gripping-beast motif. The animal with its mask-like face and ribbon-shaped body must obviously be related to, if not derived from, the small filigree, orans-like, human figure, which can be seen inset into the button of the disc-on-bow brooch from Broa, Halla, Gotland (pl. XXV c) and which occurs as an almost Borre-like creature below the suspension loop on some of the Gotlandic bracteates (pl. XXXIII a) and on the Mårtens drum-shaped brooch (pl. XXX f–h), which were probably made when the Borre style was no longer fashionable, but which have a symmetrical composition. This tendency to symmetry can also be seen when an animal version of this motif is executed in a base material on a small gilt bronze mount from Östborg, Frol, Levanger (pl. XXVIII g). The animal masks themselves should probably be derived from indigenous ornament: they are only slightly more stylized than some of the masks in the Broa find (pl. XXI c–f).

89

So far the Borre style can easily be understood in relationship to its precursors, but the other motifs are more difficult to interpret and this is particularly true of the ring-chain design, the origins of which are obscure. It does not occur in this form in any earlier Scandinavian context and it is certainly not known outside Scandinavia. Interlace patterns, as we have shown, were an integral part of pre-Viking and early Viking ornament but, although we have a similar pattern to the Borre motif on the borders of the eighth century brooches from Svejstrup and Lyngby, Denmark,[1] the parallel is not convincing enough to enable us to say with certainty that this is the prototype of the motif. Perhaps a clue to the immediate origin of the design is to be found in the general appearance of the back of one of the 'baroque' animal-headed posts in the Oseberg find (pl. XIII b). If we ignore the details of the ornament, and concentrate on the general aspect of the design, a series of hollow-sided lozenges can be seen, separated from each other by bands, the whole pattern crowned by an animal-head in relief and *en face*. The idea of an interlaced pattern with intervening lozenges was not, then, very far from the mind of the Viking artist. This is not to say that the motif was derived directly from the Oseberg piece quoted here, but rather that all the conditions necessary for the creation of this type of interlace existed in Scandinavia when the Borre interlace was introduced. There is a good deal of individuality in the objects decorated in the Borre style, they were obviously made by a group of craftsmen who had imagination and who were gradually breaking away from the existing art of the area. There is no other available explanation for the origin of the Borre interlace and this theory is but a tentative attempt to fill the gap. It has often been said that the prototype of the Borre ring-chain occurs in the Hiberno-Saxon area, but unfortunately no satisfactory parallels have been produced; an indigenous origin seems therefore to be the most likely.

A common feature of strap-ends, decorated with ring-chain interlace, is a terminal animal-head. It might be possible to see here an adaptation of an English design, for numerous strap-ends of similar form are found in English ninth-century contexts (pl. XXX e). They are smaller than the Borre objects but this is because they were probably not used as bridle mounts. A few are decorated with interlace, but a feature of the English strap-ends (it occurs on about half of the known examples) is a terminal animal mask of rather similar form to those found on the Borre strap-ends. It is tempting to think that an English strap-end formed the model for the Borre type. Anglo-Saxon strap-ends are known in Viking contexts in Scandinavia—at least three have been found in Norwegian Viking graves—and there is no reason why the idea of the English object should not have provided an inspiration for a northern artist. The clumsiness of the double strap-ends found at Borre is coincidental; it is surely due to the adaptation of an object for use in a context which bears no relationship to its original purpose. Single strap-ends, of the long, narrow form, are, of course, known—from Birka, Gnezdovo and Gokstad (pl. XXX b), for example—but neither type ever became really popular in Scandinavia.

The three mounts from Borre which bear representations of backward-looking

[1] Arbman (1937), pl. 44.

animals fall into a group which cannot be paralleled elsewhere. They appear to have no relationship to anything that occurs in earlier Scandinavian art. They are unique to the Borre workshop—and were undoubtedly made by the same man and belong to the same bridle as the other mounts in the find. They have been compared to certain mounts from the Gokstad grave (pl. xxx *a*) which are ornamented with lion-like animals. The Gokstad pieces themselves bear no relation to any other Scandinavian style.[1] The parallel is not convincing as the stylization does not take the same form; there are no spiral hips on the Gokstad animal and the treatment of the body is altogether different, both in decoration and form. It is tempting to say that there was an Anglo-Saxon or Celtic prototype for the Borre animal; the spiral hip, for example, is a typical insular motif and backward looking animals are extremely common in insular art. But there is no evidence for such a derivation, in fact both spiral hip and backward-looking animal occur in earlier Scandinavian contexts. The animals should probably be interpreted as an unique and short-lived feature of an individual craftsman of the Borre workshop. The motif apparently never infected the Borre style deeply and soon became submerged in the general development of the animal ornament of the period.

The backward looking animal of the Borre mounts is probably related to the three-dimensional animals, occasionally found on oval brooches, but more commonly on a series of fantastic silver brooches of which a number are known from central Sweden[2] (cf. pl. xxxi *c*). The two most important brooches are one from Jelets, Voronez, Russia (pl. xxxi *d*), and one, probably from the Swedish island of Gotland, in the British Museum (pl. xxxi *a*). The brooches are decorated with plastic animal and human figures. On the British Museum brooch four animals alternate with four standing human figures, whose hands grasp what may be either a forked musical-instrument or a forked beard. The Jelets brooch, although incomplete, is a much more formidable affair; it bears, contorted and twisted all over its surface, a whole menagerie of three-dimensional animals. The highest point of the brooch is crowned by a backward-looking animal, with spiral hips and hatched mane, which may well be related to the animals on the mounts from the Borre grave. The clue to the art-historical position of these objects lies in the incidental ornament. On the Jelets brooch a rather modified form of the usual Borre interlace can be seen, the modification perhaps justifying Arbman's tentative suggestion[3] that the brooch was made in the Viking colonies of Russia. The British Museum example, however, demonstrates an undoubted Borre gripping-beast combined with the features and technique of the Borre interlace pattern. This rather unattractive, but fascinating, series of objects provides an impression of the three-dimensional art of the late ninth and early tenth century.

The chronological position of the Borre style is not easily resolved. Typologically it is certainly of later date than the Oseberg find. The gripping beasts have become rationalized and the tendency towards the art of the post-Oseberg, Jellinge group, which has

---

[1] It is generally accepted nowadays that the Gokstad pieces are based on English prototypes, cf. Arbman (1961), fig. 33, and Hougen (1931–2), 82, but what the prototypes are we are at a loss to understand.
[2] Listed by Stenberger (1947–58), i, 49 n. [3] Arbman (1959).

been noticed in the Værne Kloster spur, and which can be seen in a number of other pieces, as on the pendants from Östborg, Frol, Levanger (pl. xxvIII *d–g*) or the elaborate ring-headed brooch from Birka, Sweden (pl. xxxI *b*), obviously set it apart from the Oseberg series. However, we know that the style is fairly close in date to the Oseberg find. This is demonstrated by the Gokstad grave, which contained objects decorated in the Borre style, as well as tent supports (pl. xvIII) closely related in style to the animals on the Oseberg bed-posts (pl. xvII). It is true that the Gokstad heads are more developed and are embellished with a freer use of curves and lobes, but the general similarities are undeniable. It is impossible to say whether the Gokstad tent supports (pl. xvIII) were made five years or fifty years after the Oseberg objects, all that can be said is that there is a lively traditional connection between them. On this basis it would be impossible to date the introduction of Borre motifs into Viking art to any period closer than the last half of the ninth century.

A firmer date for the Borre style is provided elsewhere. A number of objects decorated in this style occur in the well-known Norwegian hoard from Hon, which is the only mid-ninth century Scandinavian hoard which contains both coins and ornamental metalwork. Its deposition has been dated by coins to *c.* 860. Such accurate dating is perhaps questionable as all the coins have been adapted, by the addition of small loops, for use as pendants in a necklace; but it is reasonably certain that the necklace was made up all at the same time and must be dated before 860.[1] Among the objects adapted for use in the necklace are various pieces decorated in the Borre style, particularly a group of silver-gilt, cast pendants (which have loops of exactly the same type as the coins) and a gold boss (pl. xxIx *f-g*) decorated in filigree with Borre style gripping-beasts, and another piece of filigree work (pl. xxIx *h*) decorated with a form of the Borre ring-chain pattern. This hoard provides fairly conclusive evidence for the dating of the introduction of the Borre style at least as early as the middle of the ninth century. This date might be even earlier, for some of the Borre style objects were cut about without reference to their pattern and adapted from their original use before becoming part of the necklace (e.g. pl. xxIx *f*): they may thus have been of some age when they were adapted to their secondary use.

The earliest Danish hoard to contain an object decorated in the Borre style comes from Vester Vedsted, Ribe. A small, round, gold mount from this hoard is decorated with three Borre animals with heads towards the centre (pl. xxIx *l*). It is executed in plain and beaded filigree wire and is further embellished with granulation. In one minor feature the ornament is not completely typical of the style, for the body of the animal curves above, and not beneath, its head; there can, however, be no doubt that the object

---

[1] The necklace thus becomes a closed find within the hoard, and the date 860 is more justified when applied to the necklace than to the rest of the hoard. Mr R. H. M. Dolley and Mr K. Skaare have kindly confirmed the date of the gathering together of the coins, and at the present moment there seems no call to doubt the numismatic evidence. Sceptics of this sort of coin dating are referred to an argument in a similar case—the Sutton Hoo hoard—ably presented by Mr Grierson (Grierson 1952)—all the arguments used by Mr Grierson in this paper are valid, in a modified way, in a discussion of the dating of the Hon hoard.

belongs to the Borre series. The latest coin in this hoard was struck for Nasr ibn Ahmad of Samarkand and is dated AD 916/917 (*A.H.* 304). The hoard was, therefore, probably deposited before 925.

Two hoards of mid-tenth century date contain objects decorated in the Borre style —Vårby, Södermanland, Sweden, deposited *c.* 940, and Gnezdovo, Russia, deposited *c.* 953. These hoards contain, besides Borre style material, objects decorated in the Jellinge style (pl. XXXII *b*), while some of the objects from the Gnezdovo treasure[1] are decorated in a combination of both styles, a feature already noticed at Östborg and Hon.

As well as pendants decorated with the Jellinge and Borre style, the Vårby necklace also includes a series of pendants bearing degenerate foliate motifs (pl. XXXII *c*). These objects were almost certainly made in the Viking colonies of Russia. Recent finds demonstrate that a considerable number of craftsmen were working in metal and producing objects at Kiev not unrelated to some of the Vårby objects.[2] It is possible that the Borre and Jellinge objects found at Vårby and Gnezdovo were made in the Viking settlements in Russia.[3] The close correspondence in the quality of the metal and in the quality of the gilding and finish of the various objects in the Vårby hoard supports a postulated Russian origin for the whole hoard.

The late date of these hoards need occasion no surprise, for objects decorated in the Borre style occur in a number of hoards of the late tenth century, as for example at Nonnebakken in Denmark (pl. XXXIV *b*).[4] It is obvious that the Borre and the Jellinge styles lived together in harmony until well on into the tenth century.

At this point we must discuss shortly the use of plant ornament in Scandinavia in the late ninth and early tenth centuries. The pendants from Vårby decorated with foliate ornament (pl. XXXII *c*), which were probably made in the Viking colonies of Russia, were based on south-eastern European prototypes and are an isolated phenomenon in Scandinavian contexts. Otherwise plant ornament, as has been shown in the previous chapter, occurs rarely in Scandinavia during the early Viking Age and, when it is found, it most often imitates the Carolingian acanthus ornament, achieving in the process a rather rugged and untidy stylization.[5] One piece, however, a rich brooch from Mosnæs, Norway (pl. XXXII *f–g*), imitates a vine scroll of the Northumbrian, or Anglo-Saxon type. The fact that the object was made in Scandinavia is indicated by the presence, between each arm on the back of the brooch, of a Borre style animal mask of a form that is completely Viking. Plant ornament derived from both Carolingian and insular sources did, then, occur in Scandinavia towards the end of the ninth century, where it is particularly common on trefoil brooches. It is strange that, until almost the end of the tenth century, plant ornament is rarely found together with animal ornament. The Mosnæs brooch provides one of the few examples where the two motifs occur together, and even on this example the animal head is discreetly tucked away on the back. Another example of the combination of the two—and one which has already been mentioned—is a

[1] Arne (1914), fig. 22. See also our pl. xxxiii *b*.   [2] Karger (1958), pl. li.
[3] Arbman (1959), 110–35.   [4] Skovmand (1942), 84 ff.   [5] Cf. Arbman (1937), 147 ff.

strap-end from Stora Ryk, Färgelanda, Sweden (pl. xxv *d*), which has a basically Carolingian acanthus motif, the side leaves of which have developed into animal heads of a rather dubious character, possibly belonging to the Borre style. This object demonstrates the Viking artist's general lack of interest in foliate ornament, perhaps even his inability to use it.

CHAPTER IV

THE JELLINGE STYLE

Because it is so diverse in motif, quality and geographical distribution it is practically impossible to define the Jellinge style.[1] The name is taken from the tenth century, Danish, royal cemetery at Jelling in Jutland and embraces the widely different ornament on two entirely disparate objects found there—a small silver cup and a pyramidal memorial stone. The cup (pl. XXXIV *a*), sometimes identified as a chalice,[2] is 4.2 centimetres high and is decorated with ribbon-like animals (fig. 43). The stone funerary monument (pl. XLIX)—it is too large to be distinguished as a tombstone—was set up

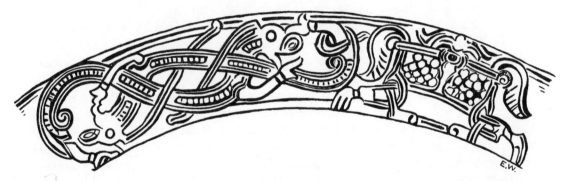

FIG. 43. The ornament of the cup from Jelling, Jutland, Denmark. Scale ⅓. *National Museum, Copenhagen.*

probably after 983,[3] by Harald Bluetooth in memory of his parents and is decorated on one face with a lion entwined by a snake (the other two faces being filled with a formalized and barbarous representation of the crucifixion and a long commemorative inscription). The animals on the cup (fig. 43) are of poor quality, while the animal on the stone is atypical, and yet these monuments form the basis for the nomenclature of much

[1] The term 'Jellinge' is retained here as against the more correct 'Jelling' (the actual spelling of the village name) as it is the common English usage. An accident of dialect in the nineteenth century introduced 'Jellinge' into archaeological terminology and there seems little point in changing an accepted label now.

[2] Schultz (1952). This identification is not altogether a happy one as no other chalice of this form is known from Western Europe or Scandinavia: but its strange form may partly be explained by the fact that the foot has been re-soldered to the bowl in modern times.

[3] For dating see below p. 120.

of Scandinavian ornament in the late ninth and tenth centuries. The Jellinge style, in its broadest sense, includes not only the ornament of these two objects, but decoration as diverse as the ribbon-like animals found on the tortoise brooch from Morberg, Røken, Buskerud, Norway (pl. xxxiv *d*), the fabulous beasts on the casket from the treasury of the German cathedral of Bamberg (pl. liv), the ornament of much of the Viking sculpture of the Isle of Man (e.g. fig. xlv *a*) or the sword guards illustrated in pl. xlvii *c–d*.

An attempt has been made to break away from this confusing terminology by retaining the term 'Jellinge style' for the ribbon-like animals of the type found on the Jellinge cup and defining a late tenth century style—the Mammen style. This style is named after a Danish grave-find which included an iron axe inlaid in silver with a substantial, semi-floriate animal. This stylistic division will be used here and this chapter will be mainly concerned with the ribbon-like animals of the Jellinge style. It is, however, impossible to discuss one of these two styles without occasional reference to the other and the main features of the Mammen style must be summarized here. The typical animal is that found on the Mammen axe and, although we shall see that it has certain atypical overtones, it seems reasonable to use this animal as an exemplar of the Mammen style.

The animal (pl. lii) is a biped—it is sometimes distinguished as a bird—and its head is rather small in relation to its substantial body. It has a lip-lappet, a double-contoured body, a spiral hip, and is completely and irrevocably interlaced with ribbon-like tendrils. If this animal is compared with the lion of the Jellinge stone (pl. xlix), which with all its assurance and grandeur is clearly distinguished as the self-satisfied product of a courtly sculptor, we can see that the two animals, which look so dissimilar, are closely related in ornamental detail. The animal on the stone has a more correct heraldic stance: it is a real lion with four enormous claws and a mane. Like the animal of the Mammen axe, however, it has the same double contour, spiral hips and lip-lappet: it has a comparatively small head and, like the Mammen animal, is caught up in an interlaced band (which in this instance takes the form of a snake). One or two foreign influences are to be seen in the make-up of both these animals—particularly noticeable are the acanthus-like fronds, of Carolingian or Anglo-Saxon origin, which here make their first appearance in Viking art—but in the main most of the details of the ornament are indigenous to Scandinavia. The stance and form of these two animals have long puzzled art-historians who have tried to derive them from all over Europe and Asia: but their prototypes are clearly to be seen in earlier Scandinavian ornament. They can be compared, for instance, to animals which occur on the runner of the fourth sledge (pl. xvi *a* and fig. 23) and on one of the terminals of a bed-head (fig. 17 *b*) from the Oseberg ship burial. Here are animals with a similar stance, similar small head, double contour and all-embracing ribbon ornament. Even refinements of detail—the broken curve of a pigtail and the foliate off-shoot, for example—can be seen in both places. Again the stance is very similar to that of the animal on the wooden lid from Gokstad (pl. xix *b*), which has a long tradition behind it. The contacts are very obvious and, although the design may have been slightly influenced from elsewhere in Europe, the native Scandinavian elements are too obvious to be ignored. Other details, which tell the same story, are clearly to be seen—for example, below the hip of the animal on the Mammen axe is the open, heart-shaped field, which was so typical a feature of Style E.

This, then, is the Mammen style. We cannot separate it completely from the Jellinge ribbon style (it occurs alongside the ribbon style, for example, on the remarkable horse collar (pl. xxx *b*) from Søllested in Denmark) and it is an unsatisfactory label, but the term is necessary if we are to discuss the tenth century with any degree of clarity.

We must turn now to the true Jellinge style, which can best be defined by describing a typical example of the style. A clear example of this motif is provided on the well-known horse collar from Mammen, Jutland, Denmark[1] (pl. xxxv *a*). The animals are cast in slight relief on the series of gilt-bronze plates let into the (now restored) wooden body of the collar. The head is in profile and has an open mouth, lip-lappet, almond-shaped eye and a head lappet, or pigtail, which interlaces with the body. The ribbon-shaped body is double-contoured and is filled with transverse billets. The foreleg emerges from a spiral hip and has a two-clawed foot. The hind-leg has an angular joint and a backward-bent, three-element foot. The tail, which terminates in three feather-like elements, interlaces with the body of the next animal.

The Jellinge style stands in a special relationship to the Borre style, but its origins are to be found in Oseberg and in the ornament of Styles D and E. One of the objects found in the Gokstad barrow (pl. xxx *d*) has ornament closely related to that found on the horse collar—it is decorated in fact with a Jellinge animal—but the open front-hip of the animal is clearly a survival from Style E. A similar relationship can be seen on a brooch from Birka (pl. xxxiii *d*), where the lappet passes through the opening in the body of an animal which is also undoubtedly a Jellinge creature. These objects must be typologically early in the Jellinge series and, indeed, the presence of a Jellinge object in the Gokstad burial is indicative of a date in, say, the last half of the ninth century for the deposition of the object. But even in the more normal Jellinge style animals there are plenty of features which are clearly drawn from Style E, as for instance the feather-like terminals of the tails of the animals on the Mammen horse collar, which hark back to the tendril-like offshoots of the older style. The ribbon-shaped animal of the Jellinge style is clearly derived from native prototypes: the correspondence of the Jellinge animals with those found on the Oseberg cart (pl. x) is particularly striking, while the flow of the lines of the body is perhaps reminiscent of the Style D animals of the Skabersjö brooch (pl. IV *a*). The Jellinge creatures are clearly in the mainstream of Scandinavian animal styles.

The close relationship between the Jellinge and Borre styles is patent. It has been shown that the animal-heads on the spur and strap-end from Værne Kloster are of a type not commonly found in the Borre style—that they are related to the animal-heads of the Jellinge style. This is particularly noticeable on the strap-end, where the lappet and the ring at the neck are entirely typical of the Jellinge style. Similar heads occur on other pieces which can only be identified as belonging to the Borre style with a

---

[1] Found in the same parish, but not in association with the Mammen axe (pls. LII and LIII).

certain amount of equivocation. Two Swedish silver brooches—from Ödeshög, Östergötland, and Östra Herrestad, Skåne—together with a bronze object from Mammen, Denmark, demonstrate the connection between the Jellinge and Borre styles with admirable clarity, in that they are each ornamented with motifs from the two styles.

The ornament of the Ödeshög brooch (pl. XXXIII *e*) is executed in silver filigree wire on a roughly moulded silver base-plate. The central feature of the brooch is a modified form of the Borre ring-chain motif, which is flanked on either side by an animal with a head in profile. Each animal has a pigtail with a sharp angle on its outer edge at the point where it emerges from the head. The body of the animal is ribbon-shaped and the front hip has a spiral hook. The angled pigtail, the spiral hook, the head in profile and the shape of the animal's body are reasonably typical Jellinge features. In fact, the animal, while not exactly typical of the Jellinge style, demonstrates very clearly something distinct from the Borre style but is at the same time associated with ornament that is undoubtedly in the Borre tradition.

The second object in this group comes from the same grave as the Mammen horse collar; it is a die[1] from which was pressed a thin metal base of a similar, though smaller, version of the Ödeshög brooch. At either end of the object (pl. XXXIII *c*) can be seen the typical ring-chain of the Borre style, while in the centre are two splendidly typical Jellinge ribbon-like animals, complete with spiral hips and lappets on the head and upper lip.

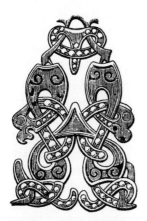

FIG. 44. Ornament from an arm of the trefoil brooch from Östra Herrestad, Skåne, Sweden. Scale: ⅔. *Statens Historiska Museum, Stockholm.*

The Jellinge element can clearly be seen on the brooch from Östra Herrestad, Skåne, Sweden (fig. 44). The bodies of these animals, however, are arranged in a pseudo-ring-chain ornament which is strongly reminiscent of the Borre style, while the thickening of the body certainly harks back to the older Scandinavian styles.[2] At the same time, while the animal-heads lack the lip-lappets so typical of the Jellinge style, they are very close in form to those on the Jellinge cup itself.

An interesting Borre–Jellinge overlap is provided by the small, sub-triangular mount of bronze from Gnezdovo (pl. XXXIII *b*): in all technical respects—the beaded border, the transversely nicked contours of the animal, the materials used, the quality of the workmanship, etc.—this mount belongs to the Borre style. The relationship of head and hips might also be identified as a detail of Borre ornament, but the animal is, in most of its detail, typically Jellinge. The lip-lappet, the pigtail interlaced round the neck, the interlaced ribbons, the hatched body and the spiral hip are Jellinge features. A similarly confusing mixture of styles is provided by the miniature weather-vane (pl. XXXII *e*) from Rangsby, Saltvik on the Finnish island of Åland.

[1] This object was first classified as a die by Brønsted (1936), 106: his identification has been largely ignored by later writers.   [2] Arbman (1961), 133.

An interesting aspect of the Borre-Jellinge relationship is the general arrangement of ornament on certain silver disc brooches. A typical example is that from Tråen, Buskerud, Norway (pl. XXXIV e); the heads of the three animals are in the centre of the brooch and the bodies interlace with each other round the rest of the field. The animals are typical of the Jellinge ribbon style, even to the lip-lappets of the classical form. The heads, although portrayed in profile, are in the same position as the heads on the brooch from Vester Vedsted (pl. XXIX l), which we have seen to be a typical Borre piece, and the position of the bodies shows a similar relationship. The Tråen and Vester Vedsted objects are but typical of a number of disc brooches decorated in the two styles and are obviously related to each other in lay-out, if not in actual motif. Some brooches even show a mixture of the two styles, while retaining the same arrangement of the field of decoration.

We have attempted to show the continuity in Scandinavian art from the Vendel period to the tenth century and, at the same time, we have tried to show the close chronological relationship between the Jellinge and Borre styles. The few examples we have chosen to demonstrate our theories could be multiplied many times, and casual references below will reinforce our argument. Let us now examine the Jellinge style in greater detail.

So far the animals on the rather run-of-the-mill quality horse-collar from Mammen have been taken as typical of the Jellinge style. It would perhaps be fairer to the Viking craftsmen to glance briefly at more competent examples of their artistic achievement before passing on to a discussion of the relationships of the style which is perhaps best seen on the pair of horse-collars from Søllested, Fyn, Denmark (pl. XXXV b).

The best preserved (pl. XXXV b) of the two collars is 44·5 cm. long. It is of wood, mounted with gilt-bronze panels and mouldings. The wood has largely decayed away, but it has been possible to reconstruct its original form. At each end of the wooden bow are gilt-bronze terminals which take the form of grotesque, formalized animal heads, with slightly open mouths, two enormous semicircular ears, and large, staring, lentoid-shaped eyes (pl. XXXVII c). The eyebrows, the up-turned terminals of the lip and the ferocious teeth of the upper jaw are inlaid with silver plates, which are in turn inlaid with dots and zigzag patterns in niello. On the cheeks and forehead are a series of small birds and animals executed in low relief, with scaled bodies and floriated tails: the eyes of some of these creatures are inlaid with blue glass. The lips and snout of each terminal animal-head are formed of an elaborate interlace pattern, the contour lines of which, like the contours of the eyebrows, are nicked to imitate filigree. The surface is in no place completely flat, it is articulated by the natural curves of the animal-head and by artificial concavities in the breadth of the interlace ornament. In this way a satisfying mobility is achieved.

The same nicked technique, which may well be derived from the similar feature in the pure Borre style, is used on the bodies of the ribbon-like animals which decorate the ridge piece of the collar. Most of these animals (pl. XXXVII b) have a backward-turned head with open mouth, lentoid eye and lip-lappet. They usually have spiral hips and the lappet and tail interlace with the body, sometimes terminating in frond-like motifs; the feet have an almost foliate quality. In one panel (pl. XXXVII d) are a pair of birds similar to those on the animal heads.

On the sides of the collar were a series of thin, pressed gilt-bronze mounts in the form of formalized human masks, with dwarf-like hands raised towards the mouth. But the two fine interlaced openwork creatures in the centre of the ridge piece are perhaps the most competent piece of work on the whole object (pl. XXXVII a). Their common body forms a loop for the reins and is carefully panelled. The long interlacing lappets are organically connected with the flanking panels of the ridge of the collar, in that they pass into the mouths of the plastic animal heads which terminate each ridge. The taut, brilliant economy of the ornament of these objects is a striking tribute to the high standard of the Viking craftsmen who made them—as a piece of casting alone the objects are a considerable technical achievement while, as a piece of applied art, they are almost without rival in contemporary Europe. Barbaric they may be, but, with the exception of the rather badly composed panel which contains the two birds, they must rank as one of the major achievements of European metalwork.

A number of similar horse-collars have been found in Denmark, they come from the island of Als,[1] from Møllemosegaard and from Mammen (pl. XXXV a), but normally a much simpler form, with a single gilt-bronze central mount, is all that occurs. The best-known collars are those from Mammen (pl. XXXV a), which, although of poorer quality than those from Søllested, have many points of interest. We have already described the animal ornament of these objects. Among the other motifs on the collars is one of a man being swallowed by a snake-like animal (pl. XXXVI a), which may represent either the Norse mythological tale of Odin being swallowed by the Fenris wolf or the Christian story of Jonah and the Whale. Immediately next to this scene is a representation of a human figure holding a crook-headed stick (pl. XXXVI c); this may be a bishop, but the dress reflects the style of many small brooches representing female figures which are found throughout the Viking period (e.g. pl. XXIV d) and may have no Christian significance at all. The animal-heads at the terminals of the collars are remarkable, for in the open mouths of the animals are gripping-beasts (pl. XXXVI b). They are in some respects poor apologies for gripping-beasts, but gripping-beasts they are, spread-eagled across the gaping mouths of each animal head. This element links, in the clearest possible way, the Jellinge and Oseberg groups and demonstrates again the inherent continuity between the different styles of Viking age Scandinavia.

It is impossible to proceed further in a discussion of this style without turning our attention to the British Isles—an area which yields a surprising amount of material decorated in a style which is very close to the Scandinavian Jellinge style.

Naturally, in a country that was conquered and ruled by the Vikings, a number of imported objects of pure Jellinge style are found. Typical of these imported objects is the terminal of a sword scabbard from the Viking capital city of York (fig. 45). Although the style of this object has certain Borre style elements, it can be compared most easily

[1] Worsaae (1865), fig. 7.

in both quality and motif with the ornament on the oval brooch from Norway illustrated in pl. XXXIV *b*. Other archaeological material (metalwork, stone sculpture, etc.), although hinting at its Jellinge connections, does not reflect the Scandinavian style very closely.

In order to understand the Jellinge phenomenon in England, it is necessary to look shortly at the pre-existing art of the British Isles. Although the great days of seventh and eighth century insular art, when the whole of Europe looked for inspiration to the British Isles, had long since passed, British art of the ninth century was, if rather decadent and no longer very influential, at least competent, precise and lively. Like their Scandinavian contemporaries the Anglo-Saxon and Hiberno-Saxon artists (i.e. artists from Ireland, Northern England and Scotland) were producing an art based mainly on formalized animal patterns with an admixture of interlace. In metalwork we might take as typical of Anglo-Saxon ornament the small lively animals, executed in silver against a nielloed background, which occur on a number of mounts and other objects in the hoard from Trewhiddle, Cornwall (fig. 46), which must have been

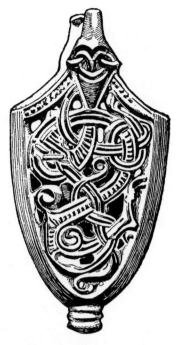

FIG. 45. Sword scabbard chape from York. Scale: ¼. *Yorkshire Museum, York.*

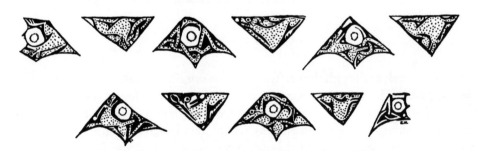

FIG. 46. Ornament from a silver drinking-horn mount from Trewhiddle, St Austell, Cornwall. Scale ¼. *British Museum.*

made in the middle of the ninth century.[1] The Trewhiddle style is related to, and is probably the origin of, the style which flourished in Ireland at this period.[2] Similar ornament occurs in the manuscripts of the ninth century, for example, in the Gospel Book, British Museum MS., Royal I.E.VI,[3] while in sculpture the elegant animal style

[1] The hoard was buried with coins dating its deposition to *c*. 875, cf. Wilson and Blunt (1961).
[2] Cf. MacDermott (1955).　　　[3] Zimmermann (1918), pls. 290 and 291 *a*.

of the Cropthorne stone cross[1] shows the same style in another medium. It was the fine quality of this competent animal style in both England and the Hiberno-Saxon area which led many scholars to the conclusion that the Scandinavian Jellinge style was derived from insular prototypes. In this book we have tried to emphasize the continuity of the indigenous art of Scandinavia and, if we are right, the widely held theory, which would place the origin of the Jellinge style in the insular area, is wrong. In order to demonstrate our thesis more fully it is necessary to examine this insular style in greater detail.

Metal objects of English manufacture decorated in the Jellinge style are rare. It is therefore not easy to compare the insular and Scandinavian material. One of the few pieces of English metalwork which shows distinct Jellinge influence is the silver roof plate (pl. XXXVIII *a*) of a casket in the British Museum: in the triangular fields of this object are a series of animals inlaid with niello (fig. 47). The ornament is incompetently

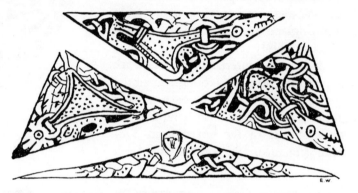

FIG. 47. Ornament from the lid of a casket, *cf. pl.* XXXVIII *a*.
Scale ⅓. *British Museum.*

and badly executed, as though the craftsman was struggling to attain a standard of which he was incapable. The animals lack any sort of charm, but are full of interest for the art-historian. They have many reminiscences of the Trewhiddle style. The sub-triangular bodies, the speckling of the ornament, the technique of inlaying with niello, the use of the triangular fields and the beaded borders which surround the field are all derived from the ninth century Anglo-Saxon ornament (cf. fig. 46). The Scandinavian element, however, is clearly seen—the double contour of the animals' bodies, the ring encircling the neck where the limb crosses it, the traces of the gripping-beast style in the topmost panel, all these are features derived from the Jellinge and Borre styles and have no connection with the preceding Anglo-Saxon styles. Similar attempts to graft this Scandinavian art onto the Anglo-Saxon stock are seen in a number of other pieces: on a scramasax from Sittingbourne, Kent,[2] for example, and on a disc brooch from Canterbury.[3] There can be little doubt that we can see on these objects attempts by artists

[1] Kendrick (1938a), pl. lxxx, 1.   [2] Wilson (1963), no. 80.   [3] *Idem*, (1960c).

trained in the Anglo-Saxon tradition to achieve a Viking art style. Because they could not altogether grasp the tricks of the style they failed to reach anything like perfection. Only in the Hiberno-Saxon west and north was full reconciliation of insular and Scandinavian styles achieved in metalwork, but we shall discuss this at greater length below.

If we turn now to stone sculpture a similar process of degeneration becomes apparent. The fine quality English sculpture of the ninth century gradually became debased in the areas settled by the Vikings after Alfred's treaty with Guthrum in 886. The basic difficulty in any discussion of the stone sculpture of England in the ninth and tenth centuries is the absence of any chronological fixed point. None of the Anglo-Saxon or Manx crosses are dated by inscription and the only basis for dating is style history, never a very satisfactory method to use. It is impossible, therefore, in many cases to say whether a certain type of incompetent-seeming ornament is the fumbling beginning or the degenerate end-product of a series. A case in point has been the discussion of the cross from St Alkmund's, Derby (pl. xxxviii *b* and *c*), which scholars have seen variously as an example of the English origin, or of the English degeneration, of the Jellinge style. If it were possible to date this fragment many of the problems of the Jellinge style would be solved, indeed, if it were possible to date any fragment of sculpture from the Scandinavian areas of England, many problems of chronology in relation to tenth century Viking art would be resolved.

Since no dated Anglo-Saxon sculpture from these areas survives, art-history and political history must be dove-tailed in an effort to build up a chronological picture of the Jellinge style in insular stone carving. The St Alkmund slab is related to a series of sculptures which have a certain geographical and chronological unity. These consist of a number of stone crosses from the East Yorkshire villages of Middleton, Sinnington and Ellerburn and one or two other small hamlets to the north of the Vale of Pickering. One of the series of carvings from Middleton (pl. xxxix *b*) is perhaps the most interesting, for it was carved by a sculptor who executed a series of at least five crosses at Middleton and elsewhere, all of which are decorated with what is for the greater part almost inconceivably incompetent animal ornament. The cross illustrated here, therefore, must be seen as the product of an established workshop in one of the Viking areas of Yorkshire and not just as the casual product of an untrained craftsman. Framed in a panel, on the back face of the cross, is an animal the head of which is seen from above: it has a ribbon-shaped—or perhaps one should say sausage-shaped—body entwined rather half-heartedly in interlace. The body is double contoured and has an amorphous tail and a pair of legs which bear little relationship to any normal mammalian physiological structure. The mouth is apparently set at ninety degrees to the head, and the two lips so formed appear as loops, through which the ribbon interlace passes. The animal bears no relationship to the animal ornament of the earlier stone sculpture of Anglo-Saxon England, its closest parallels are with the ribbon-like animals of the Scandinavian Jellinge style. The double contour of the body, various tricks of the interlace (particularly at the neck), and the presence of the free ring in the interlace in the bottom right-hand corner, are all directly derived from the Scandinavian styles. The strange form of the lips of the animal is a feature which distinguishes the school of sculptors of the Middleton area and may be derived from the Jellinge lip-lappet.

The Middleton cross must be seen as the product of an English craftsman struggling to attain the new style brought by his Viking masters from Scandinavia. That he was an insular craftsman is, we think, demonstrated by the fact that there are, in a number of the main the Middleton cross series, interlace patterns of a true Anglo-Saxon tradition; the ornament of these panels is much more competently executed than the other ornamental motifs on the crosses.

It has been argued, and argued cogently,[1] that the animal ornament of the Viking crosses is merely a barbaric English art revived under Viking influence, and that the animals are not necessarily of Viking origin. There is some truth in this argument, but we are not satisfied that this is the whole truth. There can be no doubt that there are English elements in this insular Viking art. We have already indicated the insular origin of the interlace designs, similarly the long-standing tradition of English animal ornament could not altogether be ignored by the craftsmen who carved these stones, but this is not merely the revival of a barbaric art, it is the introduction of a new style. The old traditions can be dimly perceived below the ornament of the new style, but the new forms and the new style are the important elements of the art. It is imperative, therefore, that we attempt to identify the sculptors who carved these crosses.

It is easy to forget that, apart from certain carvings on the Swedish island of Gotland, stone as an important medium for ornament was almost completely unknown to the Scandinavians before the tenth century. The Danish Vikings came to a land rich in stone-carving, to a land where the ninth century stone sculptor was using an art which the Vikings (who had an artistic ancestry in common with the Anglo-Saxons) could appreciate. It seems reasonable that in an area of primary Danish settlement (i.e. an area which had a Danish population within a generation of Halfdan's settlement and Guthrum's treaty) crosses like those at Middleton were made to the order of Viking settlers, whose only experience of sculpture may have been of wood-carving. These settlers had great confidence in their own taste and insisted on the craftsmen producing art in a Viking image. The craftsman, who carved the crosses for the settlers, apparently tried to achieve a style which his patrons, unversed in a stone sculptural tradition, would appreciate. He used certain motifs of his native Anglo-Saxon traditions, and used them to some effect; at the same time, however, he tried to adapt a completely foreign animal ornament to a medium for which it was not designed. He was not a genius and his animal ornament did not evolve into anything remarkable, yet he ultimately succeeded in obliterating almost all traces of the native Anglo-Saxon animal motifs. The almost universal bad quality, bad proportions and misunderstood use of Jellinge animal ornament in the north of England, is perhaps due to the fact that the school of sculptors in that area produced no first-rate artist, who might have developed an individual, outstanding style, or compiled the pattern book which could have inspired his contem-

[1] E.g. by Kendrick (1949), 92.

poraries to create a consistent animal style of high quality, as in late seventh and early eighth century England.

This is not to deny the fact that some Viking crosses, for example the famous Collingham shaft (fig. 48), are executed very competently. The deep rounded carving of this cross, while not attaining the quality of the slightly earlier, purely Anglo-Saxon, crosses, demonstrates the competence of the sculptor, who, as Brøndsted pointed out,[1]

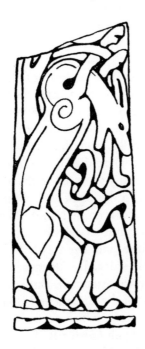
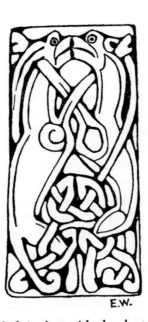

FIG. 48. Ornament from a cross-shaft in the parish church at Collingham, Yorkshire.

successfully contrives to combine Anglo-Saxon and Viking motifs. Returning to the St Alkmund cross shaft (pl. XXXVIII b and c) from Derby, it becomes reasonably obvious that this fragment is the product of a fusion of styles. The animals on two faces are very clearly influenced by the Jellinge style in their double contouring and ribbon interlace— at the same time the detail of the head and the stance of the animals is much more closely allied to Mercian sculptured animals of the ninth century—the most distinguished examples of which are seen at Cropthorne, Worcestershire.[2] The other two sides show a more degenerate Jellinge style, more nearly related to the Yorkshire series and particularly to the Collingham shaft.

It is interesting that some close parallels to this cross are found in Gloucestershire (pl. XXXIX a), it is just possible that they were erected by Vikings in the troubled times in that area between 885 and 900. But it may equally well be, however, that the Anglo-

[1] (1924), 192–194.   [2] Wilson (1960a), pl. 66.

Saxons themselves developed a taste for this style, for in the heart of Wessex, at Rams-
bury, West Camel and Colerne,[1] are found stones decorated with great competence in a
sub-Viking style, while a coped tombstone at Bexhill, in Sussex, is decorated with crude
Jellinge-derived ornament,[2] closely related to the ornament of the Sittingbourne
scramasax.[3] The Colerne fragments bear ornament which, in much of its detail, is closely
related to southern English art of the eighth century, but the interlace, particularly on
the more defaced fragment, is clearly of Scandinavian inspiration. We may see here a
late eighth or an early ninth-century attempt by the Anglo-Saxons to adapt Viking art
to their own use, at a period when their own art, judging from the rare surviving
material, was particularly sterile.

So far we have only considered sculpture from the primary area of Viking settlement.
This treaty area of the Alfred–Guthrum agreement is known, after the five main centres
(Derby, Stamford, Nottingham, Lincoln and Leicester), as the Five Boroughs. The
Five Boroughs formed, together with Yorkshire, the Danish area of settlement. This
area was completely distinct, politically and ethnically, from the north-west of England,
which was settled by Norwegian Vikings most of whom had come from Ireland in the
early part of the tenth century and who were, for many years, on terms of strained peace,
or actual war, with their neighbours to the east. In this area, as Collingwood pointed
out many years ago,[4] a different sculptural tradition is to be found. The centre of this
region,[5] from the art-historical point of view, is Cumberland, although Westmorland,
Cheshire, Lancashire, Dumfries, West Yorkshire and even North Wales produce
monuments in some quantity which tell the same story. In this area, as in the area of
Danish settlement, most of the crosses bear interlace ornament. But some of the Norse
crosses of this region are chiefly remarkable, from the ornamental point-of-view, for
the figural scenes, both Christian and pagan in content, which occur in panels on them.
The most important monument is naturally that from Gosforth. This cross is unique.
It is complete and is the largest surviving piece of pre-Norman sculpture in England—
so large in fact that it is useless to illustrate it as a whole in this context. It bears interlace
patterns and, sometimes in panels, scenes from the life of Christ and from the Voluspá,
the pagan Norse cycle which tells the story of the world from its creation to its destruc-
tion. The crucifixion (pl. XL), which appears on the east face of the cross, is contrasted
with the pagan scenes (pl. XLI) on the other faces and perhaps represents the triumph of
the Church, through Christ's death, over the pagan world.[6]

Similar narrative Christian scenes appear in panels on many of the Irish high crosses
of ninth and early tenth century date, and it is presumably from this area that the crosses
of Cumberland, and the neighbouring counties, are derived. Some of the scenes which

[1] Baldwin-Brown (1937), 280–286 and pls. cix and cxii and Kendrick (1938a), pl. lxxxiii.
[2] Kendrick (1949), pl. lvi.   [3] Wilson (1963), no. 80.   [4] Collingwood (1927), 120 ff.
[5] The authors wish to acknowledge the help given them by Mr Richard Bailey of University College,
Bangor, in this portion of the discussion. He has read this section in draft and placed his unrivalled knowledge
of this material at our disposal with great generosity. We would stress, however, that the opinions we
express here are our own and that our interpretations differ, to a minor extent, from those of Mr Bailey.
[6] Cf. Berg (1958), for an iconographic interpretation of the cross.

occur on the Irish monuments are repeated on the Northumbrian ones, the scene of the hart and the wolf (or 'hart and hound', as it is commonly known) which is a well-known symbol of the struggle between good and evil, occurs, for example, on the crosses from Ahenny and Castledermot in Ireland[1] and in a very similar form on the Dacre cross in Cumberland (pl. XXXIX c). The scene of Adam and Eve, if such it be, on the Dacre cross is also found on Irish crosses. Other scenes also occur on both Irish and western English crosses of this period—Cain and Abel, the Crucifixion, etc.

Narrative sculpture had not occurred in any quantity in Anglo-Saxon contexts since the early eighth century and the only possible derivation of this type of motif must be from Ireland, from which area the Norwegian settlers of north-west England had come. The chronology of the Irish high crosses is obscure and the allegation that the name Flann, recorded by Petrie in the nineteenth century on *the Cross of the Scriptures* at Clonmacnoise, can be identified as the King of Munster who died *c.* 904, may be open to doubt, but there seems little reason to deny that the high crosses flourished in the late ninth and early tenth centuries. Such a date fits well with the chronology of the Northumbrian series, which is discussed below. The Irish crosses are more sophisticated than their Northumbrian counterparts; the standard of their carving is much higher and the figural scenes, which decorate them, are more easily understandable. It would be a reasonable typological thesis to presume that the competent narrative scenes of the Irish crosses are the origin of the Northumbrian series.

One of the coarsening influences in the art of the Cumberland series is undoubtedly Viking. Certain human figures are shown with a dress that is typically Viking. The long trailing gown on the right-hand figure below the Crucifixion on the Gosforth cross (pl. XL) is a recurrent feature of Viking representational art (cf. pl. XXIV c).

At the same time there is much that is Anglo-Saxon in the sculpture of Cumberland and the neighbouring counties. The interlace ornament and the form of many of the crosses are derived from English prototypes; on one of the Penrith crosses, known as the Giant's Thumb, there is even a rather degenerate vine-scroll[2] which has an obvious Anglo-Saxon ancestry. Scandinavian influence is only strong in the choice of mythological subject and in its figural style. Occasionally Jellinge style elements can be seen, minor motifs among a mass of Scandinavianized Anglo-Saxon and Irish ornament—a spiral hip on one of the Lancaster crosses,[3] sub-Anglian animals bound in Jellinge interlace at Waberthwaite,[4] the free rings round the limbs and interlace of the extraordinary 'Bound Devil' on the Kirkby Stephen cross shaft (pl. XLIII a), and so on—but such features of pure Jellinge origin are uncommon. The tenth century art of north-west England seems to have been a completely home-made Viking art, based almost in its entirety on the traditions of Irish and Anglo-Saxon sculpture. It was a Viking art, but one outside the mainstream of development.

This art produced its 'sports', such as the 'hog-back' tombstones, like those from Brampton (pl. XLII a), with their quaint semi-naturalistic animals (in this case bears)

[1] Henry (1933), pls. 36 and 46.
[3] Ibid., fig. 171.
[2] Collingwood (1927), fig. 162.
[4] Ibid., fig. 177.

which grip the ends of the coped tomb. The Brampton tombstones are in Yorkshire and serve to demonstrate how the Danes and Norwegians in the north soon developed a common art—for tombstones of a similar form occur on both sides of the Pennines. A mixture of style and motif occurs on the more normal cross shafts and can already be discerned at a very early stage of Viking settlement, for the Yorkshire cross, Middleton A, which is carved by the same man as the cross illustrated in pl. XXXIX *b*, has a hart-and-hound scene on the back,[1] which is best paralleled west of the Pennines, whence it probably came. The sculpture of practically the whole of the North of England in the last three-quarters of the tenth century is a mixture of styles, relieved by a few highly individual local schools. The fact that the mixture of eastern and western styles survived into the eleventh century is demonstrated by the Leeds cross, which bears scenes drawn from both sides of the Pennines together with an interlace pattern in a late tendril style.[2]

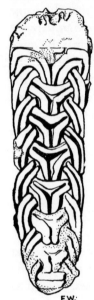

An important ornamental element in the Anglo-Norse sculptural series of the Cumberland area—and one that is found as far away as Penmon in Anglesey[3]—is a symmetrical ring-chain ornament which we will refer to, for reasons which will shortly become obvious, as Gaut's ring-chain. It is a highly individual motif consisting of a regularly interlacing chain, constructed with a midrib made up of a series of hollow-sided truncated triangles (cf. above the panel illustrated in pl. XL). There is perhaps an echo in this motif of the ring-chain of the Borre style,[4] indeed the motif itself is found on a Borre strap-end, from Sundvor, Rogaland, Norway (fig. 49). This comparison fits chronologically, but the analogy should not be pressed too far. Gaut's ring-chain is best seen as a local product of the Anglo-Norse settlers of north-west England. It usually occurs on sculpture, but is also to be seen on the Hesket sword-guard in silver plate.[5]

FIG. 49. Strap-end from Sundvor, Rogaland, Norway. *Stavanger Museum*

The motif is also found on the stone slabs of the Isle of Man (e.g. pl. XLIV *b*), where there had long been a lively sculptural tradition, based mainly on Celtic, but to some extent also on Anglian, prototypes.

Most of the crosses of the Viking kingdom of Man are carved in low relief on the comparatively soft, slate-like stone of the island. The technique, as Arbman has pointed out, is closely allied to that of the wood-carver. Unlike the crosses of the Anglo-Saxon area, they are carved—shaft and head—on the surface of a rectangular slab and only on a few late examples does the wheel-like head stand free from the shaft of the cross.

---

[1] Binns (1956), fig. 9.   [2] Collingwood (1927), fig. 193.   [3] Bu'lock (1958), fig. iv, *a*.
[4] Cf., for example, the hollow-sided truncated triangle in the Borre interlace on the bronze brooch from Stokke, Norway. Shetelig (1920), fig. 310.
[5] Cowen (1934), fig. 2.

The starting point for any study of these crosses is a stone from Kirk Michael (fig. 50), in the north-west of the island. It bears an inscription in Scandinavian runic characters which, translated, reads:

Melbrigði, son of Aðakan [the] smith, erected this cross for his . . . soul, but Gaut made this and all in Man.

Gaut's proud boast may have been, in a sense, true, when he carved the Kirk Michael stone, for, although there are a large number of such cross slabs in the Isle of Man, it is typologically quite probable that the series of slabs carved by Gaut were the first Scandinavian crosses to be erected in the island. Another cross, at Kirk Andreas, gives more information about Gaut: he was known as Gaut Björnson (he was therefore the son of a Viking) and lived at a place called Kuli, which has been identified with a farm called Cooley in the parish of Michael.

Gaut, although a competent craftsman, was not a brilliant innovator and his pattern book was very restricted. There are no animals in the ornamental repertoire of his signed crosses and he seems to have been primarily interested in interlace patterns.[1] Chief among these patterns is the ring-chain motif, which we have encountered in Cumberland and which bears his name. In fact, as Mr Bailey has pointed out to us privately, all Gaut's motifs, with the exception of the pattern at the end of the arms (which is probably derived directly from the Scandinavian Borre style), are found in the north-west of England. Even the assymetrical interlace pattern, which is seen in its typical form at Kirk Michael (fig. 50, a), is found in Westmorland at Lowther.[2] Although this motif is probably distantly related to the vine-scroll, the small tendrils which curve round the stem, with their nicked contour, and scroll-like terminal, echo a similar feature in the Scandinavian ornamental repertoire (cf. pl. XXXVII b).

Gaut was, then, greatly influenced by the sculpture of north-west England, and may indeed have come as a refugee from that area,[3] but he was obviously in closer touch with the art of the Viking homelands than were his contemporaries in the north-west, as is demonstrated by the motif at the end of the arms which appear to have Borre-like fore-runners. The full strength of the Scandinavian stylistic tradition in the Isle of Man is, however, more apparent on other Manx Viking slabs. Not only are Viking stylistic elements present on these stones, but complete scenes, and in some cases cycles, from Scandinavian mythology occur. The story of Sigurd is especially popular and occurs in a number of guises in the Manx series, particularly on the later crosses. The human figures, as at Gosforth, tend to be modelled on Viking rather than English prototypes, as on one of the stones from Jurby, where the woman with long pig-tail and trailing

---

[1] A cross, which has animal ornament and which might well have been carved by Gaut, it has at least three of his motifs, is that from Treen Church, Nappin, Jurby: cf. Kermode (1907), pl. xxxiii, 78. Other crosses perhaps carved by Gaut are listed by Shetelig (1948).

[2] *Royal Commission on Ancient and Historical Monuments, Westmorland*, pl. 5, top left.

[3] See below p. 114 f.

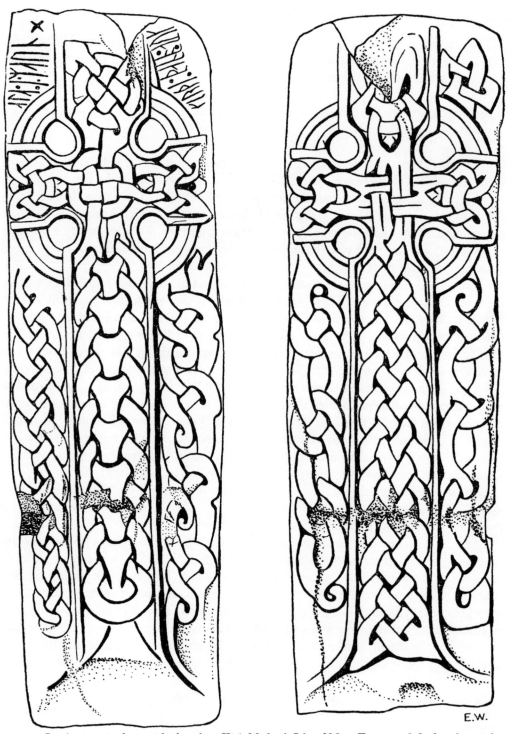

FIG. 50. Gaut's cross in the parish church at Kirk Michael, Isle of Man. Face *a* to left, face *b* to right. Cf. pl. XLIII *b*.

dress is closely related to the small, silver female figures, which were used as personal ornaments in Scandinavia (cf. pl. XXIV c). The animals in most of the strictly narrative scenes could also be derived from Scandinavian sources, but some of the motifs, particularly the 'hart-and-hound', suggest an origin in Cumberland or Ireland for some, at least, of the more naturalistic beasts. It is interesting to note in this context that the Manx narrative scenes differ from both their Cumberland and Irish counterparts in that they are not placed in small rectangular panels on the shaft of the cross. Because the crosses are carved in relief on flat slabs of stone, there is space available for decoration elsewhere and the scenes tend to occur in the space on either side of the main stem of the cross.[1] Occasionally, however, these narrative scenes contain animals which are little more than Jellinge ornamental motifs: for example, on the Sigurd slab from Andreas,[2] Sigurd is shown slaying a dragon which would be quite at home on a piece of tenth century metalwork with no apparent mythological significance. But usually the animals belonging to the ornamental series occur apart from the narrative scenes. Such narrative scenes are not, of course, new to Viking art, examples have been quoted from

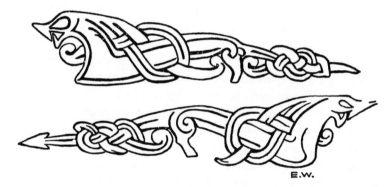

FIG. 51. Ornament from a cross slab in the parish church at Kirk
Michael, Isle of Man.

the Mammen horse-collar and from the Oseberg wagon, but, as such scenes were probably most often represented in wood in Scandinavia (other than in Gotland, which does not provide valid comparisons) we have little comparative material of an earlier date than the introduction of stone carving into the Scandinavian peninsula in the late tenth century.

Two examples of the purely ornamental animal style are all that can be discussed in the present context, one occurs on a slab from Kirk Michael and the other on the Thorleif slab from Kirk Braddan. The animals of the Kirk Michael slab (fig. 51) have many of the features of the typical Jellinge style (the spiral hip, the double contour, the

[1] There are exceptions, e.g. the Sigurd stone from Ramsey, Kermode (1907), pl. xlvi, where the whole of one face, as far as it survives, is decorated with a narrative scene.
[2] Kermode (1907), fig. 95a.

interlaced lappet and the lip-lappet) but certain details of the head (the almond-shaped eye pointing towards the snout and the tooth in the lower jaw) show influences from the succeeding Ringerike style.[1] It is possible that this stone is fairly late in the Manx series, but the interlace in the arms of the cross show that it is very closely linked to the tradition of the Gaut crosses.

The stone raised at Kirk Braddan, by a Viking named Thorleif to a son who had a Celtic name, Fiacc, is perhaps more typically Viking (fig. 52). Fiacc may have been a second or third generation colonist, Thorleif had probably married a native Celtic woman from Ireland or the Isle of Man, and, even if this is not so, the juxtaposition of names makes it probable that when the cross was raised the different racial communities in the island were being fused into one. This cross is probably later than Gaut's series and most of the ornament reflects very closely the Scandinavian Mammen style. The ornament of the decorated side panel (fig. 52a), however, is derived directly from the art which inspired the ribbon-shaped animals of the true Jellinge style, the head has a lip-lappet and the body makes a regular, wavy line along the length of the cross. The animal has a pointed oval eye and a lappet interlacing with the neck. Elements of the older Style E can be seen in the feathered extensions which occur throughout the length of the panel. The animals on the two faces of the cross are of the more substantial type of Mammen style animal, which will be discussed below. Their double contoured bodies are pelleted in exactly the same manner as the bodies of the animals on such objects as the Bamberg and Cammin caskets. The same feathered Style E feature noted on the side panel can also be seen here; the spiral hip has grown in importance, the lappets interlace and the eyes are almond-shaped. An interesting feature is the double spiral over the body of the second animal from the bottom on face b, which is almost exactly paralleled on the Levisham, Yorkshire, slab (pl. XLII b). Another Kirk Braddan slab, ornamented by the same hand, is illustrated in fig. 55.

The art of the Manx crosses never developed very far beyond the Jellinge and Mammen phases. Certain features of the ornamental repertoire, as we have seen, reflect in some measure the succeeding Ringerike style, but they are confined to a few monuments, and to a few details on these monuments, and need not concern us here.

These insular styles, both English and Manx, are of extreme importance in any attempt to estimate the chronological structure of the Jellinge style. Before returning to the Scandinavian material, the insular material must be placed in some sort of geographical and chronological sequence. The insular objects can, to a certain extent, be placed against a reasonably well-documented political background. A combination of political and archaeological evidence enables us to reconstruct, within certain rather elastic limits, a tentative chronology for the insular Jellinge style.

The earliest Jellinge sculpture in the British Isles probably occurs in the Anglo-Danish area. Between 876, when Halfdan planted Danish settlers in Yorkshire, and 886, when the Alfred–Guthrum treaty was concluded, most of the north-east and east

---

[1] This was pointed out by Professor Arbman in a lecture to the Society for Medieval Archaeology, in Douglas in April 1961.

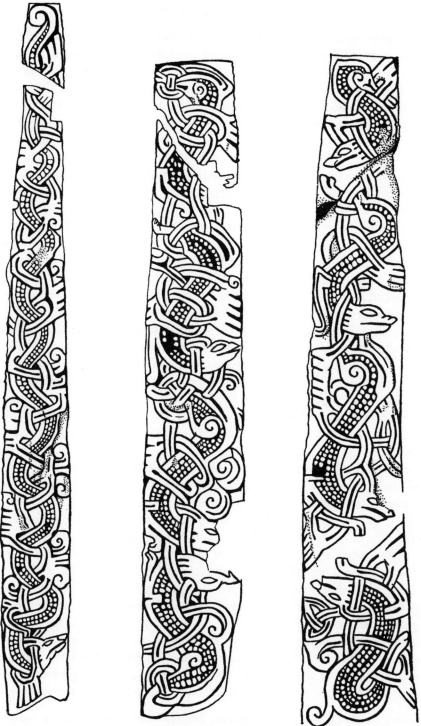

FIG. 52. Ornament of the stone erected by Thorleif at Kirk Braddan, Isle of Man.
Braddan Old Church.

Midlands came under Viking control. The Danes settled down alongside the local population, marrying the local girls, taking over a certain number of local farms and adopting, in some measure, the Christian religion. They remained, however, largely a Danish political entity and only adopted certain Anglo-Saxon traits. One of the things they took over from the native population was, as we have shown, stone sculpture. They gave it new motifs and in many ways debased the native tradition. There seems no reason why such sculptures as the St Alkmund cross (pl. xxxviii, *b* and *c*) should not belong to the period of primary settlement. It seems quite probable that most of the Middleton monuments and many of those in the surrounding villages were erected to the memory of the first Viking settlers, or of their sons, within a generation or two of the treaty with Alfred. If such be the case, many of the Viking influenced sculptures of the Danish area must be seen as the product of the late ninth and early tenth centuries. The crosses of this area were apparently little influenced by the sculptures of the Anglo-Norse areas of north-west England until, say, the second quarter of the tenth century, and it seems reasonable to suppose that a strong Anglo-Danish school of stone carving was established before the various wars and conquests brought the two Viking elements into close contact towards the end of the first quarter of the tenth century.

Turning now to the Norse areas, there seems to be a reasonable amount of evidence that the settlement in Cumberland, Westmorland and the surrounding counties did not take place until after 900. The area was colonized from Ireland and we have tried to show the various Irish influences in the sculpture. It would be reasonable to date much of the Anglo-Norse sculpture of this area to the first half of the tenth century. During the second quarter of the tenth century the styles of the north-east and north-west of England appear to have interlocked and certain common traits appear on both sides of the Pennines.

The connections between the Isle of Man and the Anglo-Norse area of north-west England are reasonably evident in the sculpture. Gaut's ring-chain motif, if we except one or two extraordinary outliers in unlikely places like Väsby, Skåne, Sweden (pl. xliv *a*),[1] is exclusively confined to these two areas. The strong Viking elements of the animal style of the Isle of Man, which were not present in Cumberland, are probably due to a close contact between Norway and the Irish sea in the tenth century—a contact which enabled the Viking colonists to keep *au fait* with the art of the homeland. Arbman[2] is probably right in saying that the Manx Viking sculptures were all executed within two or three generations of the settlement of Man (for many motifs are seen on both the typologically early and late stones), and the later artistic elements in the Manx art makes it reasonably certain that it was derived from north-west England and not vice versa. Arbman's idea, that the influences made themselves felt in the Isle of Man after the defeat of the Vikings at the battle of Brunanburh in 937, is most probably correct. We have seen that Gaut, who seems, typologically, to be one of the earliest sculptors

---

[1] Strömberg (1955). Cf. also Gällstad, Sweden, Baldwin-Brown (1937), pl. lxxxii, and other twelfth century fonts in Norway, e.g. Nicolaysen (1881), pl. II, which imply a re-introduction of the motif.
[2] In the lecture quoted above.

working in Man, had a Viking name and was the son of a father with a Viking name. Gaut or his father (or both of them) could have fled from Cumberland (where Gaut almost certainly had learnt his trade) to the Isle of Man after the political catastrophe of 937, which destroyed consecutive Viking power in England. It would be difficult to envisage a much later date than the middle of the tenth century for the earliest animal decorated slabs of the Isle of Man and it would seem reasonable to suppose that the last truly Viking crosses—those decorated in the Mammen style—were carved there during the first quarter of the eleventh century.

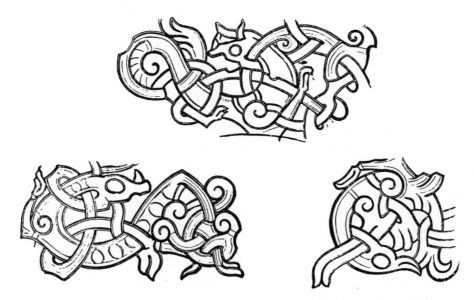

FIG. 53. Ornament from the bosses of penannular brooches from Skaill, Orkney. *National Museum Edinburgh.*

These political and historical considerations are to a certain extent supported by the English archaeological finds. The closeness in many technical and ornamental details of the shrine plates in the British Museum and the Sittingbourne scramasax to a number of objects in the Trewhiddle hoard, which was buried *c.* 875, suggests most strongly that elements of the Jellinge style were already present in the insular metalwork towards the end of the ninth century, while a find from Skaill, Orkney, demonstrates that a highly developed Jellinge style—already verging on the Mammen style—was present in the British Isles before 950. The Skaill find comprises one of the largest hoards ever found in British soil, it contained about ninety silver objects, mostly armrings, ingots and brooches and coins, which date the deposition of the hoard to *c.* 950. Among the finds are a number of so called 'thistle headed' brooches of penannular form, of a type which was probably developed in the Hiberno-Saxon area before the beginning of the tenth century (fragments of similar brooches were found in the hoard from Cuerdale, Lancashire, which was buried *c.* 905). On the terminals of a number of the Skaill brooches is engraved classic Jellinge-style ornament (fig. 53), mainly portraying animals, but including a man and a bird. They are executed in a highly competent manner and were obviously made in a British workshop for, not only are the brooches of an Hiberno-Saxon type but, as Arbman has pointed out, 'the sharp, angular nature of the interlace and the double lappets . . . [are] typical of what might be called "insular Jellinge style" '[1] and it is even possible that the brooches of the Skaill hoard were of some age when they were buried.

In 1880 Sophus Müller wrote the basic book on early Scandinavian art and put forward the theory that the Jellinge style owed much to Irish (what we should now call Hiberno-Saxon) influences. Brøndsted contradicted this theory in 1920 and attempted to show that these influences were in reality Anglo-Saxon, showing that there was practically nothing in late ninth or early tenth century Hiberno-Saxon ornament that could possibly have influenced Scandinavia. Other scholars searched for major influences in the Orient and others have seen the Jellinge style primarily as an indigenous art, built on pre-existing native traditions.

We have attempted to show that most of the elements of the Jellinge style are derived from native Scandinavian traditions, which stem back to the beginning of the ninth century, when there may well have been some direct, or indirect, insular influences in Scandinavia.

That certain ornamental motifs are derived from the non-Scandinavian area in the late phases of the Jellinge style cannot be denied, but these motifs were quickly absorbed into the pure Viking tradition and, with few exceptions, soon became completely divorced from their original context and meaning. However, a series of brooches from Scandinavia are decorated in a Jellinge style which seems to be of Anglo-Saxon inspiration. Although few such brooches are known, they do occur, not unsurprisingly, on the Swedish island of Gotland, one of the richest areas of the tenth century Viking world, and the insular influences are most easily seen on the brooch from Austris (pl. XLVI) on that island. On this brooch is a speckled animal ornament, executed in silver and niello, with rather incoherently interlaced limbs, which is very close to the upper shrine plate in the British Museum (pl. XXXVIII a). Another feature of this brooch is the series of inlaid gold panels, decorated with animal ornament, executed in a granulated technique. The filigree contour of each animal confines a body filled with a large number of small globules of gold. This technique may have an insular origin, as it is known in the insular area at this period. It occurs on the well-known Alfred Jewel[2]—a piece of ninth century English jewellery—and is also found on an Irish brooch[3] which cannot be easily dated, but which is probably contemporary with the object from Austris. At the same time a note of caution must be sounded, for the same technique is found in Gotland on ninth century bracteates (pl. XXXIII a) and the technique of granulation on the Austris brooch is much more likely to be founded on the native tradition, but it seems unlikely that the nielloed ornament of the Austris brooch could be of purely Scandinavian origin.

[1] Arbman (1961), 139.   [2] Kirk (1948).   [3] de Paor (1958), pl. 49.

Objects decorated with nielloed ornament showing Anglo-Saxon connection of this sort are rare, and the problem of its origin is complicated by the fact that niello was not a new material in Scandinavia, where it is found in a number of ninth century contexts. It is often difficult, therefore, to decide whether nielloed ornament is of English or Scandinavian inspiration in the tenth century. The button-on-bow brooches and the late drum-shaped brooches from Sweden are decorated quite profusely with silver and niello panels, the art of which can usually be related to the indigenous art of Scandinavia, but which may sometimes have English overtones (pl. XLVII a), while on the fragment of a stirrup from Stenåsa, on the Swedish island of Öland, for example, is a degenerate animal of the more substantial Jellinge type. The ornament, which is incised in bronze, is inlaid with niello and bears a strong, superficial relationship to the animals of the British Museum casket plates. Further, the four, slightly curved lines, which give a certain roundness to the belly of the animal, perhaps reflect the nicks which occur in the contour of certain ninth century English animals.[1] But the dangers of using such a comparison are great, for we are dealing with two different materials (bronze and silver) and two entirely different techniques (engraving and reservation against a niello background): furthermore, it seems reasonably obvious, from the proto-Ringerike interlace in the top right-hand corner, that the Stenåsa fragment is perhaps nearly a hundred years younger than the casket plates.

One fact remains, however, the Austris brooch, and probably some other pieces, were manufactured under strong English influence. That English influence was making itself felt in Scandinavian metalwork in the tenth century is demonstrated in a number of ways. The penannular brooch, for example, which was such a popular piece of jewellery in the early tenth century in Scandinavia, is an insular form and it is particularly interesting to see how the insular thistle-headed brooches were copied and modified throughout Scandinavia. Similarly, English moneyers in this century visited Scandinavia and minted coins over there. In other artistic media there are traces of English influence, the sculptor who carved the stone from Väsby, Skåne, for example, used Gaut's ring-chain ornament in a manner as competent as any of the insular craftsmen to whom it was a normal decorative motif.

The Austris brooch, the Väsby stone and their Scandinavian cousins are, however, isolated phenomena for on them, unlike the majority of Scandinavian artistic products of the Viking period, native ornamental elements are subordinated to external influences. It is interesting that the external influences should be 'insular Scandinavian' rather than purely 'insular', for these objects might be the products of returning expatriate craftsmen. This is not to deny the presence of external influences in tenth century Scandinavian art, but such influences are rarely seen. The indigenous elements in Viking art must once again be emphasized.

Before turning to a discussion of the Mammen style we must summarize our arguments concerning the early Jellinge style and place the style in a firm chronological sequence. We have tried to show how the style grows directly out of Styles D and E,

[1] Discussed by Wilson (1964), 25.

using as illustrations such objects as the Gokstad strap-end. The insular material was then discussed and developments of the style in the Danish and the Norwegian areas of England and in the Isle of Man were demonstrated.

On this basis a reasonably consistent chronology can be built up. The occurrence of a Jellinge type strap-end in the Gokstad burial provides a date in the last half (probably in the third quarter) of the ninth century for a Jellinge style object, for the close relationship between Oseberg and Gokstad will not allow too much of a chronological gap between the two ship burials.[1] Secondly, if it is accepted, as we think it must be accepted, that the Jellinge style develops directly out of Styles D and E, there can be no confusion caused by an attempt to derive the style from the British Isles. All the Jellinge ornament in the British Isles is derived from Scandinavia and there is a reasonable amount of evidence in favour of a development of the insular Jellinge style in the Danelaw and Yorkshire within a generation of the immediate settlement of these areas (i.e. 875–900). The evidence of the insular metalwork, and particularly of the ornament of the Sittingbourne scramasax and the British Museum casket plates, also points to a date before, or about, 900 for the introduction of the style into England. It is also to be noted that a well-developed Jellinge style was present on the brooches of the Skaill hoard when it was deposited in 950. The probability that the Manx crosses can all be dated between, say, 940 and 1000 gives us some clue to the longevity of the Jellinge style, at least in the Viking colonies, a pattern which is repeated in the Scandinavian hoards, containing brooches decorated with the Jellinge style, which run well on into the end of the tenth century.[2] Otherwise, however, coin dating is of little use in dating the beginnings of the Jellinge style, as the earliest hoards to contain Jellinge objects do not occur before the middle of the tenth century.[3]

It would seem, then, that the Jellinge style developed slowly in the middle of the ninth century, alongside the Borre style, out of the pre-existing Scandinavian styles and continued, with few changes, until well into the second half of the tenth century, when, as we shall see, it tends to merge into the Mammen style, which must now be discussed.

[1] It should be pointed out that the Jellinge object in the Gokstad mound was found while tidying up the site many years after the barrow was excavated [Hougen (1931–32)], but there is little reason to doubt that the object belongs to the original find and was missed by the nineteenth century excavators.

[2] E.g. Tolstrup, Denmark, Skovmand (1942), fig. 9, dated 991–94; Sejrø, Denmark, Skovmand (1942), fig. 23, dated after 953 and Tråen, Norway, dated c. 1000 (pl. xxxiv e) and Södra Byrummet, Sweden, dated c. 1050, Stenberger (1947–58), ii, fig. 88 and pl. 219, 2.

[3] Vårby, Sweden (c. 940) (pl. xxxii a–c) Skaill, Scotland (c. 950) (fig. 53) and Gnezdovo, Russia (mid-tenth century) (pl. xxxiii b), are the earliest hoards containing objects decorated in the Jellinge style.

CHAPTER V

THE MAMMEN STYLE

Scandinavian art of the late tenth and eleventh centuries runs smoothly in its set sequence—the Mammen, Ringerike and Urnes styles succeed each other, sometimes overlapping, but each quickly developing its individual characteristics. The smoothness of the succession demonstrates, in the clearest possible manner, the continuity of Scandinavian ornamental tradition in the late Viking Age. In this chapter we shall trace the development of the Mammen style into the Ringerike style, which is gradually subordinated to, though never completely conquered by, a tendril foliate ornament.

The animal—or, as it should more correctly be described, bird—on one face of the Mammen axe (the object which gave its name to the style) has been analysed in our discussion of the Jellinge style and its origins in the art of the ninth century Scandinavia have been indicated.[1] The Mammen animal is, in many respects, merely an exaggerated version of its Jellinge predecessors (pl. LII). The hips form a more convoluted or shell-like spiral, the double contouring of the body is emphasized even more firmly and every tendril is exaggerated. The most important features of the style are the more substantial body of the animal and the pelleting which fills it. Neither feature is new, for both occurred in the Jellinge style proper—the pelleting, for example, on the extraordinary house-like object on the Jellinge cup (fig. 43), and the more substantial bird's body on the Søllested horse-collar (pl. XXXII d). The floriated human mask at the butt of the Mammen axe is another motif with ancient traditions—its precursors can be seen in Vendel, Jellinge and Oseberg contexts (fig. 6, pl. XXXVII d and xv b).

Although one face of the Mammen axe displays a motif typical of the Mammen style, the other face (pl. LII) bears a design of tendrils which is more akin to the ornament of the Ringerike style. The contemporaneity of these two features is a problem which we shall attempt to answer at the end of this chapter; it is a problem that can only be solved by examining the whole corpus of Mammen art with care.

The greatest monument—however untypical—of the Mammen style is the Jellinge stone (pls. XLIX), one of the most impressive and accomplished masterpieces of Viking art, and one which had a considerable, if rather one-sided, influence throughout Scandinavia. The stone, a semi-pyramidal boulder of red-veined, grey granite, some 8 ft. high and damaged slightly at the top, stands in the churchyard of the small Danish

---

[1] See above, p. 96.

119

village of Jelling in Jutland, where it forms part of the remarkable complex of monuments (burial mounds, stone alignments, etc.) raised by the Viking kings of Denmark. An inscription in runic characters covers the whole of one face of the stone and continues at the base of the other two faces. It reads, in translation:

> King Harald ordered this stone to be raised in memory of Gorm his father and Thyra his mother: [he was] that Harald who won all Denmark and Norway, and made all the Danes Christian.

The Harald referred to in the inscription is Harald Bluetooth, King of Denmark from 940 to 985. It has been argued that the last line of the inscription, which tells of Harald's achievements, was added at a date later than that of the erection of the stone.[1] Although this may be true, it seems probable that the additions were made only a short time after the original inscription had been carved, for there is little palaeographical difference between the two series of characters—merely some minor variations in punctuation—and the lower part of the inscription was almost certainly carved by the sculptor of the main text. If the reference to the conquest of 'all Denmark' in the inscription refers to the expulsion of the German rulers from Hedeby in 983, the stone must have been erected between that date and Harald's death in 985. The broadest date which can be allowed for this stone is between 965, when Harald became Christian, and 985, when he died.

The two main ornamental faces of the stone are carved in soft low relief. Each scene is set within a framework of simple plaits which form a three-looped knot at each corner. On one face (pl. XLVIII) is a representation of the crucified Christ, carved in a formalized manner. The figure is stiff and flat, the legs and arms are strap-like and the face is devoid of expression; there has been no attempt to achieve naturalism. The figure is bound in an untidy ribbon-like interlace, centred on a ring which binds the trunk of the figure. The ribbons interlace symmetrically with the body, but escape from the symmetry to fill the fields, giving off tendril-like extensions at certain points. The most accomplished face of the stone portrays an elegant lion, entwined gracefully with a snake (pl. XLIX). The lion has a comparatively small head, pointed ears, a lip-lappet and a floriated lappet springing from the top of the head. It is double-contoured and spiral-hipped, has large claw-like feet and a tail which develops into a great acanthus leaf after interlacing with the snake. The animal has an almost heraldic attitude (lion passant) and the artist has brilliantly conveyed, with great economy of line, the impression of the beast's strength. The lion and snake scene is a magnificent piece of work, executed by a master craftsman who was as completely at home with this motif as he was unhappy and ham-handed in carving the bound Christ on the other face.

The bound Christ is a new element in Viking art. Although representations of the crucifixion do occur in the tenth century Scandinavian contexts, they are usually cruciform metal pendants, occasionally bearing the figure of Christ: nothing comparable to

---

[1] Cf. Lindqvist (1952), 197 ff., and Christiansson (1953), 72–101.

the Jellinge Christ is known. The crude attempt of the artist of the Jellinge stone to represent the folds of the dress dimly echoes similar features in Western European ivories and manuscripts; but the Jellinge figure is so far removed from such sources that it is impossible to trace its origins. Nevertheless, the presence of Carolingian, Ottonian, or Anglo-Saxon influence is adequately demonstrated by the acanthus-like character of some of the escaping tendrils of the interlace.

Although the bound Christ is found elsewhere in the Christian art of the period,[1] the 'bound devil' from Kirkby Stephen in Yorkshire (pl. XLIII a) is probably related to the Jellinge motif, perhaps through a common prototype.

Many of the ornamental details of the lion and snake face of the Jellinge stone belong to the Jellinge style. But such features—lip-lappet, double contour, etc.—are subordinated to a new and important element, the acanthus leaf, which has an Anglo-Saxon or Ottonian origin. The origin of the lion and snake design is a problem which has exercised scholars for many years. Western Europe has frequently been claimed as the source, but other areas, particularly South Russia and Byzantium, have also had their supporters. Most of these theories, however, are gravelled for lack of chronological support and by the absence of really satisfactory prototypes. The lion was a favourite subject of Western and Southern European artists from classical times onwards and the multifarious forms of the beast in these areas bear little or no relation to the Scandinavianized animal which appears on the Jellinge stone. If this motif was imported at this or any earlier period, it did not retain its original form but was barbarized and became a Viking animal. The whole aspect of the animal is Viking: even the stance, which might at first sight be considered foreign to a Viking milieu, is similar to that of the animal on the runner of the fourth sledge (pl. XVI a), on the bed-posts from Oseberg (fig. 17), on the Gokstad basket lid (pl. XIX b), on the Borre mounts (pl. XXVII a) or on some of the baroque Borre style brooches (pl. XXXI d). Most of the ornamental elements of the Jellinge stone animal were present in Viking art long before Harald erected this monument. The animal is an indigenous motif: its precursors can be seen in Oseberg, the plastic animals of the Borre style and the decoration of the Søllested horse-collar. Even the trilobate protuberances of the interlace in the crucifixion scene, about which Dr Holmqvist has made much,[2] are present in almost exactly the same form in the Oseberg style (pl. XVI a). The Jellinge stone, and the Mammen style, to which it belongs, can only be understood against the background of indigenous art. Most of its elements are Scandinavian and, where foreign forms and motifs occur, they are barbarized into an art as Scandinavian as the Vikings themselves.

The Jellinge stone was a royal monument, raised by royalty in memory of royalty: for its period it is unique in Europe. We shall show in the following chapter how it had considerable artistic influence both in Scandinavia and England, how craftsmen carved stones like that from Tullstorp (fig. 54) which, in ornament and design, are obviously

[1] E.g. at an earlier period on an Anglo-Saxon stone cross from St Andrew, Auckland, Co. Durham (cf. Kendrick (1938a), pl. 52).
[2] Holmqvist (1951), 2–3.

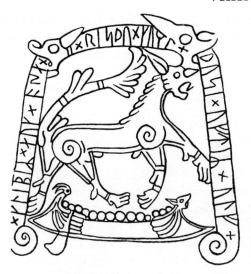

FIG. 54. Ornament of the rune-stone from Tullstorp, Skåne, Sweden.

a wealthy man's copy of the royal memorial stone at Jellinge. But for all this, the Jellinge stone itself has little immediate importance in our understanding of the Mammen style. Its unique quality emphasized, our attention must now be turned towards less exotic objects, decorated with motifs more typical of the Mammen style.

Probably the earliest object, decorated in the Mammen style, is the fragment of carved wood, discovered during the 1861 excavations of the great Jellinge barrow.[1] The fragment (pl. L) forms part of the furnishings of the tomb (sometimes identified, rather questionably, as Thyra's barrow) which contained the small silver cup mentioned above (p. XXXIV *a*). The date, purpose and meaning of the fragment is obscure. It consists of a flat piece of wood carved in the form of a bearded man. He is seen in profile and only the head and trunk survive; his tunic is decorated with billeting and defined by a broad border. A four-element ribbon crosses his stomach and the body and ribbon are interlaced by a double contoured ring. The back of the object is decorated with incised interlace patterns (pl. L *b*). Another piece of decorated wood (pl. LI), found in the grave, takes the form of an openwork tendril pattern; like the other piece it is painted in red and yellow.

The anthropomorphic carving from the Jellinge grave must be compared with the grotesque representation on a dished bone plaque from the River Thames, at London (pl. XLV *f*). The man's head is missing and only the point of his beard survives. His two legs are raised to enclose his arms and body and are interlaced with a pair of snakes. The spiral hips and shoulders, the band-like border and the pelleted body, together with the interlacing snakes, are features common to the Thames plaque and the Jellinge wood carving.

There is little sense of movement in either of these carvings: the figures are static—skilfully executed, but lifeless. This lifeless quality is not normally found in the ornament of other Mammen style objects and these two pieces should perhaps be seen as precursors of the style. They do not quite fit into the Mammen series, for even the courtly formalism of the lion of the Jellinge stone shows a sense of movement, however sedate.

The Jellinge carvings demonstrate that wood was the true medium of the Mammen style. The billeting and the broad contour are obviously well adapted to the skill and material of the wood-carver, and it is a fact that few objects of metal decorated in this

[1] Kornerup (1875).

style are known to exist; a surprising number are in wood, bone, ivory, elk-horn or other similar material. Even when Mammen artists ventured to work in stone they frequently used the technical tricks of the wood-carver. It is significant that a number of scholars have pointed to the fact that the Manx crosses, particularly Thorleif's cross (fig. 52) at Kirk Braddan (which is decorated in the Mammen style), are executed in a wood-carving technique. Wood was clearly the traditional material of the Scandinavian sculptor and it is hardly surprising that there are reflections of the Oseberg wood-carvers style in Mammen art.

The cross of Thorleif from Kirk Braddan in the Isle of Man is one of the most purely Scandinavian crosses in the Manx series and is perhaps one of the earliest examples of an object decorated in the true and lively Mammen style. One of the most famous of the Manx crosses, it was cited as early as 1868 by the great Danish archaeologist Worsaae[1] as an important parallel to the then newly-found Mammen axe. The ornamented surface is 57 in. (146 cm.) long and, carved in runes, on one of the edges is Thorleif's inscription to the memory of his son Fiacc. The ornament on the other faces bear a close affinity to the Jellinge style—the typical lappets at the lip and on the head, the spiral hip, the interlacing ring, etc., are all familiar Jellinge elements. But Mammen style elements predominate. There is a certain amount of foliate ornament of typical Mammen form, while the animals have a plain border and the bodies are filled with pelleting similar to that found on the Jellinge man and the Thames plaque. The pelleting technique is normally unsuitable for stone, having been developed for use in bone or wood, but it is a technique that could be easily adapted to the soft, fine, blue slate of the Isle of Man. Another stone from Kirk Braddan, the cross raised by Odd (fig. 55 and pl. XLV a), was almost certainly carved by the sculptor of Thorleif's cross, for the style and detail of the ornament are almost exactly similar. Another example of the Mammen animal style can be seen on the Joalf slab at Kirk Michael, while interlace executed in the Mammen technique can be seen on a number of other Manx crosses.[2] An ornamental element of certain Manx crosses is a double spiral offshoot from the band which interlaces with the body of an animal; it normally occurs in the hollow of a U-shaped back and is a particularly frequent feature of Thorleif's cross. The same feature is found in Yorkshire, on the Levisham slab (pl. XLII b), for example (which is probably contemporary with its Manx counterparts), and it presumably has its origin in the tendril with scrolled terminals which issued from the back of animals decorated in the Mammen and Jellinge styles in Scandinavia (cf. pls. XXXVI b and LII).

The ornament of the Mammen series of Manx cross slabs is much closer to its Scandinavian prototypes than that of any other group of sculpture from the British Isles. Although direct influence from the Scandinavian homeland—presumably from Norway—can clearly be seen in this series, it is fair to assume that the sculptor had been trained in the Manx stone-carving traditions. These crosses are the only surviving objects decorated in the Mammen style which are demonstrably made outside Scan-

[1] Worsaae (1869).
[2] E.g. Kermode (1907), pl. I,100 A and the ornament in the shaft at Ballaugh, *ibid.*, pl. xxxii, 77b.

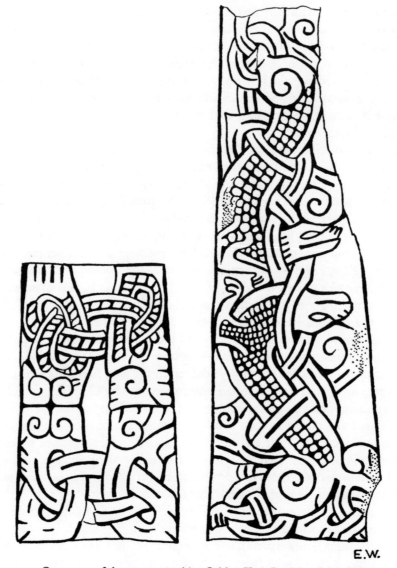

E.W.

FIG. 55. Ornament of the stone raised by Odd at Kirk Braddan, Isle of Man.
Cf. pl. XLV *a. Braddan Old Church.*

dinavia, although there is strong circumstantial evidence to suggest that certain objects from the eastern Viking colonies were made in Russia. Objects decorated in the Mammen style are not common and two of the most important monuments of the style, to which we must now turn our attention, are of German provenance.

One of these is the Bamberg casket (pl. LIV). It is now in the Bavarian National Museum at Munich but it was, until the secularization, in the Bamberg Cathedral treasury. It is sometimes known as the jewel-box of Queen Kunigunde, the daughter of Canute the Great, and it is not impossible that it at one time belonged to this lady, who married the German Emperor Henry III in 1036. Unfortunately the story—however attractive —cannot be proved, for the casket is not documented until 1743; but the association of Queen Kunigunde with Bamberg, together with the fact that the casket is of Scandinavian workmanship, lend a certain authentic air to an otherwise improbably coincidental story.

The casket is square in plan and has a slightly pitched roof: 10·4 in. (26·5 cm.) long and 5·1 in. (13 cm.) high, it consists of an oak box covered with thin, carved sheets of walrus ivory. These sheets are clasped by gilt-bronze bands, which are nailed to the wooden base. The lid is reinforced and decorated with ridge poles set saltirewise with a spherical crystal separating four animal heads in the centre. A bird's head at each terminal of the ridge pole faces inwards towards the centre. The animal and birds heads are in high relief and are floridly formalized. The other strips of gilt bronze are decorated with a formal tendril pattern, or an irregular Scandinavianized interlaced version of it, reserved against a punched background. The hinges and the lock are comparatively modern replacements (the original key-hole is a T-shaped slot in the lid), while a number of pieces of cast bronze are missing from the space between the arms of the saltire on the lid.

The ivory panels are skilfully decorated in a lively version of the Mammen style. In one of the fields of the lid, for example, is a human mask of triangular form, the moustache, hair and beard of which are produced into fantastically elaborate scrolls and tendrils, the broader band containing the familiar pelleting so typical of the style. Other panels contain birds and animals (in pairs or singly), all caught up in the great convolutions of the tendrils and leaf-like interlace. The right-hand panel on the lid of the box, for example, bears the representation of a fierce creature with lip-lappet, spiral hips, large feet, interlacing tendrils and a tail terminating in an acanthus leaf. Like all the carving on this box, this creature has a movement and freshness which has been missing from Viking art for more than a hundred years.

Mammen and Jellinge features are present abundantly in this object. The gilt-bronze animal and bird heads of the ridge-poles, with their upstanding semicircular ears and beaded tendril-like lappets, are very close in form to the terminal animal heads of the Jellinge style horse-collars and very obviously have an origin in the Borre, if not in the Oseberg, style. The interlaced semi-foliate pattern of some of the bronze strips is related to the ornament on the lips of the Søllested collar terminal and to a similar motif on Gaut's cross at Kirk Michael on the Isle of Man (fig. 50).

The ornament of the ivory plaques exhibits similar traits and relationships. Jellinge details, such as the lip-lappet, and complete Jellinge motifs, such as the bird which is derived from the same source as the birds on the Søllested horse-collar terminals (pl. xxxvii d), combine well with such Mammen features as the shell spiral hip, the pelleted animal bodies, the acanthus leaves and the profusion of interlaced semi-foliate ornament. There is an ebullience in this ornament never encountered in the Jellinge style, an ebullience entirely typical of the Mammen style.

The Bamberg casket is rich and beggars description. It sits solid and four-square in its show-case in the Museum, giving an impression of strength entirely proper to its character as a jewel-box. It is rightly regarded as one of the masterpieces of Viking art: barbaric, vulgar and ostentatious, it is nevertheless a satisfying object which a queen would be proud to own.

The much larger casket, once in the treasury of the Cathedral at Cammin in Pommerania, may well have come from the same workshop as the Bamberg casket.[1] Unfortunately this object was destroyed during the Second World War and neither of the authors of this book have seen it; our knowledge of the object rests, then, on pictures, casts and the notes of our more fortunate colleagues. The casket (pl. LV) was shaped like an inverted boat with squared-off bow and stern and was made of wood overlaid with twenty-two sheets of elk-horn, bound into position by engraved gilt-bronze bands, which terminated on the roof in plastic animal and bird heads. The central panel, on one side of the top, formed a lid and was fastened by two hasps, which engaged with locks in a rectangular plate on the front of the object. The casket was much larger than the companion piece from Bamberg—the measurements (probably accurate to the nearest centimetre) given by Goldschmidt[2] are: length 24·8 in. (63 cm.), height 10·2 in. (26 cm.) and width 13 in. (33 cm.). The gilt-bronze strips were engraved with a rather more numerous set of motifs than occurred on the Bamberg casket; for, as well as conventional and Scandinavianized tendril designs of the type met with on the Bamberg casket, there are ribbon interlacing patterns and a wide variety of scrolled leaf patterns. The patterns on the strips were sometimes set against a pointillé background, sometimes against a plain one. The animal heads which protrude, gargoyle-like, over the edge of the casket, which face the ridge-pole of the roof, or terminate the hasps, were close in design and technique to those on the Bamberg casket, and were of similar quality. Many small details of these heads, the spiral nostrils of the animals and the upstanding ears for example, relate the Bamberg and Cammin animal heads extremely closely—although there was more variety on the Cammin example. The horn plates bore all the features of the plates on the Bamberg casket; there were, however, additional motifs—a series of small panels, for instance, carved with purely foliate motifs, but generally speaking its decoration is very close to that of its Bamberg contemporary. There are stylistic minor differences, but the close correspondence between the two objects is remarkable. The main difference between the two is the slightly less chunky quality on the carving of the Cammin object, which may be due to the much thinner material used; this difference can be seen if we compare the human masks represented on both objects (pls. LIV *a* and LVI *a*).

[1] The late Professor Shetelig, whose knowledge of Viking antiquities can never be rivalled and who carried his knowledge lightly and with imagination, made a typically bold attempt to identify the Cammin casket with the casket presented by the Norwegian King Sigurd the Crusader to the Church of the Holy Cross in Kongehelle, and subsequently stolen by the Vends when they sacked the town in 1127 (Shetelig 1932–3). This was characterized by its author as a 'guess' (Shetelig (1949), 136), but it is a happy theory which, although it can never be proved, enlivens our view of Viking art and represents, at least, the importance of the object.   [2] (1918), ii, 59.

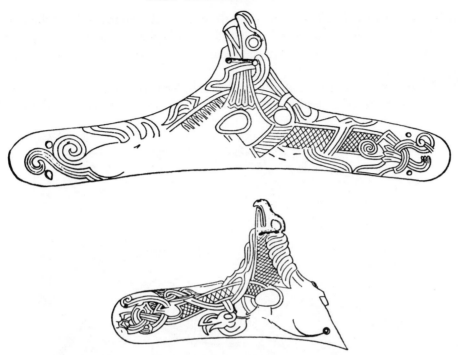

FIG. 56. Two saddle mounts from Šestovitsy, Černigov, Ukraine, U.S.S.R. *Černigov, Archaeological Museum.*

There are other objects decorated in this style, but not very many of them. There is the so-called sword of St Stephen in Prague Cathedral, very much worn but with definite elements of the style,[1] a Morse ivory object from Kastager Strand, Utterslev, Norre, Denmark (pl. XLVII *b*),[2] which has a distinctive Mammen feature—the small semicircular break in the contour of the ribbon—which can be seen on the Braddan stones (figs. 52 and 55) and the Mammen axe, and a bone fragment from Lund, Sweden,[3] with a formalized interlace pattern related to, but more sober than, the interlace patterns of the two caskets and such objects as the Gnezdovo bone object[4] or the saddle mounts from Šestovitsy, in the Ukraine (fig. 56),[5] which may have been made in the Viking states in Russia, but which exhibit clearly most of the features of the Mammen style in a rather formalized fashion. From Denmark comes a gilt-bronze horn mount from Århus,[6] decorated with a frieze of double-contoured, spiral-hipped birds, set against a punched background. The ornament is perhaps more clearly equivalent to the succeeding Ringerike style, but retains sufficient Mammen detail to be included here. Also decorated in the Mammen style is a fine elk-horn sword-pommel guard from the ancient Swedish town of Sigtuna (pl. XLVII *c* and *d*), and a fragment of bone from Reistad in

[1] Paulsen (1933a), pl. ix, 2 and fig. 11.   [2] National Museum, Copenhagen, inv. no. c. 5408.
[3] Goldschmidt (1918), pl. lxii, 188.   [4] Arne (1914), fig. 19.   [5] Arne (1931), 297.
[6] Lindqvist (1931), 144.

north Norway, which Dr. T. Petersen rightly associated with the style of the Bamberg casket.[1] It is, however, a recent find which illuminates the style more clearly than any other—the bone sleeve found at Årnes, Nordmöre, in northern Norway early in 1962 (pl. XLV *a–e* and fig. 57).[2]

The Årnes sleeve is quite small, only 6·0 cm. in length; it is formed of a section cut from the long-bone of a largish animal—a cow or pony, perhaps—and the whole

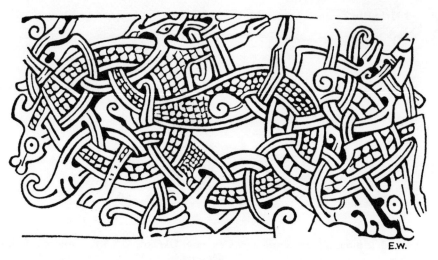

FIG. 57. Ornament from the bone sleeve illustrated pl. XLV *b–e*; from Årnes, Stangvik, Nordmöre, Norway. Scale: ⅓. *Videnskapsselskapets Oldsaksamling, Trondheim.*

surface is covered with carving in low relief. It is stained with iron and has small rivet-holes along the borders. The ornament is closely comparable to some of the freer panels of the Cammin casket: the bodies of the three interlaced animals are filled with the same pelleting, there is the same spiral hip, the same double contour and, as on one of the panels on the roof of the Cammin casket, the U-shaped animals loop together with each other and with bands of interlace ornament. Certain details of the ornament of this piece, however, are not far removed from features of the Ringerike style. This is particularly true of the form of some of the leaves which no longer have the rather fleshy quality of the leaves on the two caskets, but have instead an elongated tautness not seen before in this art. The less substantial bodies and the general lay-out of the field occur in a number of Ringerike contexts and the Årnes object must be seen as an intermediary stage in the process of development to the full Ringerike style, the earliest stage of which can be traced on the Bamberg and Cammin caskets.

[1] Th. Petersen (1936).
[2] We are grateful to Dr S. Marstrander of the Norske Videnskapers Selskab Museum in Trondheim for allowing us to publish this object here.

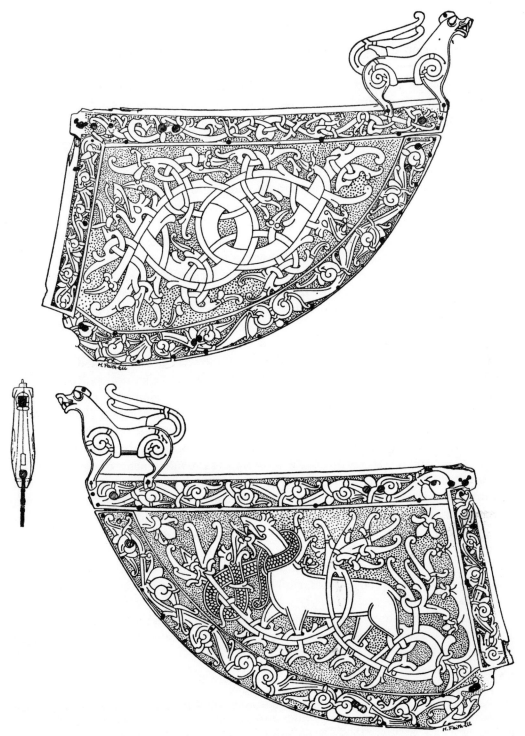

FIG. 58. Ornament from a gilt-bronze weather-vane from Källunge, Gotland, Sweden. *Gotlands Fornsal, Visby.*

The pattern on the Årnes object is best paralleled on one face of a weather-vane (fig. 58), which was still in use as late as 1930 on the spire of Källunge church, in the Swedish island of Gotland.[1] This object is one of a number of similar weather-vanes which have been discovered in Scandinavia and discussed in some detail.[2] The Källunge vane is entirely characteristic of its type and is probably the earliest of the series. It consists of a thin gilt-bronze plate of sub-triangular form engraved with zoomorphic patterns. The plate is bound with thicker engraved strips; it is hinged on the shorter side and crowned at the tip by a splendid animal cast in the round. On one face two serpentine animals are looped together and produce an untidy muddle of interlaced tendrils. These elongated tendrils are even more pronounced on the other face, where they develop out of the interlace surrounding a form of the lion and snake motif of the Jellinge stone. In this object, the Mammen style has almost completely disappeared—having given way to a fully-fledged Ringerike ornament.

It is often difficult to separate the Mammen and Ringerike styles; the overlap, which can so clearly be seen on the Årnes object, occurs frequently in Mammen style contexts. In order to understand the Mammen style, therefore, it is useful to examine, at this point, a typical Ringerike monument so that such objects as the Årnes bone sleeve and the Källunge vane may be seen in proper perspective.

No object could be more typical of the Ringerike style than the Alstad stone from the Ringerike area of Norway. The geographical and art-historical position of this stone will be discussed in the next chapter, here it is taken simply as a sample of the Ringerike style. The stone, which is now in the University Museum (Universitetets Oldsaksamling) at Oslo, is perhaps the most important of the Ringerike series (fig. 59). It was first described and illustrated by the great Scandinavian polymath Ole Worm as early as 1643,[3] and it is surely one of the most impressive monuments of the Viking Age remaining in Norway. It stands nearly 9 ft. high and both faces are covered with ornament and inscriptions. The stone was originally raised by a man called Jørun in memory (possibly) of Ql-Arnir, and an inscription was later added by a certain Igle to commemorate his son Thorald. Below a great displayed eagle on one face is carved a pictorial representation of the Sigurd Saga, which we have seen to be a popular subject in Viking sculpture.[4] The horses and other animals carved on this stone are closely related to the animals (lions, horses, etc.) which occur on the various objects decorated in the Mammen style.

The animals are more lively than most animals decorated in the Mammen or Jellinge styles, but it is the other side of the stone which demonstrates the true features of the Ringerike style.

[1] Roosval (1930).   [2] Brøgger and Bugge (1925) and Bugge (1931).
[3] For full history and description see Jacobsen (1933).
[4] Jacobsen (1933), 31, interprets it as follows (in translation): 'Below a large ornamental bird, possibly of symbolic import, is a man on a horse—with a hawk in his hand and followed by his dogs. The man is possibly Sigurd setting out on his fateful journey. Beneath this scene is a horse without a rider: Grane coming home after the death of his Lord. Lastly comes a man riding with a mighty raised weapon: which could be the murderer, Høgne.'

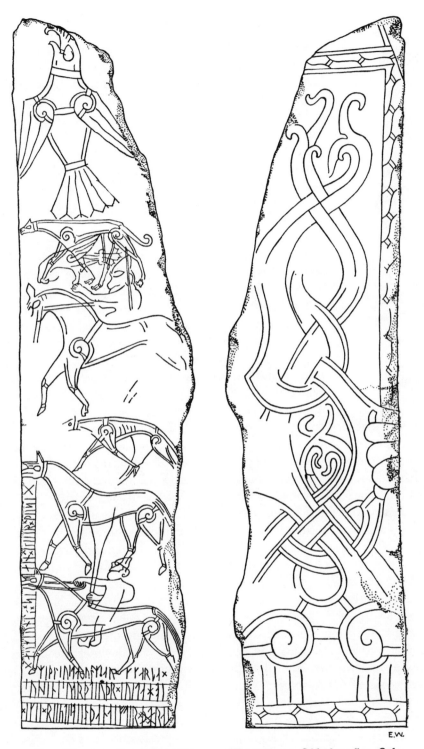

FIG. 59. The stone from Alstad, Norway. *Universitetets Oldsaksamling, Oslo.*

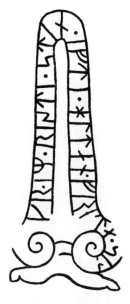

FIG. 60. The design of a runestone from Göt-lunda, Västergötland, Sweden.

Here can be seen a great swirling tendril motif, long, taut and typical of the Ringerike style. Also typical of the style are the two shell spirals at the base of the design, which have their origin in the animal hips of the Jellinge and Mammen styles and first occur in this position in the Borre style as, for example, on the miniature weather-vane from Rangsby, Finland (pl. XXXII *e*). The same feature can also be seen in numerous contexts as far apart as Winchester, the cultural capital of England (pl. LIX *c*). Mammen itself (pl. LIII) and, in a very debased form, on the very different Swedish runestones (cf. fig. 60).

This short excursus into the Ringerike style allows us to grasp more clearly the true chronological and stylistic implications of the Mammen style, which must be seen as a bridge between the Jellinge and Ringerike styles.

The Mammen style is usually identified as a Danish style, partly because of its close and undoubted relationship to the Jellinge stone, partly because of the identification of the Bamberg casket with a Dane, Queen Kunigunde, and partly because of the Danish provenance of the Mammen axe and the various Jellinge antiquities. If the corpus of material decorated in the Mammen style is regarded objectively, it can be clearly seen that there is no evidence to support an exclusively Danish origin for the style. A good number of objects decorated in this style have been found outside Scandinavia and it is not always possible to say where they were made. There seems little reason to doubt the fact that the Šestovitsy saddle mounts were made in Russia and there can, of course, be no doubt that the Manx crosses were carved in the Isle of Man. Further, although the Gnezdovo mount and the Thames plaque may have been made in Scandinavia, they might equally well have been made in the Viking colonies where they were found. The Bamberg casket is associated by tradition with Queen Kunigunde, but even if it did belong to her, it may well have come from any part of her father's kingdom, which extended from North Cape to the Isles of Scilly. The Cammin casket has no known history and similarly there is nothing to help us trace the original homeland of the St Stephen's sword in Prague. In Norway two pieces, the Reistad fragment and the Årnes sleeve, come from the north of that country, while the sword guard from the ancient Swedish town of Sigtuna was found well outside Danish territory. Very little is left, therefore, to Denmark other than the Jellinge pieces, a bone strip from Lund, the walrus ivory object from Kastager Strand, the Århus horn mount and the Mammen axe. If the zoomorphic ornament on the Mammen axe had corroded away and only the ornament on the back of the axe had remained, archaeologists would undoubtedly have classified it as of the Ringerike style (indeed it is a typical example of the bridge between the Mammen and Ringerike styles) and its Danish character would not have been pressed.

Almost anything can be proved by distribution maps based on such a sporadic occurrence as this: consequently we have not attempted to plot the find spots on a map of Europe, but the lack of a sufficiently large body of material decorated in the Mammen style in the Danish homeland, or in the strongly Danish province of Skåne, would seem to demonstrate the misleading nature of the Danish label for the Mammen style. It would seem reasonable to suppose that the style was universal in the Viking world— perhaps inspired from Denmark, where the related Jellinge style reached its heights of achievement, but spreading to Central Sweden and the north of Norway and to the colonies in Russia and the British Isles. This style was the crucible from which the fully fledged Ringerike style emerged.

It is even more difficult to propose a chronological position for the Mammen style. Most of our evidence is of a negative variety, depending on the dating of the succeeding Ringerike style. A significant clue is provided in the Isle of Man, where Ringerike features, present in embarrassing quantities in much of Mammen ornament elsewhere, are merely incipient. The evidence of the manuscript material would suggest that the Ringerike style was present in the British Isles as an established force as early as the first quarter of the eleventh century and, although it does not really occur in Ireland until the second quarter of the eleventh century, the lively contact between Norway and the Isle of Man would suggest that the Ringerike influences would be felt there much earlier than in Ireland, which seems to have been but little receptive of Viking artistic ideas in this period. On balance, then, the Mammen style, in so far as it can be distinguished from the Ringerike style, on such pieces as the Thames plaque and the Manx crosses, was probably flourishing as a separate, but strong, influence as late as the first quarter of the eleventh century. The earliest date for the appearance of the style is not easily arrived at, the fact that it is foreshadowed on such pieces as the Jellinge cup (fig. 43) and the Søllested horse-collar (pl. XXXVII c) would indicate a slow development. The reasonably firmly dated Jellinge stone (983–5) would indicate that the style had already been established for some time when the stone was erected. We would therefore postulate that the Mammen style be bracketed somewhere within the very wide limits of the last half of the tenth and the first quarter of the eleventh century.

The vocabulary of art-history is circumscribed and it may be wrong to distinguish the Mammen style as a 'style' in the sense that Borre or Jellinge are 'styles'. The Mammen style seems to be little more than a conglomeration of various technical features which adapt the art of the period to its own lineaments. But the Mammen style is more than a motif, more than a co-ordination of a few technical tricks, it stands by itself as an art and as such can only be distinguished within the limits of the art-historian's language as a 'style'. It is a style in that it treats different motifs in a specific and uniform manner, whether that motif be Jellinge or Ringerike. At the same time it is a style which links the motifs and styles of Jellinge and Ringerike and the transition between these two styles, seen in Mammen, enlightens our view of both its predecessor and its successor.

CHAPTER VI

THE RINGERIKE STYLE

The Ringerike style takes its name from the district of that name a few miles north of Oslo. Here, and in the immediately adjacent districts,[1] were found a handful of carved stones (from Vang (pl. LVII), Alstad (fig. 59), Tanberg, Strand and Dynna) which are entirely typical of the style. We have described one of these stones—that from Alstad— at some length,[2] as a typical representative of the Ringerike style and we have seen how one of its faces bears animals, the double contouring, spiral hips and acanthus-like tendrils of which all demonstrate the origin of the Ringerike animals in ornament of the Mammen style. We have also mentioned and discussed one of the motifs on the Källunge weather-vane (fig. 58), which is simply a livelier version of the lion and snake motif found on the Jellinge stone.

The Jellinge stone is a nodal point in any discussion of the Ringerike style, for it seems very probable that it provided the literal prototype for all the single, large, lion-like animals which appear in Ringerike stone carving.

The Scandinavian settlers had, as we have shown, little or no experience of orna-mental stone carving before their arrival in the British Isles. In fact, if the competently carved stones of Gotland are ignored, it would be difficult to name even half a dozen stones, earlier than the Jellinge stone, which bear any major design other than a plain runic inscription[3] or simple magical symbol.[4] Stones like that from Väsby, Sweden (pl. XLIV a), if indeed it is to be dated earlier than the Jellinge stone, are so obviously influenced from the British Isles that they need not be considered here; while the Tu stone from Norway,[5] which has two poor human figures carved on it, and which is sometimes dated earlier than the Jellinge stone, could quite as easily be of later date. There seem, then, to be few tenth-century stones in South Scandinavia and Norway decorated with any substantial ornament, and we can safely say that no stone in these areas, before the erection of the Jellinge stone, has a lion, or other large beast, as its main decorative motif.

Boulders, while not uncommon in Denmark (they are nearly all glacial erratics), have a fascination for the Danish mind. Even today it is quite common for the discovery of a

---

[1] See Bugge (1904). [2] p. 130 f.
[3] A single example is the stone from Möjbro, Uppland; Jansson (1962), pl. 3.
[4] Jacobsen *et al.* (1942), pl. 29, 79. [5] Olsen and Shetelig (1909), fig. 1.

large boulder to be reported in a local newspaper. This interest in large lumps of rock has a long history: for example, one of the marvels of the royal castle at Kronborg from 1577 to 1597 was a large stone—the 'Lappesten'—which Frederik II had moved from its find place to Kronborg—a considerable distance. The moving and setting in place of this stone was recorded by an inscription carved on its face[1] and it is mentioned in descriptions and even appears in engravings of the castle until 1597 when Christian IV had it broken up to make a bridge at Frederiksborg.[2] It is not impossible that stones had a similar fascination for the Danish Vikings and that, immediately Harald had erected the Jellinge stone, it became an object of wonder to the Danish population, so that every important Dane would want to have a similar stone erected to his memory. Such a thought process may explain the many memorial stones erected throughout Denmark in the late tenth and early eleventh centuries, whence it may have spread throughout the Scandinavian peninsula. Only a handful of stones decorated with large animals survive, but it is interesting that the new motif had such a widespread distribution.

Perhaps the most remarkable example of a direct imitation of the lion and snake scene of the Jellinge stone is the famous slab, perhaps part of a stone sarcophagus, found in the churchyard of St Paul's Cathedral in London in 1852 (pl. LVIII a). It is one of the finest examples of Viking stone carving known outside Gotland, indeed the squarely-cut background of the design is extremely reminiscent of the similar technique which occurs particularly on the Gotlandic stone from Grötlingbo.[3] A possible Swedish origin for the craftsman who carved the St Paul's stone is further indicated by the runic inscription on the side, which might well be of Swedish rather than Danish type.[4] The stone itself is small, varying between 21 in. (54 cm.) in length at the top and 22·5 in. (57·5 cm.) at the bottom. It has a plain flat border with a pear-shaped lobe (a common Ringerike feature) terminating a knot in the border at the two top corners. The scene portrayed on the stone is of a backward-looking animal entwined by an elaborate snake-like animal. The animal is crisply cut: the great spiral at the hips, the eye, the mouth, the divisions between the claws, etc., are accurately and carefully delineated by V-shaped incisions. The outline of the animal is square-cut and the background is removed to the depth of this line. The most remarkable feature of the ornament is the treatment of the tendrils. The ears of the animal takes the form of long tendrils with tightly curled ends, while the body of the snake, which interlaces with that of the main animal, degenerates into a series of similar tendrils, including a splendid knot of them above the rump of the main animal.

The frame and the ornament of the St Paul's stone were originally painted in colours which have since deteriorated so that they are hardly recognizable today unless the surface of the stone is dampened. Much of the paint now visible is a dull umber colour, this may well have acted as a gesso-like base for the main overlaying colours, which

[1] 'Anno 1577 Fredericus 2, Daniae Rex curavit hoc Saxum a primo suo loco, ubi vicissim alius subrogatus est lapis, ad hoc devolvi locum.'   [2] Cf. Pedersen (1920), 64 and Pedersen (1926), 315–16.
[3] Lindqvist (1941), fig. 152.   [4] Jacobson, et al. (1942), 478 f.

can best be seen on the head. The main colour appears to have been blue/black, but many details—the teeth, eye, tongue, spiral hooks and lappet, for example—are picked out in a brown/yellow colour. The body and the head of the snake were apparently speckled with carefully painted circular white spots.

This stone has all the attributes of the Ringerike style—the long drawn out tendrils of the lappets and interlace, the mobile animal and the pear-shaped feature of the two upper corners (derived from the central element of the Viking interpretation of the acanthus leaf). The Swedish overtones of the ornament are demonstrated by the knot around the front knees of the animal, which is almost exactly paralleled (in a slightly less florid form) on the Swedish runestone from Lyrestad, Rogstorp, Västergötland[1]: the ultimate origin of the design is, however, clearly that of the Jellinge stone.

The St Paul's stone and the weather-vane from Källunge, Gotland (fig. 58), show the lion and snake motif in its purest Ringerike form: a slightly more developed expression of the same design occurs (pl. LVIII b) on one of the other Swedish weather-vanes (from Söderala, Hälsingland), while the design on the Vang stone from Norway might also be related to it.[2] The motif was always popular in medieval Scandinavia and indeed became the main motif of the Urnes style. On the runestones of South and East Scandinavia the snake is separated from the body of the lion and becomes the frame of the picture, its body serving as the confining element of the runic inscription, as at Sørup, Tullstorp (fig. 54) and Norra Åsarp. It would be a bold man who would say that the crosses, which appear in such profusion on many of the Scandinavian runic stones, are derived from the crucifixion scene on the Jellinge stone, but it is quite possible that Harald set the trend when he erected the Jellinge stone.

The content of the true Ringerike style, then, begins to emerge. There are three main elements: the lion, the snake and the extended, sometimes slightly fleshy, tendril. The lion, or (as it is sometimes called) 'the Great Beast', which occurs in various forms on a number of stones and other objects, is often drawn with a freedom and skill which is breathtaking. The artistic achievement of the metalworker who engraved the animals of the Heggen vane (pl. LIX a and b and fig. 61), for example, was considerable: the two animals portrayed here, even though perhaps more to the taste of the student of *art nouveau*, delight the modern eye by the economy with which a rich effect is presented. If this is a high point in the surviving art of the Ringerike style, the stone carvings come not far behind: the Vang animal (pl. LVII), the Norra Åsarp animal (fig. 62b), even the animals from the Stora Ek (fig. 62a) and Tullstorp stones (fig. 54) have a mobile quality missing from the more pedestrian and stolid—if no less competent—art of the Jellinge and Mammen styles.

The snake is the second main element of the style—often encircling the field, sometimes linked with one or two fellows, it becomes the *leitmotif* of the stone-carver of

---

[1] Junger (1940), pl. 15.

[2] This interpretation may not hold good if Almgren's theory that the Vang stone is one side of a church portal is correct (Almgren (1944)). There seems no inherent reason to deny the theory and Gjærder, (1952), 33, in his standard work on medieval doorways in Norway, appears to accept it.

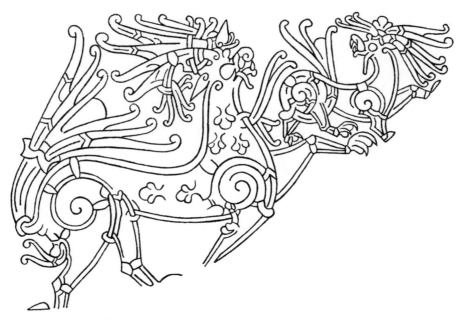

FIG. 61. Ornament of the weather-vane from Heggen, Norway. *Universitetets Oldsaksamling,* *Oslo.*

Sweden, Denmark and even Norway. It is hardly difficult to draw a snake, but details of some of the snakes from the runestones, as for example those in fig. 63, show that the artist, with his usual economy of line, occasionally turned a snake's head into a masterpiece. The snake as a symbol of evil, which we presume it must be in the lion and snake designs, may have been confused with the great snake, Midgardsorm, which, according to Norse mythology, encircles the earth and which has an important function at the end of the world—it is therefore of some significance on a memorial stone.

The third main ornamental element of the style is the elongated, fleshy scroll, often with an angular, or scrolled, thickening half-way along its outer contour and with a

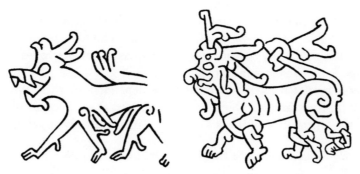

FIG. 62. Animals inscribed on rune-stones at (*a*) Stora Ek, and (*b*) Norra Åsarp, Västergötland, Sweden.

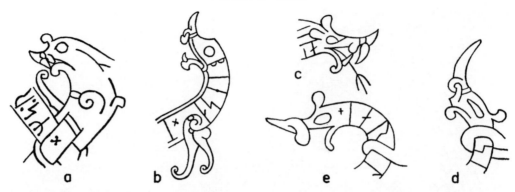

FIG. 63. Snakes' heads from Swedish rune-stones, showing the development towards the Urnes style: (*a*) Boge, Gotland, (*b*) Ockelbo, Gästrikland, (*c*) Strängnäs, Södermanland (Sö.279), (*d*) Strängnäs, Södermanland (Sö.276), (*e*) Vallentuna, Uppland (U.212).

tightly curled terminal. This motif is derived from the acanthus elements of the Mammen style and ultimately has its origin in the Ottonian or Anglo-Saxon world. The increasingly ragged and extended quality of the acanthus ornament of the manuscript art of the late tenth century, which is particularly seen in southern English manuscripts,[1] presumably influenced the Ringerike style directly. The increase of the power of Christianity in Scandinavia with the consequent introduction of books—some presumably illuminated—provided a medium for the diffusion of motifs, which were adapted successfully to materials other than vellum, with all the usual self-confidence of the Viking artist. That Ringerike influences were felt in southern England has been demonstrated by the St Paul's slab (this influence will be discussed more thoroughly below); this stone shows, in fact, that there was a community of artistic taste in England and Scandinavia in the early eleventh century, which is seen wherever the two styles overlap and mix. The long tendrils drawn by the manuscript artist were ideally suited to the medium to which their Scandinavian adapters turned their hands: it would be difficult to imagine, for example, a more competent piece of wood-carving than the simply engraved Ringerike tendrils which appear on panels from the ancient Viking farm at Flatatunga in Iceland (pl. LX).[2] The ornament of the Vang stone (pl. LVII) demonstrates a similar mastery in stone sculpture, while the achievement of the metalworker of the Söderala weather-vane (pl. LVIII *b*) shows how the tendrils combine well with a design which is basically zoomorphic—over-fussy to modern eyes, even degenerate, but a competent technical achievement.

All the other details of Ringerike ornament are dependent on these three motifs; the pear-shaped motif, for example, which has been noticed at each corner of the St Paul's slab, is merely the central lobe of the acanthus leaf (it was already apparent in the welter

[1] E.g. in the Anglo-Saxon charter of the New Minster, British Museum MS, Cotton Vespasian A.VIII (Kendrick (1949), pl. ii).
[2] For full discussion of these pieces and a complete photographic survey, see Eldjárn (1953); see also Mageröy (1961).

of foliage motifs on the Cammin and Bamberg caskets—pls. LIV and LV), while the floriated cross (which is often the only ornamental feature within the border formed by the inscription of the runestones) is often embellished with tendrils which are completely typical of the Ringerike style. Even when narrative scenes are carved on standing stones or, as sometimes happens, in the living rock, the animals and trees are treated as individual pieces of Ringerike ornament, rather than as a narrative composition. The horse, tree, wolf and snake of the famous Swedish Sigurd carving from Jäder in Södermanland (pl. LXI a) demonstrates this very clearly. This fact is confirmed by the character of the 'Gök stone' from the nearby parish of Härad (pl. LXI b), which is a copy of the Jäder stone by an artist who treated the scene as ornament, and not as a narrative, to such an extent that certain motifs become completely meaningless.

Many of the runestones were originally painted; on some the fact that they were painted is even recorded in the inscription.[1] The colours of the St Paul's stone have already been described in some detail. The colours usually used in Sweden are chiefly brown, red, blue and black.[2] Unfortunately many stones have been repainted in modern times and the colours seen today may not be those which were the original Viking colours. However, a lucky find of about sixty fragments of runestones, built into the wall of the church at Köping, on the Swedish island of Öland, has provided a considerable amount of evidence concerning the painting of the stones. The Köping stones are in a remarkably fresh condition and must have been broken up soon after they were erected. A preliminary report[3] on the find has shown that the chief colours are red and black (red lead and soot) and that not only were the carved lines painted, but the whole area between the lines was also painted. On a number of stones alternate words in the inscription were painted red and black. Where the stones were carved in low relief (like the St Paul's stone) the background was generally painted black while the ornament was painted red—a feature which occurs in wood in the rather later piece of carving from Hørning, Denmark (frontispiece, see below p. 153). That this was not always the case is demonstrated by the Ringerike gravestone from St Lars church, Linköping, Sweden, which was discovered in 1957. On this stone the surviving paint showed that the colour was closely related to those at Köping: the background at St Lars, however, was apparently left plain.[4] When Professor Jansson's final publication appears we are promised a review of the painted runestones of Scandinavia; it is likely that many preconceived ideas will have to be reconsidered and it is therefore wiser to refrain from pursuing this matter further here.

Many of the ornamental elements of the Ringerike style appear—in a slightly developed form—on the jewellery of the period. Owing to the gradual introduction of Christianity into Scandinavia, after the middle of the tenth century, the Christian rite of unfurnished burial replaced the pagan rite of a furnished grave with its accompanying

[1] Conveniently listed in Jansson (1962), 149–152.
[2] E.g. Lindqvist (1917–24), 48–50; Hallström (1931); Christiansson (1959), 37–38 and Jansson (1962), 147–155.
[3] Jansson (1954).   [4] For reconstruction of colours cf. Jansson (1962), pl. before p. 153.

personal equipment and jewellery. As a result nearly all the surviving jewellery decorated with Ringerike style ornament has been found in hoards, and there is a consequent decrease in the number of objects of base metal decorated in this style, while many fewer small personal objects survive than in previous periods. In fact, in our study of the Ringerike style, we rely on a completely different type of material to that encountered previously. It is difficult, therefore, to make qualitative judgments in any comparison, say, of the Jellinge and Ringerike styles. The kind of material that began to appear in the late Jellinge phase of Viking art now predominates—memorial stones, ivory carvings, the ornament of weapons, even the ornament of buildings, replace the ornament of the brooches and other personal jewellery which, with the exception of the Oseberg ship and the Gotlandic picture stones, dominate the earlier part of this study.

The most completely typical Ringerike style animal on a piece of jewellery is that engraved on the round silver brooch from the Swedish Espinge hoard (pl. LXII c). This animal appears almost sedate by comparison with the animals on the runestones, but in form it is at a much later stage of development than, say, the Stenåsa stirrup fragment (pl. LXII a), which was discussed in relation to the late Jellinge style. Long tendrils—the hall-mark of Ringerike—are present on this object alongside many other minor features of the style. Very different is an openwork brooch, in the form of a crested bird, from a hoard found at Græsli in the north of Norway (pl. LXII b). The bird is by no means typical of the Ringerike style, but the central pear-shaped lobe of the tail betrays its stylistic relations. By the same token it is possible to recognize certain circular brooches, decorated with silver filigree wire, as objects decorated with a modified form of a Ringerike motif. Only the pear-shaped acanthus lobe identifies the brooch from Årstad in Norway[1] with the Ringerike style, the brooch from Hornelund, Denmark (pl. LXII f), however, shows slightly more of the Ringerike detail—tendrils, for example, as well as the pear-like central lobe of the formalized leaf ornament. The small gold brooch from Vestvik, Beistad, Nord Tröndelag, Norway (pl. LXII e), betrays its Ringerike character by the tendril-like tail-feathers of the bird. Other brooches, such as the penannular example from Kyrkebinge in Gotland,[2] demonstrate the tendril feature more clearly, together with a very developed animal ornament, which is rather atypical of the style, but which occurs on a number of other brooches of the same, but rather less elaborate, form found in Gotland hoards.[3]

Certain charming, but unique, objects demonstrate the achievement of the metalworker in the field of personal jewellery: particularly fine is the dished, circular brooch of silver from Gerete, Gotland (pl. LXIII c), with its three interlaced animals and the acanthus knots with their attendant tendrils, which might best be compared with the similar feature on the St Paul's slab; while the restraint of the armlet from Undrom, Boteå, Sweden (pl. LXII d), with its three-dimensional Ringerike animal head and its engraved and nielloed tendril ornament, delights the eye and emphasizes the skill of the silversmith. An outstanding piece of plate from the Gotlandic hoards is the fluted silver

[1] Petersen (1928), fig. 123; Petersen (1955), pl. 52.   [2] Holmqvist (1951), fig. 41.
[3] Stenberger (1947–58), ii, fig. 286 and possibly fig. 284.

bowl from the Lilla Valla, Rute (pl. LXIII *a–b*). This vessel, which might be dealt with as an Urnes object, contains amongst its ornamental repertoire enough Ringerike features to be considered in this context. By the restraint of its decoration it is perhaps one of the most pleasing pieces of Viking metalwork to survive; for once in Viking art the ornament is very much secondary to the form of the object (this is, however, merely the subjective judgment of modern taste). Two charmingly naïve crucifix figures of silver filigree (pl. LXIV *a–b*) show in the treatment of Christ's hands distinct tendril elements of Ringerike origin—although with a distinct flavour of the Mammen fleshiness. They were found in a hoard in Trondheim, Norway.

The metalwork described in the last paragraph comes largely from hoards containing coins. These objects are, therefore, of some importance in the dating of the style, and we shall return to them below. But for our present purposes the date for the main *floruit* of the style in Scandinavia can be taken as the first half of the eleventh century.

It will be noticed that we have deliberately chosen, as one of the most important examples of Ringerike ornament, the design on the slab from St Paul's churchyard in London, an object found far outside the Scandinavian homeland. It must, however, be remembered that, when the St Paul's slab was carved, England formed part of the vast Anglo-Scandinavian Empire of Canute the Great; England was, therefore, in one sense a Viking country and produced—alongside its native styles—a typically Viking art.

A small number of objects decorated in purely Ringerike style have been found in England, and in many cases it would be difficult to decide whether they were made in England or in the Viking homeland. Such a piece is the magnificent bronze strip from Winchester, sometimes identified, for no apparent reason, as part of a weather-vane (pl. LIX *c*), which bears a design of florid tendrils, growing out of double shell spirals in the centre of the panels. The metal is oxidized to a mature green, but traces of the gilding which originally enriched the object can be seen within the finely engraved lines. The design, which is preserved against a background of punched circles, bears no trace of any zoomorphic characteristic beyond the shell spiral which, in its original form, was an animal's hip. Many of the true features of the Ringerike style —tendrils, pear-shaped lobes and shell spirals—are present on this object and the quality of the ornament stands comparison with the best pieces of Scandinavian Ringerike metalwork; it is undoubtedly the finest piece of its style found in the British Isles. It is impossible to say whether this object and, indeed, other objects, such as the bone pin from the Thames (fig. 64), and the bronze plates from Smithfield, London,[1] were made in England or in Scandinavia; for Anglo-Saxon craftsmen were obviously quite as capable as their Scandinavian colleagues of producing a piece of Ringerike decoration. The Anglo-Saxon scribe who carefully drew out the design of a book-cover, or box, (pl. LXIV *c*) on a spare space in the Caedmon manuscript, now in the Bodleian library at Oxford, was obviously quite a capable artist who, in his use of both Ringerike scroll work and Winchester-style rosettes, showed himself to be the master of both barbarous and sophisticated motifs.

[1] Wheeler (1927), fig. 21, and Paulsen (1933*a*), fig. 4.

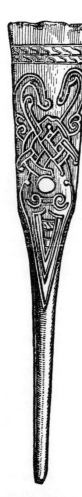

There is an undoubted affinity between the Ringerike and Winchester styles; it is an affinity which must stem from the origin of the attenuated fleshy scroll of Ringerike art in the southern English material, or from the common origin of this element of English and Viking ornament on the Continent. The English artist was clearly inspired by Viking art in the same way as the Viking artist was inspired by his English contemporaries. Unfortunately we have little material from the south of England of sufficiently high quality to demonstrate the complete mastery of Viking motifs by English artists. Many of the objects made in England in the Ringerike style, by artists who were definitely English, are of rather poor quality. Objects of high quality, such as the St Paul's slab (pl. LVIIIa), the Leeds cross-shaft,[1] the Otley slab (pl. LXV a) (which is a very fine and typical piece of Ringerike carving), the Winchester panel (pl. LIX c) and the Smithfield objects may well have been made by Scandinavian, rather than English, craftsmen. Our knowledge of the English Ringerike style rests, then, largely on minor or second-rate pieces.

Such a minor piece is a small bone comb, of unknown provenance, in the British Museum[2]; it is unique as the only three-dimensional object ornamented with both Anglo-Saxon and Ringerike ornament. On one face (pl. LXV b) is a Ringerike snake of slightly tame appearance, while on the other (pl. LXV c) are a pair of contorted Anglo-Saxon animals of a typical late tenth- or early eleventh-century form. A more important piece, but, even so, not of first-class quality, is the large disc brooch, nearly 6 in. in diameter, which was found with a hoard of coins of William the Conqueror at Sutton, Isle of Ely (pl. LXVI a), at the end of the

FIG. 64. Bone pin from the River Thames at London Scale c. ⅔. *British Museum.*

seventeenth century. Its Anglo-Saxon origin is attested by the lengthy inscription on the back, and its inferior quality is proclaimed by the incompetent Ringerike style ornament, with certain Winchester overtones in the foliate details, of the front. Here are snakes and animals of typical Ringerike type, creatures which are little more than rather miserable versions of the animals on the Alstad stone (fig. 59). A rather more competent rendering of a Ringerike motif occurs in the well-known manuscript Ff.1.23 in the University Library, Cambridge. The initial letter *d* illustrated here (pl. LXV d) is perhaps the most accomplished piece of drawing in a rather second-rate manuscript and the snake, which forms the letter, is as fine as many of its Scandinavian brethren and in stance and ferocity it reminds one of the quasi-snake on the St Paul's slab. One of the features of this snake is the pear-shaped eye, with the point towards the snout, which is a typical feature of the Ringerike style.

[1] Kendrick (1949), fig. 16.   [2] Wilson (1960b).

There is little sculpture of this style in southern England. The oft-quoted fragment of a slab from Bibury, Gloucestershire, now in the British Museum (pl. LXVIII), demonstrates in its foliate character only a weak reflection of the Ringerike style which inspired the design. The double-contoured animals below the mask are flaccid and almost too featureless to be anything but the acme of provinciality. The masks alone given an unconvincing barbaric strength to the sagging remnants of a poor combination of the Winchester and Ringerike styles. This is a very different style from the often illustrated, purely Viking, Ringerike ornament of the coping stone of a grave from St Paul's churchyard, London, in the British Museum.[1]

Other elements of the Ringerike style have been alleged in English manuscript sources, but, apart from certain scraps of interlace ornament in the Bodleian Library manuscript, Junius 11[2] and some rather doubtful 'Scandinavianisms' cited by Wormald in the British Museum MS., Cotton, Claudius B. iv[3] and certain other places, they do not amount to much.

We have mentioned two pieces of stone-carving from the north of England—Otley and Leeds—and in an earlier chapter we have discussed incipient Ringerike features amongst the stone sculptures of the Isle of Man,[4] one might also draw attention to Scottish finds.[5] Particularly worthy of mention is a carving in stone from Dòid Mhàiri, Port Ellen, on the Hebridean island of Islay (now in the National Museum of Antiquities of Scotland).[6] This slab has a rather clumsily constructed Ringerike tendril pattern on either side of a wheel-headed cross, and, since the Maeshowe carving,[7] which is sometimes said to be Ringerike in style, is actually twelfth century and has only superficial Ringerike characteristics, the Dòid Mhàiri stone is the most important object of this style found in Scotland.

In Ireland the Ringerike art occasionally achieves a high standard, as on the shrine of the crozier of the Abbots of Clonmacnoise (pl. LXVII and fig. 65). This is perhaps the finest example of the Irish facet of the Ringerike style, but it is late in the series and stands out against a background of fragmentary and rather second-rate pieces. Such a piece is the Misach, a book shrine with many later accretions but with three surviving Ringerike panels. One of these panels (pl. LXIII d) is embellished with an interlaced animal pattern, executed with a formal symmetry unknown elsewhere in contemporary Viking art. The end panels are decorated with typically ragged Ringerike animals, which sprout tendrils in all directions, and they can hardly be characterized as brilliant expressions of the style, for the heads are weakly delineated and the ribbon interlace is coarse in quality and poorly executed. A slightly more competent Ringerike design can be seen on two nielloed gilt-bronze panels on the shrine of the Cathach (pl. LXVI b). Each of these

---

[1] Kendrick (1949), pl. lxviii. [2] E.g., ibid., pl. lxxiii, 2. [3] Wormald (1952), 67.
[4] Cf., for example, the crosses at Michael (Kermode (1907), pl. xl) and Onchan (Kermode (1907), pl. xxi, 59a).
[5] Cf., for example, the gilt-bronze strap-end from the Viking settlement of Jarlshof, Shetland (Hamilton (1956), pl. xxix, 1), which was probably made in Scandinavia, but which is of exactly the same technique as the Winchester weather-vane.
[6] Stevenson (1958–59), 53. [7] Mackenzie (1936–37).

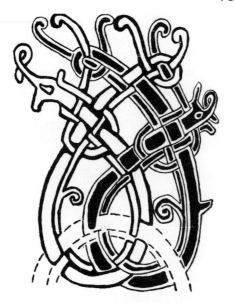

FIG. 65. Animal ornament from the crook of the crozier of the Abbots of Clonmacnoise. Pl. LXVII. *National Museum, Dublin.*

bears a raised Ringerike pattern of classic design—consisting of two interlaced, looped animals, with typical, if rather stylized, heads. The pattern, like all good Ringerike ornament, is asymmetrical and is embellished with the typical tendrils of the style. An inscription records that the shrine was made for a certain Cathban O'Donnell, perhaps at Kells, between 1062 and 1098, but in view of the numerous accretions to the shrine in the later Middle Ages, it is not easy to decide whether the Ringerike plates formed part of an earlier shrine or are contemporary with the inscription.

The crozier of the Abbots of Clonmacnoise (pl. LXVII and fig. 65), or rather the metal casing which enshrines it, is of a much higher quality than the two book shrines and the various other Irish Ringerike objects. The tendril ornament, however, has lost some of the raggedness of the high Ringerike style and the whole design is well on the way towards the ultimate smoothness of the Urnes style. The head of the bronze casing, which enshrines the original crozier, is embellished by inlay executed in silver and niello. The inlay, with the addition of some engraving, delineates a number of snake-like animals looped together in a fashion similar to that found on the Misach shrine. The motif is more or less the same as that which we have seen in Scandinavia (on the Källunge vane, fig. 58, for example) and shows the influence of the Scandinavian Ringerike style on its Irish contemporary. The lower part of the upper knop of the crozier (pl. LXVII) is decorated with standing beasts, cast in high relief, which may be related to the free-standing animals of some of the Scandinavian weather-vanes. They are the nearest we get in the Irish material to the great beast of the Jellinge/Vang/ Tullstorp type.

A group of Irish stone crosses discussed by Mr Liam de Paor[1] have certain claims to the Ringerike label. They are far outside the main stream of Ringerike art and are of interest in that they are the only sculptural representatives of the style in Ireland.

Irish Ringerike material is all of a relatively late date. The occurrence of Gaut's ring-chain, the Manx Jellinge motif on the Soiscel Molaise,[2] which is dated between 1001 and 1025, indicates that the Ringerike style may not have been introduced until about the middle of the century. If this is the case, and this date can only be accepted tentatively, it may well be that the two Ringerike panels on the shrine of the Cathach were made in the late eleventh century. It would seem, then, that there can be little

[1] (1955–56).   [2] Mahr and Raftery (1932–41); i, pl. 57, 2.

doubt that the Ringerike style was introduced into Ireland at a very late stage in its development and there can be no doubt that features of the style occur well on into the twelfth century, for the Ringerike tendrils occur in an obscure position on the well-dated cross of Cong (pl. LXXVI).

We must now consider the chronological position of the Ringerike style in Britain and Scandinavia. Dr Holmqvist, in an attempt to prove his thesis that the Ringerike style is of English origin, has changed the accepted date of the Caedmon manuscript, placing it at about 1000.[1] He has further dated the St Paul's slab 'to about the middle of the eleventh century'. The first date, in a period when palaeographical chronology is well documented, is improbable, while the second date shows, we think, too little consideration for the political and cultural conditions pertaining in England. Dr Holmqvist is of course right in emphasizing that the best dating evidence is provided by the English manuscripts which contain elements of the style. Most of them are of about the same date as the Cambridge University Library MS., Ff.1.23, which is assigned on palaeographical and other grounds to the second quarter of the eleventh century,[2] and by implication to a rather early date in that quarter.[3] It would seem reasonable to suppose that the Winchester–Ringerike *rapprochement* took place during the reign of Canute (1016–35) and that it would hardly have survived the francophile taste of the sycophantic courtiers of Edward the Confessor, who succeeded the last Danish King of England in 1042. It is conceivable, but hardly likely, that certain fine pieces of Ringerike decorated material were produced in England during the reign of the Confessor, but it must be assumed that such a completely Scandinavian piece as the St Paul's stone was produced by a Viking craftsman for a Viking—an unlikely event after the reign of Harthacnut.

Evidence from Scandinavia is more difficult to assemble and summarize. Unfortunately no ornamented stone decorated in the Ringerike style is firmly dated by its inscription, and any attempt to provide accurate dating is doomed to failure on the grounds of subjectivity.[4] The style was probably introduced after the erection of the Jellinge stone (983–5), and the harmony demonstrated between the Mammen and Ringerike styles might indicate that the style came into being only shortly after this date. For the rest we must rely for our chronology on objects found in coin hoards, but it must be emphasized that the fixed points so provided are the latest possible dates only. The hoard from Espinge, Hurva, Skåne, which contains the brooch adorned with a splendid Ringerike beast (pl. LXII c), was deposited c. 1048[5] and most other hoards containing Ringerike material must be dated to the years about the middle of the eleventh

[1] Holmqvist (1951), 47 ff. He is supported by Nordenfalk (Grabar and Nordenfalk (1957), 187).

[2] Wormald (1952), 59.   [3] Ibid., 62–63, under no. 14.

[4] One of the most reasonable attempts to date a stone to within a decade concerns the Swedish Yttergärde stone. The inscription tells of three named Danegelds, paid to a farmer named Ulv. This stone is often dated to 1020–30 on the basis of the Danegelds (cf., e.g., Jansson (1962), 53–55). But it is impossible to say when Ulv died and the attempt to date the stone cannot be accepted.

[5] This dating, and the numismatic dates which follow, were kindly supplied by Mr R. H. M. Dolley of the Coins and Medals Department of the British Museum.

century—Lilla Valla, Gotland, which demonstrates the dying kick of the style (pl. LXIII *a*), to *c*. 1050, Gerete, Gotland (pl. LXIII *c*), to *c*. 1055, with rather later outliers at Græsli, Norway (pl. LXII *b*), which is dated to *c*. 1085, and Sutton, Isle of Ely (pl. LXVI *a*), which must be dated to about the same period. Two earlier hoards, Årstad, Norway (deposited *c*. 1030), and Kännungs, Gotland (deposited *c*. 1025), contain circular brooches decorated with filigree designs, which are related to the Ringerike style. There are other hoards containing Ringerike material which could be listed here: some of them, like the great Johannishus hoard from the Swedish province of Blekinge, are of no use for dating purposes, as their coins are so diverse and are spread over a long period of time (more than a hundred and fifty years in this case); others tell exactly the same story as those quoted.

On the basis of the English and Scandinavian evidence, it would seem reasonable to accept the traditional view that the Ringerike style emerged towards the end of the tenth century and lasted into the third quarter of the eleventh century. The Irish material can only be seen as the remains of a dying art; and the lack-lustre style of the shrine of the Misach demonstrates the style sinking into symmetry, a fatal sign in any northern animal art style. In Sweden the shadow of the Urnes style is clearly seen on the rune-stones, where the sleek, smooth, almost decadent, last flicker of Viking art now comes to the fore.

With the end of the Ringerike style the truly barbarian, self-confident art of the Viking is ended, all that it left is the ultimate refinement of over-specialization. It was soon to become a flaccid art, without meaning or strength, an art which could only be rescued by adding barbarism to the Romanesque style, which was gradually introduced into Scandinavia from the south and west.

CHAPTER VII

THE URNES STYLE

The Urnes style takes its name from the decoration of the small church in the Norwegian village of that name in the province of Sogn. The building is a stave-church; that is to say, that its walls consist of the vertically placed tree trunks split into two. The timbers of the ancient church, many of which were decorated externally, were re-used when the building was reconstructed in the middle of the twelfth century. Only a few of the original decorated portions of the building survive—the portal, the door, two planks in the north wall of the church, the north-west corner post and the gables at the east and west end of the church. Two distinct techniques were used by the sculptor of the Urnes church: carving in low, flat relief on the door and the gables (fig. 66), and carving in high, round relief (4·7 in. or 12 cm. deep) on the portal, the planks and the pillar (pl. LXIX).

Three motifs were used by the Urnes sculptor: (a) a standing quadruped, (b) a snake-like animal with a single foreleg and a hind-leg, which is indicated only by the terminal foot and an angular break in the curve of the body, and (c) a very thin inter- lacing ribbon which sometimes has an animal head. The animals have a distinctly sinuous form, the bodies swell and curve and the few angularities only serve to emphasize the undulating character of the motif. The animals interlace together biting each other at the neck, while the thin ribbons form an interlace pattern which is a *leitmotif* of the composition. The few distinct zoomorphic features which have survived conversion into this sinuous medium are familiarly Viking; chief among them are the spiral hip and lip-lappet of Jellinge origin, and the pointed eye of the Ringerike style, which now fills almost the whole of the animal head. New details include the delicate treatment of the feet, and the hook-like extension of the lower jaw, which, at Urnes, provide the chief reflections of the extended tendril of the Ringerike style. The interlace is rarely fussy, but forms large loops of even, almost monotonous, curves.

A characteristic, but by no means universal, feature of the Urnes style in its Scandi- navian homeland is the 'combat' motif. Each animal bites its neighbour. This feature is clearly related to the combat motif, if it can be so called, which was so frequent a feature of the Mammen style (cf. the Jellinge stone, pl. XLIX). The elements in both cases are the same, an animal and a snake, the fact that at Urnes itself animal occasionally bites animal deserves little emphasis, for the sinuous quality of the creatures sometimes makes it hard to distinguish snake from animal.

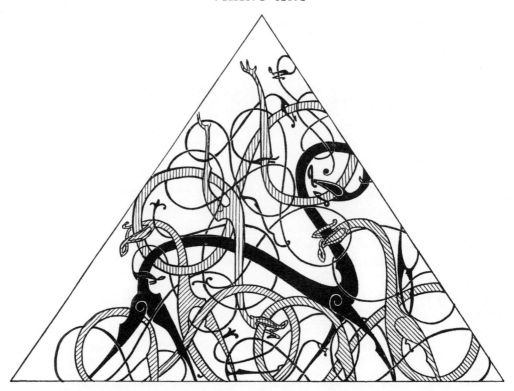

FIG. 66. Ornament of the west gable of Urnes church, Norway.

Wooden carvings in the same style have been found in a number of Norwegian churches. Fragments were found, for example, on odd pieces of wood recovered under the floor-boards of the churches at Hopperstad, Sogn, and Torpe, in Hallingdal,[1] while the planks on either side of the doorway of the church at Bjölstad, Heidalen, in Gudbrandsdal (pl. LXX) provide a more substantial monument of the style. The two planks were moved to Bjölstad from the older church at Nordre Prestgar at some time in the sixteenth century. The Bjölstad panels are less accomplished—probably more degenerate and later—than the Urnes panels, but the design of the animals is basically the same. Other panels from Rinde and Söndre Gate, Trondheim, are similarly decorated, but add little to our overall understanding of the Urnes style.

The splendour of the carvings at Urnes is not found elsewhere in Norway: this small church is the only place in Western Scandinavia where the high quality of Viking art of the late eleventh century can be appreciated. This quality is not even reflected in the metalwork, which so often in the past has been the only medium by which a style could be judged, for apart from a handful of openwork brooches, like that in pl. LXXIII *f*,[2] there

---

[1] Shetelig (1909), figs. 5 and 6.
[2] Petersen (1955), figs. 98 and 99. The piece illustrated in our pl. LXXIII *f* is in the Danish National Museum and has no recorded provenance.

is precious little metalwork ornamented in this style from Norway. The accidental survival of the wood carving reminds us again of the precarious nature of many of the judgments we have been forced to make in cases where metal is the only significant surviving medium of a style. When presented with such a magnificent find, in such an outlandish part of Norway on a comparatively small church, it is perhaps not completely idle to speculate concerning the quality of the carvings in long-vanished metropolitan buildings, built under royal patronage. Such speculation cautions us in qualitative judgments concerning the rôle of the Urnes style outside Norway, where little Urnes woodwork survives.

It must always be remembered that the name of this style is coincidental and does not necessarily imply a Norwegian origin for the art. The name was first used by Shetelig[1] in a discussion of the ornamental group dependent on Urnes, at a period when the style had hardly been recognized elsewhere, and it has been retained here despite the fact that the origins of the style can best be seen in Sweden, to which country attention must now be turned.

Little wooden material decorated in this style survives in Sweden, the few remaining pieces seem atypical—as for example the two panels taken from Guldrupe church in Gotland[2] and now displayed in a practically inaccessible position in Gotlands Fornsal, Visby. These panels are probably degenerate examples of Urnes style ornament, for the animal head tends towards the Romanesque. Our knowledge of the Swedish Urnes style depends largely on the decoration of stone and metal. In both these mediums—but chiefly in stone sculpture—the Ringerike origins of the Urnes style are clearly seen. Once again the development of a Viking style out of its predecessors can be clearly demonstrated in the abundant surviving material. We have no hesitation in assigning little importance to external artistic influence in the development of the style.

In the previous chapter, the identification of the Lilla Valla bowl (pl. LXIII a) as an object decorated in the Ringerike style was tentatively questioned. The ornament of this object can only be interpreted as transitional between Ringerike and Urnes. Such features as the pear-shaped lobe separating the animal heads on the rim of the vessel and the tendril-like treatment of the animal heads clearly belong to the Ringerike style. Other features clearly belong to the Urnes style: the single-limbed animals, for instance, which were present on the Urnes gable, and the split ribbon-like tail of the animal on the base of the object (pl. LXIII b) (which is seen particularly in the English material), are completely foreign to the Ringerike style.

These transitional stages in the development of the Urnes animal ornament are not only present in the metalwork, they can also be seen in the runestones. Indeed, the gradual fining of the Ringerike into the Urnes styles, on the Swedish runestones, occasionally makes it difficult to distinguish the precise art-historical position of a stone. For this reason the art of the Ringerike and Urnes styles in Sweden is often lumped together under the general heading 'runestone style'. This term has been abandoned

[1] Shetelig (1909).
[2] Moe (1955), fig. 9. For other wooden Urnes style objects from Sweden *vide* Holmqvist (1948), fig. 58–60.

here as it is of little use in treating the eleventh century art as a whole—the calibration is not fine enough. Further, the term 'runestone style' is misleading in that it places an emphasis on the most durable material—stone—and ignores the more perishable materials such as wood and metal. Further, every other late Viking style has a toponymous label and it seems pointless to break away from this practice.

It is customary to use the stone Ardre III (from the parish of Ardre in Gotland) to demonstrate the earliest stage of the Urnes style among the Swedish runestones. There seems no good reason to depart from this practice, for on this stone (pl. LXXI) can be seen the last elements of the Ringerike style—the pear-shaped lobe, separating the two adorsed animals, the tendrils of the head lappet and the jaws, and the dead hand of symmetry, which destroyed the Ringerike style, but which was ultimately derived from the graceful freedom of such motifs as that on the reverse of the Mammen axe, together with the two hip-like features in each of the bottom corners of the field. The bands split from the bodies of the animals to form a loop and this feature, as well as the even width of the single-limbed animal bodies, belong to the Urnes rather than to the Ringerike style. In fact Ardre III is little more than an interpretation in stone of the motif which appears on the Lilla Valla bowl and demonstrates the transitional phase just as well.

This transitional phase is not quite so clear on the stones from the mainland, but similar features can be seen. The head of the animal, fig. 63e, from stone U.212[1] at Vallentuna in Uppland, demonstrates a slightly more advanced development of the animal head, but the eye does not as yet monopolize nearly all the space in the head, the rest of the ornament of the stone, which is not illustrated here,[2] bears the marks of the dying phase of Ringerike symmetry and, particularly, the series of pear-shaped lobes. The same is true of fig. 63d, which portrays the head of the animal on the stone Sö.276 from Strängnäs.

A slightly later phase, more closely related to Ardre III than to the stones of the mainland, occurs in the ornament of the stone from Resmo on the island of Öland.[3] The pear-shaped lobes which embellish this object remind us of the Ringerike style, but the rest of the ornament comprises a typical interlace pattern of pure Urnes animals and ribbons, not, however, set in combat and, atypically in the Swedish runestone series, symmetrical.

This symmetry is entirely lacking in the main Swedish series, which we introduce with the stone from Stav, Roslagskulle, Uppland (pl. LXXII b), which bears a Ringerike acanthus ornament and a *soupçon* of Ringerike taste in the placing of balanced spirals in the body of the animal at the bottom of the field. This is an extremely fine, if rather erratic, representative of the Swedish aspect of the Urnes style. The animal represented here is the single-limbed creature encountered at Urnes, encircled by a large number of band-like snakes and other animals, which bite the main animal, themselves and each other. The heads of the animals show the elongated pointed eye, filling most of the

---

[1] The numbers used here and elsewhere in this chapter refer to the catalogue numbers of the stones in the Swedish runestone corpus (under authors in bibliography, U = Uppland, Sö = Södermanland, etc.).
[2] Christiansson (1959), fig. 130.　　　　[3] Holmqvist (1951), fig. 32.

head, which occurs at Urnes itself. The lip-lappet has been formalized and the head-lappet survives in only one instance—and that in a very modest fashion. The regularity of the pattern of the Urnes church decoration is absent; indeed, on this stone there is a pleasing freedom in the design, which only occasionally degenerates into fussiness. A similar stone is that from Skràmsta, Haga, Uppland (pl. LXXII a), which has a few traces of the elongated tendrils of the Ringerike style and of the elaborate Ringerike lip-lappet. Nevertheless, the whole design of this stone is of Ringerike inspiration, the two looped main animals reflect the ornamental structure seen on the Källunge vane (fig. 58), the Årnes mount (pl. XLV b–e) and fig. 57 and a number of other objects. Yet this stone is clearly an Urnes monument; the form of the snake, the shape and size of the eye and the angular break in the body just above the tail are all classic features of the style. On this stone can be seen the typical feet of the Scandinavian Urnes animals, a rather loosely constructed bifurcated foot with a rounded heel.

The final stage of the high Urnes style on the Swedish runestones can be seen at Nora, Uppland (fig. 67). Here is the classic Urnes combat motif together with features completely typical of the style: foot, eye, head, lappets, leg, etc.

From the sixth century onwards the names of sculptors occur spasmodically on the runic monuments in Sweden but, until the popularization of stone carving in Sweden in the eleventh century, it is impossible to name any group of carvings after the name of the rune carver. During the first half of the eleventh century, however, phrases like *Þorbiorn risti* (Thorbjörn cut [the runes]), become quite frequent, the rune carver's name is sometimes used in an elaborate manner:

'*Raði drængR*	'Let him read
ÞaR rynn se	who knows the runes
runum þæim	those the runes
sum Balli risti.'	that Balle carved.'

The runes were sometimes painted by another man who was of some importance. He is occasionally mentioned in the inscription, as at Gerstaberg, Ytterjärna, Södermanland, where it is recorded that Äsbjörn carved the runes and Ulf painted them. This type of inscription is rare and it is the carver of the letters, and presumably the whole design, who was important; particularly the Uppland carvers Åsmund, Asbjörn Kåresson, Äskil, Fot, Livsten, Balle the Red and, most prolific of all, Öpir.

An attempt has been made to erect a chronology of the runestones on the basis of the carvings of these men. As late as 1955 Moe[1] divided the groups up without any qualification:

(1) An initial phase, dominated by Åsmund, dated 1020–40.
(2) The classical phase, dominated by Fot and Balle, dated 1040–70.
(3) The late phase, dominated by Öpir, dated 1070–1100.

The dates stated here are hardly valid; it is impossible to be so unequivocal when the working lifetimes of the rune carvers are not known from historical sources. Moe's

---

[1] Moe (1955), 8–9.

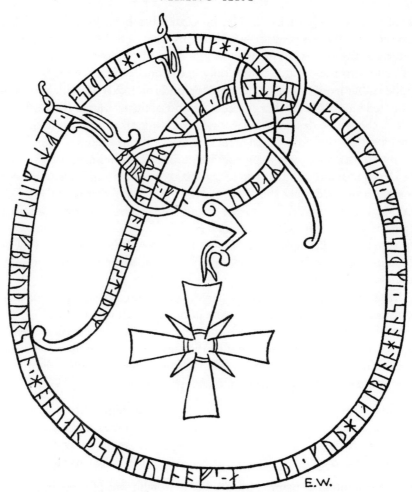

FIG. 67. Runic inscription and ornament of a stone from Nora, Uppland, Sweden

statement ignores the development of an individual's style[1] and the originality of the carvers. Nevertheless, the threefold division of the Swedish runestones, while useless in terms of absolute chronology, is useful as a vernier scale against which the monuments can be placed. Thus the initial phase represents the breaking away from the Ringerike tradition, the classical phase represents that reached on the Skråmsta stone, and the late phase is equivalent to that of the Nora stone. Such a division begs many questions, for the sequence of artistic development demonstrated on the Swedish runestones must be seen as a gradual refinement away from the florid Ringerike style to the dryness of the late Urnes style. It would be impossible to place all the Swedish runestones of the Urnes style within one of these groups, for transitional pieces would abound.

[1] Cf. U.819 and U.873, Wessén *et al.*, iii, 435 ff., and 542 ff., both stones of Balle the Red, but the latter with much earlier features than the former.

Metal objects from Sweden decorated in the Urnes style are comparatively common. Urnes motifs occur on objects of a familiar type, for example, on the back plate of a drum-shaped brooch from Tändgarve, Sweden (pl. LXXIII *a*); occasionally, however, more remarkable objects are found. Two bronze shrine terminals from Gotland (one of which is illustrated in pl. LXXIII *b*), and a number of silver objects with Urnes motifs are of finer quality. Some of the latter, like the crucifix from Gåtebo, Öland (pl. LXXIII *c*), were found in hoards and are therefore of some importance in the chronological discussions which conclude this chapter. Our main impression of the Swedish Urnes style is, however, derived from the art of the runestones: for although they have little chronological significance, they are the only monuments which enable us to appreciate the breadth and quality of the Urnes achievement in eastern Scandinavia.

Turning to the Danish influenced provinces of South Sweden and to the modern kingdom of Denmark, there is only one runestone which achieves the standard of its northern contemporaries. This stone, from Simris, Skåne,[1] must be considered as an outlier of the Uppland group, for its contemporaries in South Scandinavia have no ornamental details of any importance, or, like a small group of stones from the island of Bornholm,[2] are extremely degenerate in their decoration. Apart from a few small metal objects, of the usual openwork type (pl. LIII *f*),[3] the only considerable evidence for the presence of an accomplished Urnes style in this area is the fragment of wood, found in the last century in the church at Hørning, Denmark (frontispiece). It is a portion of the grooved beam which held the tops of the upright members of the original stave church, which on coin evidence was probably built in the first half of the eleventh century.[4] The ornament is carved in flat relief and consists of a single snake with an elegant head which is completely typical of the Urnes style. The wood is painted so that the snake is seen in red against a black background.

Despite the lack of material in South Scandinavia the Urnes style can be seen as a Viking phenomenon which dominated the whole of Scandinavia. Its seeds are to be seen in the preceding style; once again we are presented with an art which blossoms as an indigenous art. The self-confidence of Viking culture is re-asserted and the theme of this book comes full circle.

But the Urnes style, like its predecessors, the Jellinge, Mammen and Ringerike styles, was also of profound importance in the art-history of Britain. It is strange that, in a period when Viking power was waning outside Scandinavia, there should be a resurgence of Viking art in the British Isles. This revival, for it is no less than that, can only be explained as a result of the injection of a considerable amount of Viking taste into the insular bloodstream with the settlement of so many ex-Vikings—Normans in other words—in England. It seems reasonable to suppose that most of the objects decorated in the Urnes style found in the British Isles, were manufactured after the Norman Conquest of England in 1066. It is significant, as we shall show, that most of the Irish Urnes style seems to be later than the English material and we must assume that, as so often

[1] Jacobsen *et al.* (1942), pl. 795. [2] E.g. ibid., pl. 912 and 913.
[3] Ramskou (1960), *title page*, illustrates the finest of the series. [4] Krogh and Voss (1961), 20.

in the past, Ireland received its inspiration from England and converted it with great competency into an individual style of high quality.

Let us then examine this insular material. At first glance there seems to be little of importance decorated in the Urnes style found in England—little more than a handful of metal objects and one or two architectural fragments. But one of these objects is of superlative quality, even when compared with its Scandinavian contemporaries—the brooch found in the churchyard at Pitney, Somerset (pl. LXXIII e). Moe has pointed out that this fine gilt-bronze object is the 'sole Urnes monument found on English soil with a clear combat motif'.[1] It is 1.5 in. (3.8 cm). in diameter and the animal and snake, which interlace in smooth coils within the scalloped edges of the circle, are cast in openwork in the dished surface of the object. In every detail, save perhaps the foot of the animal and its scalloped border, the object is purely Urnes in style—eye, lip-lappet, hip and the angled break in the curve are all typical features of the style. A pale reflection of this object was found at Wisbech, Cambridgeshire (pl. LXXIII d), it is a small bronze object, neither gilt nor dished, interpreting the same motif in openwork, but the interlacing snake is replaced by a simple ribbon. There are a number of other metal objects from England bearing ornament in this style,[2] all of which seem to have been manufactured in this country, but the most important is the head of a crozier found in what is alleged[3] to have been Bishop Flambard's (died 1123) tomb in the chapter-house of Durham cathedral. It is of iron, covered with a thin sheet of silver; an animal design (fig. 68) is incised in the silver and inlaid with niello. The pattern is a spirited interpretation of a knotted Urnes zoomorphic pattern with many of the typical details of the style. Kendrick[4] examined this ornament carefully, in the light of English manuscript illumination, and came to the conclusion that it was, despite its many Urnes features, in a direct English tradition. It would probably be more correct to say that there already existed in England a taste for Viking ornament of this form. What is important is that this object was made for a Norman warrior-bishop—whether Flambard or not—in an important Norman see. In view of the political and cultural conditions pertaining at the time, it would seem unlikely that the craftsman who made this crozier would have been a Viking working in his Scandinavian homeland. This object was almost certainly made by an Anglo-Norman craftsman (possibly of Viking descent) within the Norman kingdom of England.

But metal-work is not the only medium in which the English Urnes style is found: here and there in widely scattered places, Jevington, Sussex, West Marton[5] and Southwell, Nottinghamshire,[6] are a few pieces of stone carved with Urnes motifs. Most typically Urnes are the animals at the feet of the figure of Christ at Jevington (pl. LXXIX a). The animal on Christ's left at Jevington is sinuous and has a pear-shaped eye and lip-lappet. At Norwich a capital, probably from the cloister of the cathedral, is

---

[1] Moe (1955), 17.

[2] Cf. Wilson (1964) nos. 33, 58 and 141, Kendrick (1949), fig. 20, b, Moe (1955), fig. 16.

[3] This identification has recently been questioned, cf. Wilson (1964), 7, the name, however, is retained here for the sake of convenience.

[4] (1938b).   [5] Kendrick (1949), pl. lxxxviii.   [6] Ibid., pl. lxxxvi.

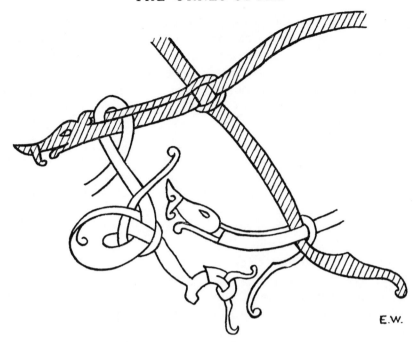

FIG. 68. Ornament from the socket of the crozier of Bishop Flambard of Durham. Scale: ⅓. *Durham Cathedral.*

decorated with two snake-like creatures, which vividly recall the Pitney brooch.[1] The Norwich capital is dated on reasonably firm documentary grounds to 1140 and with one exception, the Herefordshire school of sculpture (to which we shall return), is the last expression in England of the Urnes style. Certainly it is the last expression of the native Viking tradition in England, but before we attempt to estimate the chronology of the Urnes style, we must once again turn our attention to Ireland.

Irish art of the late eleventh century has an archaistic quality which makes it difficult to separate the different styles of ornament of which it is formed. On the Lismore crozier,[2] for example, which is dated (on the basis of an inscription) to between 1090–1113,[3] Urnes elements occur together with interlaced animal ornament which is clearly based on the ninth-century tradition present in the Kell's crozier.[4] The difficulty of identifying Urnes elements in late Irish art has mislead scholars in the past and we must examine those objects which are indubitably of Urnes derivation, in order to appreciate the true extent of its influence in Irish art.

Apart from the crozier head from Aghadoe (pl. LXXIV *a*), which is carved in walrus ivory, most of the surviving Urnes art in Ireland is executed in either metal or stone. Metal objects are perhaps the most valuable in this discussion, as many are dated by in-

[1] Zarnecki (1951), pl. 76.
[2] de Paor (1958), fig. 34*a* and *b*.
[3] Mahr and Raftery (1932–41), ii, 160.
[4] Cf. MacDermott (1955), fig. 13.

scription. Such is the case of the Shrine of St Patrick's Bell (pl. LXXV), which is more correctly, though less familiarly, known as 'the Shrine of the Bell of St Patrick's Will'. The bell itself was first mentioned in the Irish annals in the sixth century and was obviously a well-known piece when it was so richly enshrined in the early twelfth century. From an inscription on the openwork panel of the back of the shrine we learn that it was made, between 1091 and 1105, by Cu Duilig O Inmainen and his sons, probably at Armagh.[1] Unlike most of the famous Irish shrines of this period it has suffered little at the hands of later restorers. Apart from a very obvious later medieval crystal in a damaged field on the front face, the object is substantially of one period. The Urnes influence can best be seen on the crest of the bell (pl. LXXV), where openwork Urnes animal heads are mounted in cast silver on a sheet bronze background—all gilt. The elongated pear-shaped eye, which is one of the important Urnes features in the decoration of this object, is of cast glass. The long drawn out tendrils and easily applied interlace demonstrate how the ragged quality of the earlier Ringerike style is completely lost; here is all the smoothness of the Scandinavian Urnes style, with some of its disciplined sense of movement. In the right-hand upper panel of the crest can be seen a weak representation of the Urnes combat pattern: the small looped snakes in the two top corners of the field, seem to cock a snook at the degenerate animal, which appears to have exhausted itself in innumerable coils. The rest of the ornament of the shrine is pedestrian by comparison, but is of remarkably high quality. In the semicircular field under the crest at the front of the shrine (pl. LXXV a) is a carefully balanced, formalized inhabited vine-scroll containing two affronted birds. This motif has a long history in Ireland, and indeed in the whole of the ancient world from the Roman period onwards, and it is hardly surprising to see it here. The main face of the shrine comprises a panelled silver frame containing fields of gold filigree ornament; but symmetry has destroyed the live quality of the animal figures which make up much of this ornament. The symmetrical quality of this ornament is also apparent in the cast ornament on the sides, which, although quite pleasing and vital, has lost much of the barbaric charm of the style.

The other major pieces of dated metalwork decorated in the Urnes style in an Irish idiom is the Cross of Cong (pl. LXXVI). It is a processional cross, which also functioned as a reliquary for a fragment of the True Cross. According to an inscription cut in a silvered bronze plate on the side panels of the cross; it was commissioned by Toirdelbach Ua Conchubhair, King of Connacht, c. 1123. It is a splendid object, one of the finest and liveliest pieces of ornamental metalwork ever to be made in Ireland. No other piece of Irish art, other than the Tara brooch and the Ardagh chalice (which were made some four hundred years earlier), survives to witness to the skill of the Irish craftsman to a greater extent than this shrine. The front of the cross (pl. LXXVI a) is decorated with

[1] The sceptic would say that it is the bell and not the shrine that was made at this period, if the latest translation of its inscription is correct in grammar: 'A prayer for Domnall O Lachlaind [king of Ireland 1083–1121] under whose auspices this bell was made. And for Domnall, successor of Patrick [abbot of Armagh 1091–1105], in whose house it was made. And for Cathalan O Mael-Challand, steward of the bell. And for Cu Duilig O Inmainen and his sons who covered it.' But even the authors of this book would not carry pedantry thus far.

a series of gilt bronze openwork panels separated by plain silvered borders. The panels portray symmetrically-placed animals—usually in pairs, but occasionally singly. The animals have hatched bodies, the hips are usually spiraliform and the mouths occasionally bite across the body of the animal. The animals are caught in ribbon-like interlace. The ribbons in some of the panels (in the top two panels of pl. LXXVI a for example), have zoomorphic characteristics and are closely comparable to the minor animals of the combat motif on the gable of the Urnes church (fig. 66). The ribbon takes the form of an animal with pear-shaped eye, single, tautly stretched leg and foot with spiral hip, and a filament-like body exactly comparable to its Norwegian prototype. The biting animal head seen from above, which is also encountered at Urnes, can be seen in the two fields second from the top in pl. LXXVI a, where the animal bites the neck of one animal in each field. These panels are executed in a much more lively manner than is normal in Irish art, while the face of the cross was further enlivened by the presence of glass studs and nielloed roundels filled with spirals of silver wire.

The ornament of the openwork panels, which decorated the back of the cross, is much more symmetrical, but no less interesting; for here also can be seen the small, ribbon-like animals forming a background to the creatures which interlace so beautifully with each other all the way up each arm. The ribbon-like creatures no longer indulge in combat with the more ponderous quadrupeds, but their fierce little heads are clearly to be seen, sometimes in profile with a lip-lappet, sometimes (more simply) from above, with prominent eyes and mouse-like ears. In the portion of the back of the cross shown in pl. LXXVI b only two of the ribbon-like animals (those at the base of the field) have the single leg and spiral hip of the Urnes animals. Enamelled studs enliven the borders of this face and the openwork panels, like those of the front, are seen against a background of gilt bronze sheeting.

The cross appears to rest in the mouth of an animal cast in relief with inlaid, lentoid, blue glass eyes (pl. LXXVI), and the knop, which is so formed, is decorated with openwork panels similar to those on the two faces of the cross. The animal illustrated in pl. LXXVI d, for example, is clearly an Urnes creature with pear-shaped eye, lip-lappet, spiral hips and slim body: engaged with it, with its head in the bottom, left-hand corner, is a typical Urnes snake. Ringerike-like foliate motifs occur, as we have seen, below the sides of the cross, in the fields which separate the two half animal heads which form the knop (pl. LXXVI c).

An object which probably came from the same workshop as the Cross of Cong is the Shrine of St Manchan, now kept at Boher, Co. Offaly.[1] No general photograph of this object can convey the quality of its craftsmanship, but the detailed photo (pl. LXXVIII b) of one of the terminals of an arm of the cross applied to the front face of this house-shaped shrine, shows openwork animal ornament, complete with an interlaced snake, which might have been taken from the Cross of Cong. A number of bronze figures, six of which are shown in pl. LXXVIII a, are secured in a rather rough-and-ready fashion to the shrine. Cast in half-round form, they portray men, naked save for a loin-cloth.

[1] A careful study of this object was published by Kendrick and Senior (1937).

The ornament on one of these loin-cloths (third from left in pl. LXXVIII *a*) is typical Urnes ornament and we would seem to have here a very interesting occurrence of three-dimensional Irish art of the Viking period. There can be little doubt, *pace* Miss Senior,[1] that these figures are contemporary with the rest of the shrine, if not actually made for it. They appear to be saints or apostles: the figure holding an axe, second from the right in pl. LXXVIII *a*, may well be the Scandinavian St Olaf.

Another object of the same period, which is allegedly dated to the first quarter of the eleventh century by inscription,[2] is the remarkable arm reliquary of St Lachtin—one of the earliest Western European arm-reliquaries (pl. LXXVII). This naturalistic shrine shows a fore-arm with closed fingers. It is made of bronze and is inlaid with niello, gold and silver and decorated with various Urnes patterns, one of which is drawn out in fig. 69.

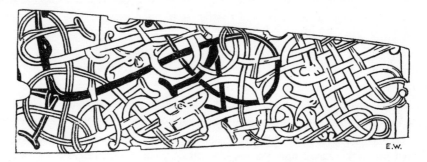

FIG. 69. Ornament from the reliquary of St Lachtin's arm. Pl. LXXVII. Scale ¾.
National Museum, Dublin.

The ornament is rather crudely executed but, if not examined too closely, gives an impression of competence. The binding-strip half-way along the arm is decorated with smoothly curving, openwork Urnes animals, while the strange binding-strip at the base is decorated with ornament which has some Urnes characteristics, but which, in some of its zoomorphic details, stems back to the single animals of ninth-century Ireland.[3] The most typical Urnes ornament is seen, however, on the plates which cover the arm: some have a symmetrical design of regularly interlacing animals, while some fields (like that illustrated in fig. 69) contain a rather more muddled, but none the less interesting, array of interlaced quadrupeds and snakes. There is, however, no combat motif on this object.

Although there are a fair number of metal objects from Ireland decorated in the Urnes style, they cannot all be discussed here and one undated object must serve to terminate the series—it comes from Holycross and it is of the highest quality (pl. LXXVIII *c*). The use of the object is not known, but it may be the mount from a lid of a small box; it consists of a convex sheet of bronze, of rectangular form, bound by narrow, incised strips. The sheet is apparently cast—it is extremely thin—and the ornament appears in low relief. The field is divided by a cross, the arms of which are filled, in part,

[1] Kendrick and Senior (1937). [2] Interpreted by Macalister in Mahr and Raftery (1932–41), ii, 161.
[3] Cf. e.g. de Paor (1958), fig. 29.

by a sub-Ringerike foliate motif typical of the style. In the four fields formed by the arms of the cross, are a series of interlaced animals of true Urnes character, some of which appear to be in combat with the others. The ornament is asymmetrical and exceptionally striking, demonstrating how even quite humble objects were decorated with skill and care by Irish artists working in the Urnes style.

The story of Irish metalwork in the period after these objects were made is the story of the disintegration of the Urnes style. On a few objects, for example the Shrine of St Dimma's book,[1] the style lingers on in a heavy-handed manner, but these objects reflect the last flowering of the great era of Irish metalwork. Once again a foreign art stimulated Irish art into producing something great and, when the artists of the Cross of Cong and the Holycross mount passed from the scene, the outstanding capability of Irish metalwork was never again seen in the Middle Ages.

In stone sculpture only one object comes anywhere near achieving the splendour of the Irish Urnes metalwork—the famous Cashel sarcophagus (pl LXXIV b). This is now preserved in the chapel of Cormac Mac Carthaigh, King of Munster, which was consecrated in 1134 with great ceremony. The double bead-and-roll of this tomb, as Mr de Paor has pointed out to us, is characteristic of Irish architecture of the middle of the eleventh century, and it is tempting to think of this sarcophagus as the founder's tomb of the great Cormac's chapel (there are good Hiberno-Saxon precedents for this usage). Whatever the case, the ornament of the main carved panel is of the familiar Irish Urnes character. The deeply carved, interlacing animals, caught up in a whirl of rather ragged interlaced snakes, exhibit many details already met with in the metalwork—the prominent eye and lip-lappet, the tightly coiled spirals and the tautly stretched leg and foot. The tails of the animals interlace with the bodies, and with the snakes, to form an untidy, ribbon-like background to the ornament. The snakes and the tails terminate in tightly rolled coils, and the snakes heads are seen from above with a pair of eyes and with the ears lying back along the body.

The pure Urnes theme of the well-dated Cross of Cong has already disappeared on the sarcophagus, the interlace is much more ragged and untidy and it would seem fair to associate it with the date of the Chapel of Cormac, and even the most cautious would place it in the second quarter of the twelfth century.

No other piece of Irish Urnes stone sculpture achieves the standard of the Cashel sarcophagus. It would seem reasonable to suppose that the purely Romanesque sculpture, which beautified the Chapel of Cormac, set a fashion for the many Romanesque churches and chapels, which were erected in Ireland in the last sixty years of the twelfth century[2] and that the Urnes style was swamped in the process, surving only in a very debased form on such objects as the Dysert O'Dea cross,[3] or as a minor motif in a grand construction, as on the capital of the outer order of the doorway at Killeshin church, as late as 1160. Like the rest of the northern world, Ireland had a foreign art imposed on it in the twelfth century: the vital native art, which had received many foreign styles

[1] Mahr and Raftery (1932–41), ii, pl. 101.
[2] See Leask (1955), *passim*.   [3] de Paor (1955–6), pl. V.

over the preceding millennium, was unable to survive this final onslaught and peters away in a whimper.

The brackets of the Urnes style are, then, very broad: geographically they extend from Sweden to Ireland and chronologically from the second quarter of the eleventh century to somewhere in the third quarter of the twelfth century. It has been shown how the Urnes style grew gradually out of the preceding style in Scandinavia and it is apparent in such circumstances that one cannot point to a single area or date for the initial phase of the style.

In Scandinavia the runestones would suggest, by their inscriptions, a date for the first phase of the Urnes style somewhere in the second quarter of the eleventh century —a date supported, but not made absolute, by the coin evidence produced by the Danish excavations at Hørning.[1] Hoard evidence leads us to similar conclusions. The ornament on the bowl from Lilla Valla, Gotland (pl. LXIII *a*) which, as we have shown, balances on the knife-edge between Ringerike and Urnes, occurs in a hoard deposited *c.* 1050. Hoards containing Urnes material, which do not occur outside Scandinavia, spill over into the twelfth century. The hoard in which the Gåtebo crucifix was found, for example, is dated to the early twelfth century, and it is of some interest that the same hoard contains a brooch (pl. LXXIX *b*) with heavy, sluggish snake patterns which represents a very late phase of Urnes ornament in Sweden (if indeed it can be called an Urnes phase at all). The roughly contemporary hoard from Old Uppsala contains a bowl with ornament (pl. LXXX) which is undoubtedly of Romanesque character. By the first quarter of the twelfth century Romanesque art started to replace the Urnes style in Scandinavia and a new vital style was developed which found its expression in monumental sculpture in the middle of the twelfth century at Lund Cathedral[2] and, at about the same time, on the group of ivories of which the British Museum chair-leg is the most outstanding example.[3]

In England it seems reasonable to suppose that the Urnes style flourished for a short period after the Norman conquest of 1066. It never made much of an impact in this country, however, until, in its final degradation, it suddenly blossomed forth and became one of the elements in the fantastic Herefordshire school of stone sculpture, of which Kilpeck is the leading example (*c.* 1140).[4] The dragons of the outer order of the magnificent portal of this church exhibit the last flickering traces of the true Urnes style.

The Irish Urnes style, such a magnificent reflection of its Scandinavian precursor, was at its greatest when the style was apparently dying in Scandinavia. The Cross of Cong is firmly dated by inscription to *c.* 1123 and is a worthy apogee of Irish Urnes art. Ireland may well have received the Urnes style about 1100, when the Bell of St Patrick's Will was enshrined, and the style apparently tails off into virtual nonentity in the third quarter of the twelfth century.

[1] Krogh and Voss (1961), 20. [2] Cinthio (1957), 205–208. [3] Lasko (1960).
[4] Professor Zarnecki tells us that he prefers this earlier date to 1150, which he used in his last published reference to the style—Henry and Zarnecki (1957–8), 24.

ENVOY

In this book we have traced the history of Viking art from its beginnings in pagan Scandinavia to its last flickering brilliancy in Christian Britain. For the last two hundred and fifty years of its existence Viking art was vital enough to influence some of the finest Western European art. Until it was finally eclipsed by the powerful new-fangled Romanesque art, Viking art retained its self-confidence unimpaired; quickly swallowing intrusive influences or motifs into its own repertoire. When it finally surrendered it was to an art attuned to Viking taste—Romanesque art: solid, sculptural and occasionally grotesque, the latter element of which must have been particularly appealing to the Viking palate.

We have stressed the lack of balance presented by the surviving Viking art, a lack of balance caused by accident of material. But it is proper that two series, the sculptures of Oseberg and Urnes, should overshadow Viking art, for wood was the material which the Scandinavian peoples were most happy to work with, and it is in the wooden furniture and folk-art of later Scandinavia that the Viking tradition is seen to survive. Viking art, however, was not merely a folk-art, it was an art which affected all levels of society, from the king with his great memorial stone to the peasant with his worn bronze brooch: all Viking society shared an appreciation of one of the most vital arts ever to appear in Europe. We who study its intricacies today cannot appreciate the thoughts which lay behind it, we can only marvel at the skill which fashioned it. If it is not to our taste, let us not condemn what we cannot understand.

BIBLIOGRAPHY

ÅBERG, N. (1921): 'Stil III och jellingestil', *Fornvännen*, xvi, 63–82.

ÅBERG, N. (1941): *Keltiska och orientaliska stilinflytelser i vikingatidens nordiska konst*, Stockholm. (*Kgl. Vitterhets, Historie och Antikvitets Akademiens Handlingar, 46:4*).

ALMGREN, B. (1944): 'Vangstenen', *Viking*, viii, 83–98.

ALMGREN, B. (1955): *Bronsnycklar och Djurornamentik*, Uppsala.

ARBMAN, H. (1937), *Schweden und das Karolingische Reich*, Stockholm. (*Kgl. Vitterhets, Historie och Antikvitets Akademiens Handlingar, 43*).

ARBMAN, H. (1940–1943): *Birka I, Die Gräber*, Stockholm.

ARBMAN, H. (1945): 'Stildrag i folkvandringstidens konst', *Fornvännen*, 88–101.

ARBMAN, H. (1956): 'The Skabersjö Brooch and some Danish Mounts; *Meddelanden från Lunds Universitets Historiska Museum*, 93–112.

ARBMAN, H. (1959): 'Skandinavisches Handwerk in Russland; *Meddelanden från Lunds Universitets Historiska Museum*, 110–135.

ARBMAN, H. (1961): *The Vikings*, London.

ARNE, T. J. (1914): *La Suède et l'Orient*, Uppsala.

ARNE, T. J. (1931): 'Skandinavische Holzkammergräber aus der Wikingerzeit in der Ukraine; *Acta Archaeologica*, ii, 285–302.

ARRHENIUS, B., and HOLMQVIST, W. (1960): 'En bildsten revideras', *Fornvännen*, 173–192.

ARWIDSSON, G. (1942a): *Vendelstile, Email und Glas im 7.–8. Jahrhundert*, Uppsala.

ARWIDSSON, G. (1942b): *Valsgärde 6*, Uppsala.

ARWIDSSON, G. (1954): *Valsgärde 8*, Uppsala.

BAKKA, E. (1958): 'The Beginning of Salin's Style I in England', *Universitetet i Bergen Årbok*. (*Historisk-Antikvarisk rekke, nr. 3*).

BALDWIN-BROWN, G. (1937): *The Arts in Early England*, vi, pt. 2, London.

BECKER, C. J. (1953): 'Zwei Frauengräber des 7. Jahrhunderts aus Nørre Sandegaard, Bornholm', *Acta Archaeologica*, XXIV, 127–155.

BERG, K. (1958): 'The Gosforth Cross', *Journal of the Warburg and Courtauld Institutes*, xxi, 27–43.

BINNS, A. L. (1956): 'Tenth century carvings from Yorkshire and the Jellinge style', *Universitetet i Bergen Årbok*. (*Historisk-Antikvarisk rekke, nr. 2*).

BLOCH, M. (1961): *Feudal Society*, (English edition), London.

BÓNA, I. (1956): 'Die Langobarden in Ungarn', *Acta Archaeologica* (Budapest), vii, 183 ff.

BRØGGER, A. W., and BUGGE, ANDERS (1925): *Bronsfløiene fra Heggen og Tingelstad Kirker*, Oslo. (*Norske Oldfunn, v*).

BRØNDSTED, J. (1920): 'Nordisk og fremmed Ornamentik i Vikingetiden', *Aarbøger for nordisk Oldkyndighed og Historie*, 162–282. (See Brøndsted, 1924.)

BRØNDSTED, J. (1924): *Early English Ornament*, London/Copenhagen.

BRØNDSTED, J. (1936): 'Danish Inhumation Graves of the Viking Age', *Acta Archaeologica*, vii, 81–228.

BRØNDUM-NIELSEN, J. (1933): 'Danske Runeindskrifter', *Runorna*, (ed. O. v. Friesen), 114–144. (*Nordisk Kultur, vi*).

BRUCE-MITFORD, R. L. S. (1949): 'The Sutton Hoo Ship Burial. Some Recent Theories and some Comments on General Interpretation', *The Proceedings of the Suffolk Institute of Archaeology*, XXV, 1–78.

BU'LOCK, J. D. (1958): 'Pre-Norman Crosses of West Cheshire and the Norse Settlements around the Irish Sea', *Transactions of the Lancashire and Cheshire Antiquarian Society*, lxviii, 1–11.

BUGGE, ALEXANDER (1905): *Vesterlandenes indflydelse paa Nordboernes og særlig Nordmændenes ydre Kultur, Levesæt og Samfundsforhold i Vikingetiden*, Christiania.

BIBLIOGRAPHY

BUGGE, ANDERS (1931): 'The Golden Vanes of Viking Ships. A discussion on a recent find at Källunge church, Gotland', *Acta Archaeologica*, ii, 159–184.

BUGGE, S. (1891–): *Norges Indskriften med de Ældre Runer*, Christiania.

CHADWICK, S. E. (1958): 'The Anglo-Saxon Cemetery at Finglesham, Kent: A Reconsideration', *Medieval Archaeology*, ii, 1–71.

CHRISTIANSSON, H. (1953): 'Jellingestenens bildvärld', *Kuml*, 72–101.

CHRISTIANSSON, H. (1959): *Sydskandinavisk stil*, Uppsala.

CINTHIO, E. (1957): *Lunds Domkyrka under romansk tid*, Lund/Bonn. (*Acta Archaeologica Lundensia, octavo series, I.*)

COLLINGWOOD, W. G. (1927): *Northumbrian Crosses of the pre-Norman Age*, London.

COWEN, J. D. (1934): 'A Catalogue of the Objects of the Viking period in the Tullie House Museum, Carlisle', *Transactions of the Cumberland and Westmorland Antiquarian and Archaeological Society*, xxxiv, 166–187.

de PAOR, L. (1955–6): 'The Limestone crosses of Clare and Aran', *Journal of the Galway Archaeological and Historical Society*, xxvi, 53–71.

de PAOR, L. and M. (1958): *Early Christian Ireland*, London.

ELDJÁRN, K. (1953): 'Carved Panels from Flatatunga, Iceland', *Acta Archaeologica*, xxiv, 81–101.

FORSSANDER, J.-E. (1937): 'Provinzialrömisches und germanisches', *Meddelanden från Lunds Universitets Historiska Museum*, 78 ff.

FORSSANDER, J. E. (1943): 'Irland-Oseberg', *Meddelanden från Lunds Universitets Historiska Museum* 130–240.

FRIESEN, O. V. (*ed.*) (1933): *Runorna*, Stockholm. (*Nordisk Kultur, vi*).

FRIESEN, O. V. (1940): *Sparlösastenen*, Stockholm. (*Kgl. Vitterhets, Historie och Antikvitets Akademiens Handlingar, 46, 3*).

GANDERT, O.-F. (1951): 'Die oldenburgischen Silberschatzfunde von Klein-Roscharden (Kreis Cloppenburg)', *Oldenburger Jahrbuch*, li, 151–206.

GJÆRDER, P. (1952): *Norske pryd-dører fra Middelalderen*, Bergen.

GRABAR, A., and NORDENFALK, C. (1957): *Early Medieval Painting, from the fourth to the eleventh century*, Lausanne.

GRIERSON, P. (1952): 'The Dating of the Sutton Hoo Coins', *Antiquity*, xxvi, 83–86.

GOLDSCHMIDT, A. (1918): *Die Elfenbeinskulpturen aus der Zeit der karolingischen und sächsischen Kaiser*, ii, Berlin.

HALLSTRÖM, G. (1931): 'Böra runstenar och hällristningar uppmålas?', *Fornvännen*, xxvi, 171–180 and 257–283.

HAMILTON, J. R. C. (1956): *Excavations at Jarlshof, Shetland*, Edinburgh.

HASELOFF, G. (1951): *Der Tassilokelch*, München. (*Münchener Beiträge zur Vor- und Frühgeschichte*, i).

HAUCK, K. (1957): 'Germanische Bilddenkmäler des früheren Mittelalters', *Deutsche Vierteljahrsschrift für Literaturwissenschaft und Geistesgeschichte*, xxxi, 349 ff.

HENCKEN, H. O'N. (1933): 'A Gaming Board of the Viking Age', *Acta Archaeologica*, iv, 85–104.

HENRY, F. (1933): *La sculpture irlandaise*, Paris.

HENRY, F. (1962): 'The Effects of the Viking Invasions on Irish Art', *Proceedings of the International Congress of Celtic Studies, held in Dublin, 6–10 July, 1959*, Dublin, 61–72.

HENRY, F., and ZARNECKI, G. (1957–8): 'Romanesque Arches Decorated with Human and Animal Heads', *The Journal of the British Archaeological Association*, 3rd series, xx–xxi, 1–34.

HILDEBRAND, H. (1883): *The Industrial Arts of Scandinavia in the Pagan Time*, London.

HINSCH E. (1958): 'Gokstadhøvdingens jaktransel?', *Viking*, 1957/1958, 175–201.

HOLMQVIST, W. (1948): 'Sigtunamästaren och hans krets', *Situne Dei*, vii, 6–107.

HOLMQVIST, W. (1951): 'Viking Art in the Eleventh Century', *Acta Archaeologica*, xxii, 1–56.

HOLMQVIST, W. (1955): *Germanic Art during the First Millennium A.D.*, Stockholm. (*Kgl. Vitterhets, Historie och Antikvitets Akademiens Handlingar, 90*).

HOUGEN, B. (1931–32): 'Studier i Gokstadfunnet', *Universitetets Oldsaksamlings Årbok*, 74–112.

HOUGEN, B. (1940): 'Osebergfunnets billedvev', *Viking*, iv, 85–124.

JACOBSEN, L. (1933): *Evje-Stenen og Alstad-Stenen*, Oslo. (*Norske Oldfunn, vi.*)

JACOBSEN, L., et al., (1942): *Danmarks Runeindskrifter*, København.

JANSSON, S. B. F. (1954): 'Om Runstenfynden vid Köping på Öland', *Fornvännen*, 83–90.

JANSSON, S. B. F. (1962): *The Runes of Sweden*, Stockholm.

JUNGER, H. (1940): *Västergötlands Runinskrifter*, i, Stockholm.

KARGER, M. K. (1958), *Drevnij Kiev*, Moscow/Leningrad. (*Akademija Nauk SSSR*).

KENDRICK, T. D. (1938a): *Anglo Saxon Art to A.D. 900*, London.

KENDRICK, T. D. (1938b): 'Flambard's Crosier', *The Antiquaries Journal*, xviii, 236–240.

KENDRICK, T. D. (1949): *Late Saxon and Viking Art*, London.

KENDRICK, T. D. and SENIOR E. (1937): 'St Manchan's Shrine', *Archaeologia*, lxxxvi, 105–118.

KERMODE, P. M. C. (1907): *Manx Crosses*, London.

KIRK, J. (1948): *The Alfred and Minster Lovel Jewels*, Oxford.

KLINDT-JENSEN, O. (1952): 'Keltisk tradition i romersk jernalder', *Aarbøger for nordisk Oldkyndighed og Historie*, 195–228.

KORNERUP, J. (1875): *Kongehøiene i Jellinge og deres Undersøgelse efter Kong Frederik VII's Befaling i 1861*, Kjøbenhavn.

KRAFFT, S. (1956): *Pictorial Weavings of the Viking Age*, Oslo.

KROGH, K. J., and VOSS, O. (1961): 'Fra hedenskab til kristendom i Hørning', *Nationalmuseets Arbejdsmark*, 1–34.

LASKO, P. E. (1960): 'A Romanesque Ivory Carving', *The British Museum Quarterly*, xxiii, 12–16.

LEASK, H. G. (1955): *Irish Churches and Monastic Buildings*, i, Dundalk.

LINDQVIST, S. (1917–24): 'Den helige Eskils biskopsdöme', *Antikvarisk Tidskrift för Sverige*, xxii, p. 1.

LINDQVIST, S. (1931): 'Yngre Vikingastilar', *Kunst* (ed. H. Shetelig), 144–147 (*Nordisk Kultur*, xvii).

LINDQVIST, S. (1941): *Gotlands Bildsteine* i–ii, Uppsala.

LINDQVIST, S. (1948): 'Osebergmästarna', *Tor*, i, 9–28.

LINDQVIST, S. (1955): 'Tre nyfunna bildstenar', *Gotländskt arkiv*, 41 ff.

MACDERMOTT, M. (1955): 'The Kells Crozier', *Archaeologia*, xcvi, 59–113.

MACKENZIE, W. M. (1936–37): 'The Dragonesque Figure in Maeshowe, Orkney', *Proceedings of the Society of Antiquaries of Scotland*, lxxi, 157–173.

MACKEPRANG, M. (1952): *De nordiske Guldbrakteater*, Aarhus.

MAGERØY, E. M. (1953): 'Tilene fra Mørðufell in Eyjafjord', *Viking*, xvii, 43–62.

MAGERØY, E. M. (1961): 'Flatatunga Problems', *Acta Archaeologica*, xxxii, 153–172.

MAHR, A., and RAFTERY, J. (1932–41): *Christian Art in Ancient Ireland*, Dublin.

MOE, O.-H. (1955), 'Urnes and the British Isles', *Acta Archaeologica*, xxvi, 1–30.

MÜLLER, S. (1880): 'Dyrornamentiken i Norden . . .', *Aarbøger for nordisk Oldkyndighed og Historie*, 185–405.

NICOLAYSEN, N. (1881): *Kunst og haandverk fra Norges fortid*, i, Kristiania.

NORDMAN, C. A. (1931): 'Nordisk ornamentik i Finlands järnålder', *Kunst* (ed. H. Shetelig), 180–201. (*Nordisk Kultur, xvii*).

OLSEN, M. (1933): 'De Norröne Runeinnskrifter', *Runorna* (ed. O. v. Friesen), 83–113. (*Nordisk Kultur, vi*).

OLSEN, M., and SHETELIG, H. (1909): 'Runstenar fra Tu og Klepp' *Bergens Museums Aarbok*.

OLSÉN, P. (1945): *Die Saxe von Valsgärde I*, Uppsala.

ØRSNES-CHRISTENSEN, M. (1955): 'Kyndby. Ein seeländischer Grabplatz aus dem 7.-8. Jahrhundert nach Christus', *Acta Archaeologica*, xxvi, 69–162.

BIBLIOGRAPHY

PAULSEN, P. (1933a): *Wikingerfunde aus Ungarn im Lichte der nord- und westeuropäischen Frühgeschichte*, Budapest. (*Archaeologica Hungaria, xii*).

PAULSEN, P. (1933b): *Studien zur Wikinger-kultur*, Neumünster.

PEDERSEN, L. (1920): *Kronborg have . . .*, Kjøbenhavn.

PEDERSEN, L. (1926): *Helsingør i Sundtoldstiden 1426–1857*, Kjøbenhavn.

PETERSEN, J. (1928): *Vikingetidens Smykker*, Stavanger.

PETERSEN, J. (1955): *Vikingetidens smykker i Norge*, Stavanger.

PETERSEN, TH. (1936): 'Rester av et skrin med belegg av benplater med skurd i Jellingestil funnet på Reistad i Frol. Nord-Trøndelag', *Det Kongelige Norske Videnskabers Selskab, Forhandlinger*, ix, no. 3, 9–12.

RAFTERY, J. (1941): *Christian Art in Ancient Ireland*, ii, Dublin. (See also Mahr and Raftery, 1932).

RAMSKOU, T. (1960): Lindholm Høje, Copehhagen. (*Nationalmuseets Blå Bøger*).

ROOSVAL, J. (1930): 'Acta angående Källunge-flöjeln', *Fornvännen*, xxv, 367–372.

SALIN, B. (1904): *Die Altgermanische Thierornamentik*, Stockholm.

SALIN, B. (1905): 'Studier i ornamentik', *Antikvarisk Tidskrift för Sverige*, xi, 1–141.

SALIN, B. (1922): 'Fyndet från Broa i Halla, Gotland, *Fornvännen*, xvii, 189–206.

SCHULTZ, C. G. (1952): 'Jellingebægeret—vor ældste kristne kalk?', *Kuml*, 187–198.

SHETELIG, H. (1909): 'Urnesgruppen', *Foreningen til norske Fortidsmindesmærkers Bevaring, Aarsberetningen*, 75–107.

SHETELIG, H. (1920): *Osebergfundet*, iii, Kristiania.

SHETELIG, H. (ed.) (1931): *Kunst*, Oslo. (*Nordisk Kultur, xxvii*).

SHETELIG, H. (1932–33): 'Helgenskrinet fra Kongehelle', *Bohuslänska studier tillägnade Landshövdingen Oscar von Sydow av Goteborgs och Bohusläns Fornminnesförening*, 28–30.

SHETELIG, H. (ed.) (1940): *Viking Antiquities in Great Britain and Ireland*, Oslo.

SHETELIG, H. (1948): 'The Norse Style of ornamentation in the Viking settlements', *Acta Archaeologica*, xix, 69–113.

SHETELIG, H. (1949): *Classical impulses in Scandinavian Art from the Migration period to the Viking Age*, Oslo.

SKOVMAND, R. (1942): 'De danske Skattefund fra Vikingetiden og den ældste Middelalder indtil omkring 1150'. *Aarbøger for nordisk Oldkyndighed og Historie*, 1–275.

STENBERGER, M. (1947–58): *Die Schatzfunde gotlands der Wikingerzeit*, Lund/Stockholm.

STEVENSON, R. B. K. (1958–59): 'The Inchyra stone and some other unpublished Early Christian Monuments', *Proceedings of the Society of Antiquaries of Scotland*, xcii, 33–55.

STOLPE, H., and ARNE, T. J. (1927): *La nécropole de Vendel*, Stockholm.

STRÖMBERG, M. (1955): 'Ein orniertes Steinfragment aus Väsby in Schonen', *Meddelanden från Lunds Universitets Historiska Museum*, 227–233.

STRÖMBERG, M. (1961): *Untersuchungen zur jüngeren Eisenzeit in Schonen*, Bonn/Lund. (*Acta Archaeologica Lundensia, quarto series, no. 4.*)

VEDEL, E. (1886): *Bornholms Oldtidsminder og Oldsager*, København.

VEDEL, E. (1897): *Efterskrift til Bornholms Oldtidsminder og Oldsager*, København.

VOSS, O. (1954): 'The Høstentorp Silver Hoard and its Period', *Acta Archaeologica*, xxv, 171–219.

WERNER, J. (1941): *Die beiden Zierscheiben des Thorsberger Moorfundes*, Berlin.

WERNER, J. (1950): 'Die Schwerter von Imola, Herbrechtingen und Endrebacke. Studien zur mitteleuropäischen und skandinavischen Metallarbeiten aus der ersten Hälfte des 7. Jahrhunderts', *Acta Archaeologica*, xxi, 45–81.

WERNER, J. (1958): 'Kirmukarmu—Monza—Roes—Vendel XIV;' *Suomen Museo*, lxv, 29–43.

WERNER, J. (1959): 'Frühkarolingische Silberohrringe von Rastede (Oldenburg)', *Germania*, xxxvii, 179–192.

WERNER, J. (1962): *Die Langobarden in Pannonien. Beiträge zur Kenntnis der langobardischen Boden-funde vor 568*, München. (*Bayerische Akademie der Wissenschaften. Philosophisch–historische Klasse, Abhandlungen–n.f., 55.*)

WESSÉN, E., *et al.* (1940): *Upplands Runinskrifter*, Stockholm.

[WHEELER, R. E. M.] (1927): *London and the Vikings*, London. (*London Museum Catalogues; no. i.*)

WIDEEN, H. (1955): *Västsvenska Vikingstidsstudier*, Göteborg.

WILSON, D. M. (1955): 'An Early Viking Age Grave from Källby, Lund', *Meddelanden från Lunds Universitets Historiska Museum*, 105–126.

WILSON, D. M. (1960*a*): *The Anglo-Saxons*, London.

WILSON, D. M. (1960*b*): 'An Anglo-Saxon Ivory Comb', *The British Museum Quarterly*, xxiii, 17–19.

WILSON, D. M. (1960*c*): 'The King's School, Canterbury, disc brooch', *Medieval Archaeology*, iv, 16–28.

WILSON, D. M. (1960*d*): 'The Fejø Cup', *Acta Archaeologica*, xxxi, 147–173.

WILSON, D. M. (1964): *Anglo-Saxon Ornamental Metalwork, 700–1100, in the British Museum*, London.

WILSON, D. M., and BLUNT, C. E. (1961): 'The Trewhiddle Hoard', *Archaeologia*, xcviii, 75–122.

WORMALD, F. (1952): *English Drawings of the tenth and eleventh centuries*, London.

WORSAAE, J. J. A. (1865): *Om Slesvigs eller Sønderjyllands Oldtidsminder*, Kjøbenhavn.

WORSAAE, J. J. A. (1869): 'Om Mammen-fundet', *Aarbøger for nordisk Oldkyndighed og Historie*, 203–218.

ZARNECKI, G. (1951): *English Romanesque Sculpture, 1066–1140*, London.

ZARNECKI, G. (1953): *Later English Romanesque Sculpture 1140–1210*, London.

ZIMMERMANN, E. H. (1918): *Vorkarolingische Miniaturen*, Berlin.

LIST OF SOURCES POST–1963

ANKER, P. (1970): *The art of Scandinavia*, i, London.

BLINDHEIM, M. (1965): *Norwegian romanesque decorative sculpture 1090–1210*, London.

CAPELLE, T. (1968): *Der Metallschmuck von Haithabu*, Neumünster.

FOOTE, P. G. and WILSON, D. M. (1970): *The Viking achievement*, London.

HÅRDH, B. (1976): *Wikingerzeitliche Depotfunde aus Schweden*, Lund.

HENRY, F. (1967): *Irish Art*, i, London.

HOLMQVIST, W. (1963): *Overgångstidens metallkonst*, Stockholm.

JANSSON, I. (1969): '*Wikingerschmuck und Münzdatierung*', *Tor* 26–64.

LANG, J. (1978): 'Anglo-Scandinavian Sculpture in Yorkshire', *Viking York and the North* (ed. R. A. Hall), London, 11–20.

LANG, J. (ed.) (1978): *Anglo-Scandinavian and Viking Age Sculpture*, Oxford (*British Archaeological Reports*, 49).

MOLTKE, E. (1976): *Runerne i Danmark og deres oprindelse*, København.

NIELSEN, K. M. *et al.* (1974): 'Jelling problems. A discussion'. *Medieval Scandinavia*, vii, 156–234.

NORDHAGEN, S. H. (1974): *Some Aspects of the Ringerike Style*, Bergen.

ØRSNES, M. (1966): *Form og Stil*, København.

ØRSNES, N. (1976): *Proceedings of the Seventh Viking Congress*, Dublin.

RAMSKOU, T. (1963): 'Stil F. En Skitse'. *Aarbøger for nordisk oldkyndighed og historie*, 100–118.

ROESDAHL, E. (1977): *Fyrkat, en jysk vikingeborgen*, ii, *oldsagerne of gårpladsen*, København.

SJÖVOLD, T. (1974): *The Iron Age Settlement of Arctic Norway*, ii.

WILSON, D. M. (1976): 'The Borre Style in the British Isles', *Minjar og menntir* (K. Eldjárn *Festschrift*) Reykjavík, 502–511.

PLATES

NOTE ON THE SCALE OF THE PLATES

Wherever possible the objects reproduced in this book are published at a scale of 1:1 and this is indicated in the caption. Where the object measures more than 30 cm. in length or width no scale is given; where it is important, measurements of large objects are given in the text. A scale placed at the end of a complete caption indicates that all the objects in the plate are reproduced at the same scale. Pls. xlvi, lxii (with the exception of *d*), lxiii*b* and *c*, lxvi*a*, lxxiii*a*, lxxviii*c* and lxxix*b* are all to scale 1:1, although they are not so marked in the captions.

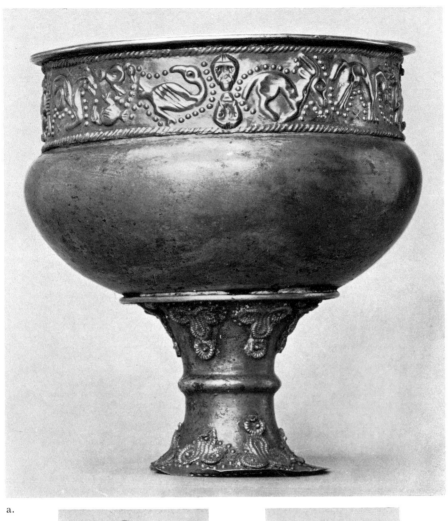

a.

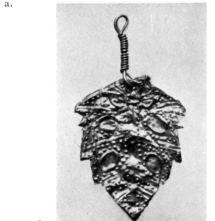

b.

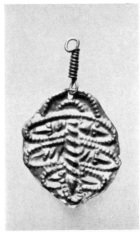

c.

Pl. I. (*a*) Silver-gilt beaker from Sjælland, Denmark. *National Museum, Copenhagen.* (*b*) and (*c*) Gold leaves from Brangstrup, Fyn, Denmark. *National Museum, Copenhagen.* 1:1.

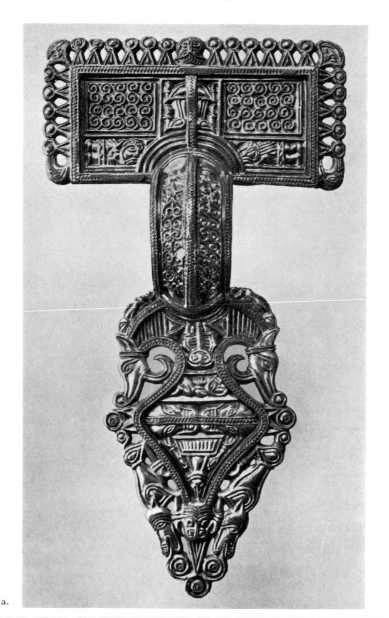

a.

b.

Pl. II. (*a*) Silver-gilt square-headed brooch from Gummersmark, Sjælland, Denmark. *National Museum, Copenhagen.* (*b*) Gilt-bronze harness mount from Vallstenarum, Gotland, Sweden. *Statens Historiska Museum, Stockholm.* 1:1.

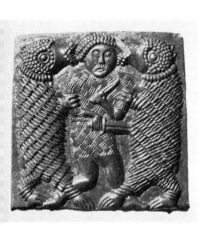

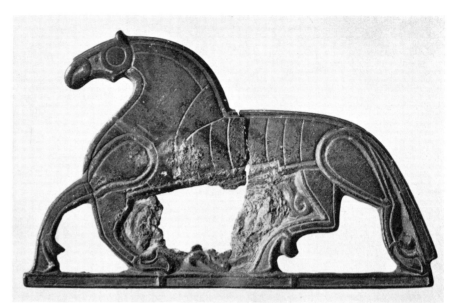

a.

b.

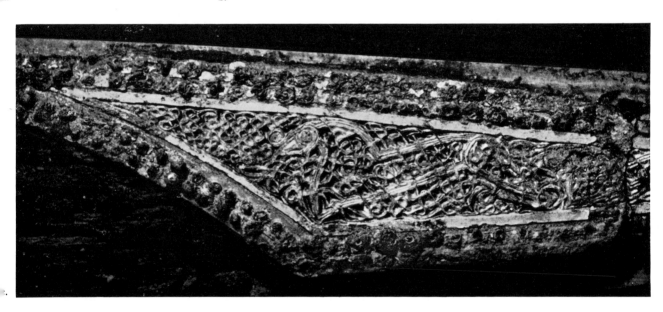

Pl. III. (*a*) Bronze die from Torslunda, Öland, Sweden. *Statens Historiska Museum, Stockholm*. 1:1. (*b*) Horse figure of bronze from Veggerslev, Jutland, Denmark. *National Museum, Copenhagen*. 1:1. (*c*) Detail of gilt-bronze mount of a scramasax from Valsgärde, Uppland, Sweden, grave 5, *Universitets Museum för Nordiska Fornsaker, Uppsala*.

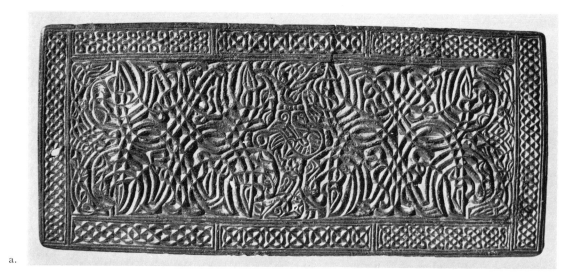

a.

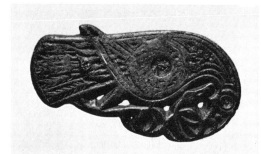

b.

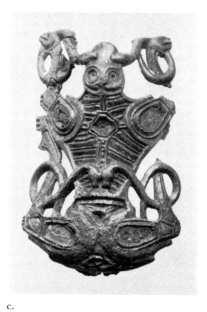

c.

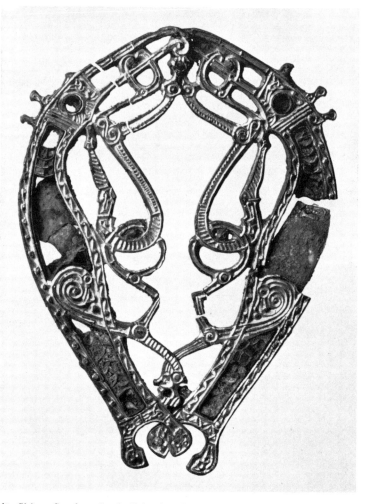

d.

Pl. IV. (*a*) Gilt-bronze brooch from Skabersjö, Skåne, Sweden. *Lunds Universitets Historiska Museum, Lund.*
(*b*) Bronze brooch from Kobbeå, Bornholm, Denmark. (*c*) Bronze brooch from Lousgård, Bornholm, Denmark, grave 12. (*d*) Gilt-bronze ornament from Lousgård, Bornholm, Denmark, grave 47. *b–d: National Museum, Copenhagen.* 1:1.

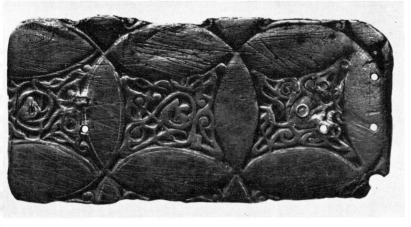

a.

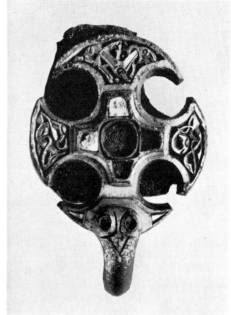

b.

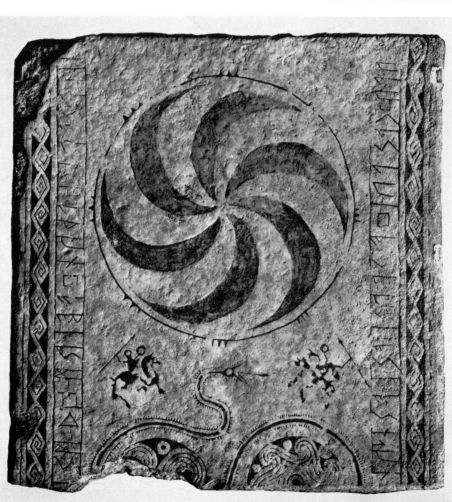

c.

Pl. V. (*a*) Gilt-bronze plate from Råbylille, Møen, Denmark. *National Museum, Copenhagen.* 1:1. (*b*) Gilt-bronze bridle mount from Valsgärde, Uppland, Sweden, grave 13. *Universitetets Museum for Nordiska Fornsaker, Uppsala.* 1:1. (*c*) Picture-stone from Martebo, Gotland, Sweden.

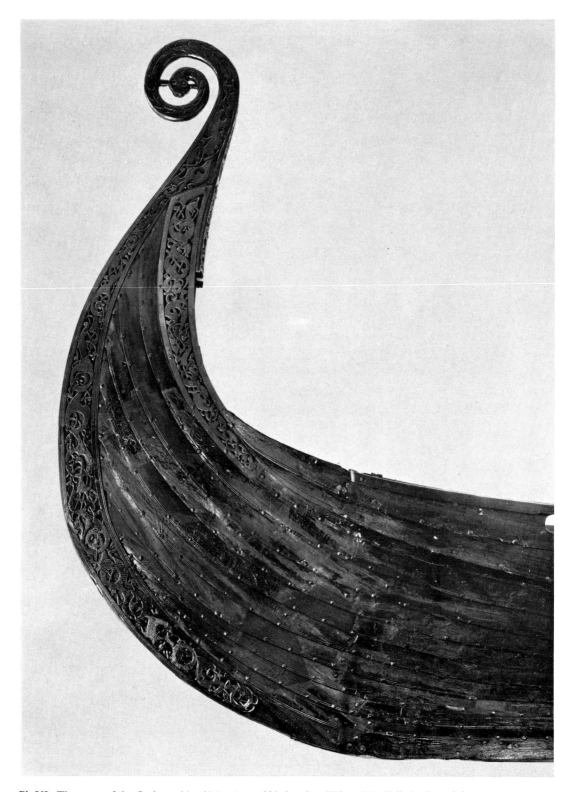

Pl. VI. The prow of the Oseberg ship. *Universitetets Oldsaksamling (Viking Ship Hall, Bygdøy), Oslo.*

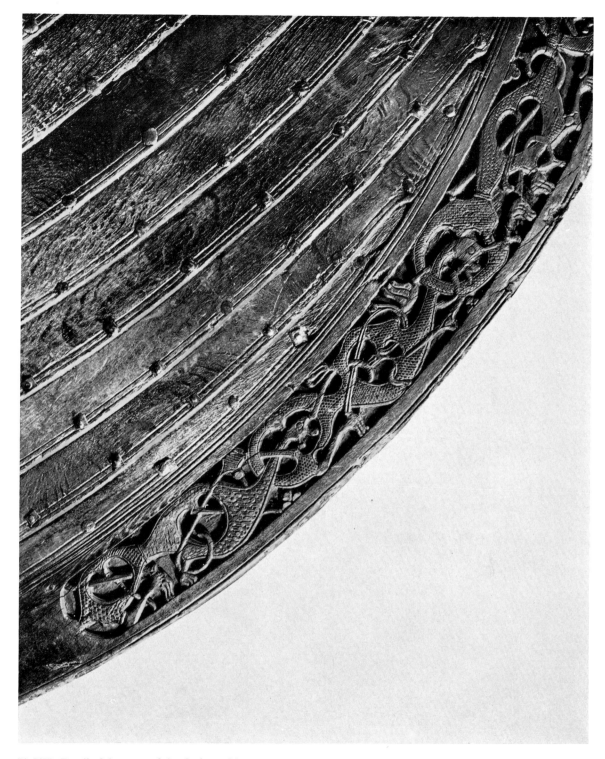

Pl. VII. Detail of the prow of the Oseberg ship.

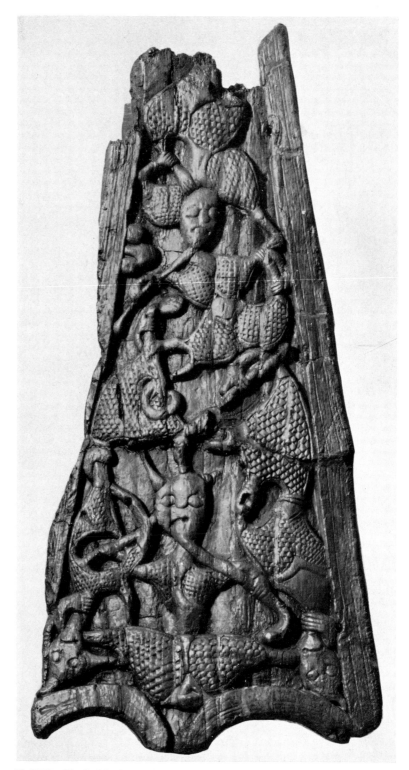

Pl. VIII. *Tingl* of Oseberg ship.

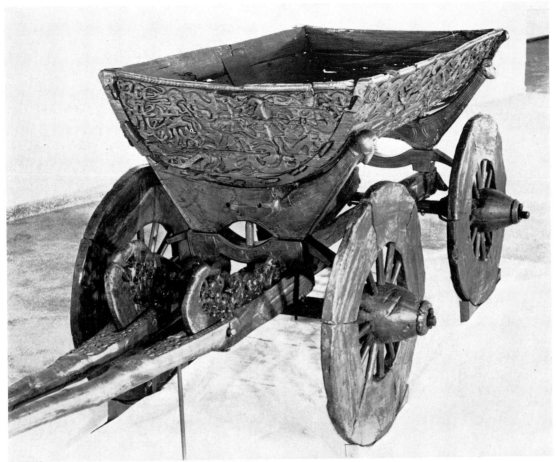

a.

b.

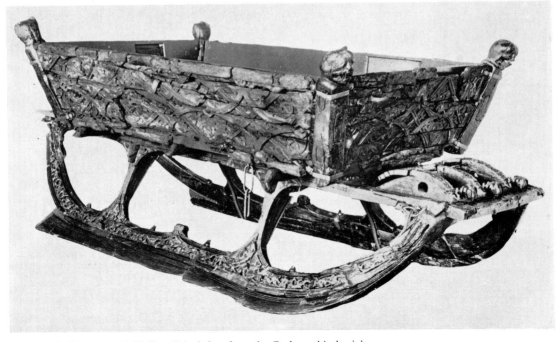

Pl. IX. (*a*) The cart and (*b*) Shetelig's sledge, from the Oseberg ship-burial.

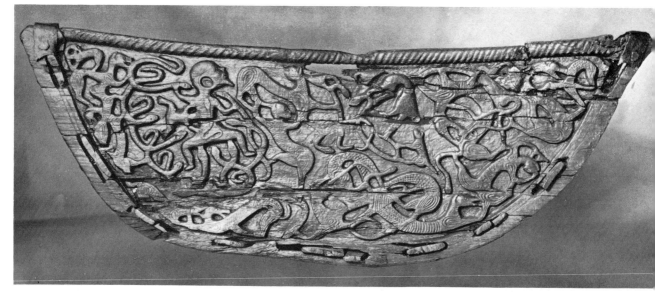

a.

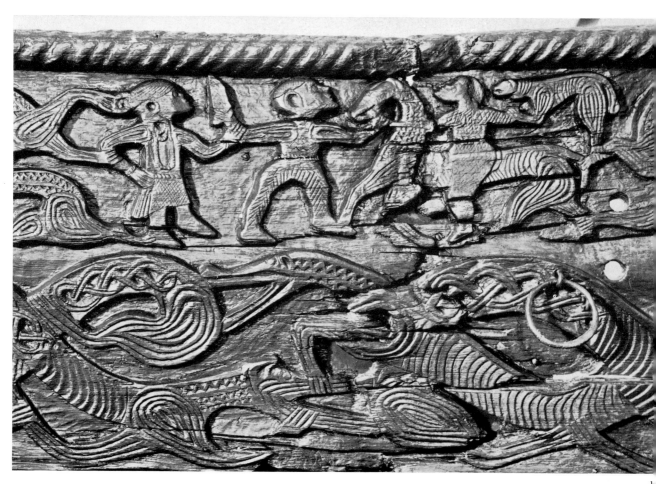

b

Pl. X. Details of cart from Oseberg ship-burial.

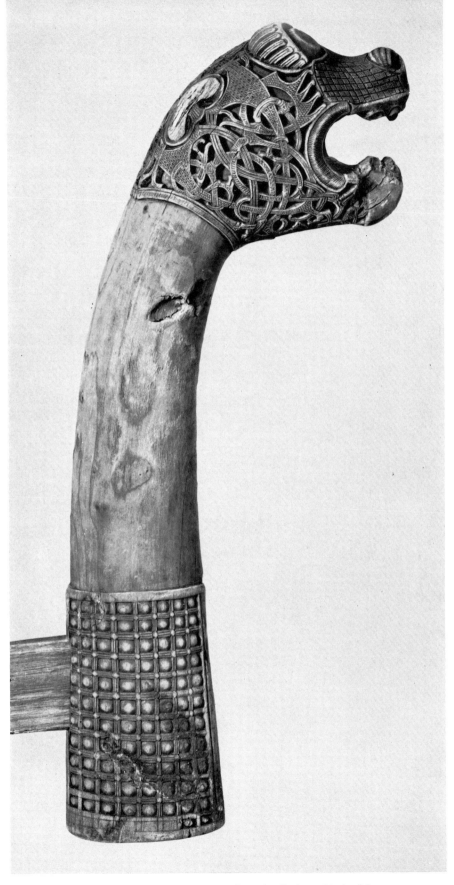

Pl. XI. The 'Academician's' animal-head post from the Oseberg ship-burial.

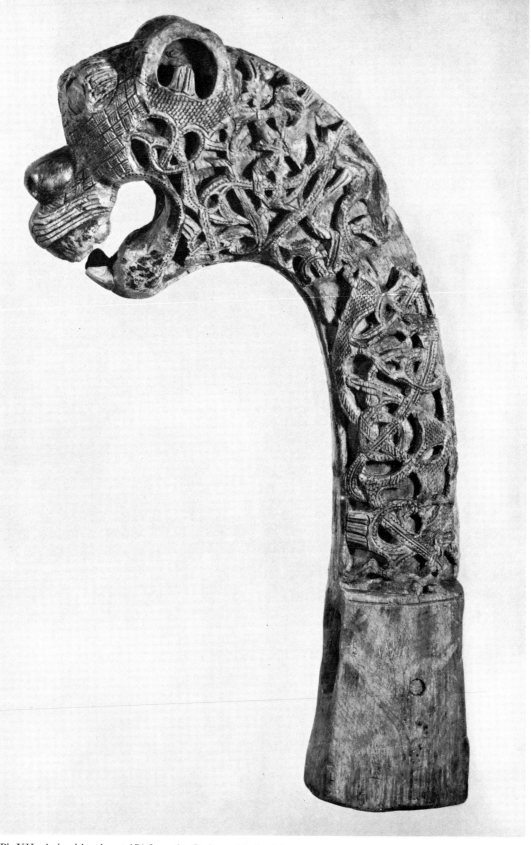

Pl. XII. Animal-head post 174 from the Oseberg ship-burial.

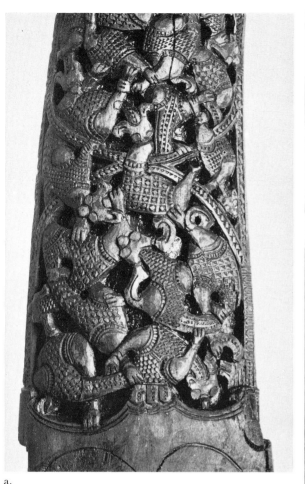

a.

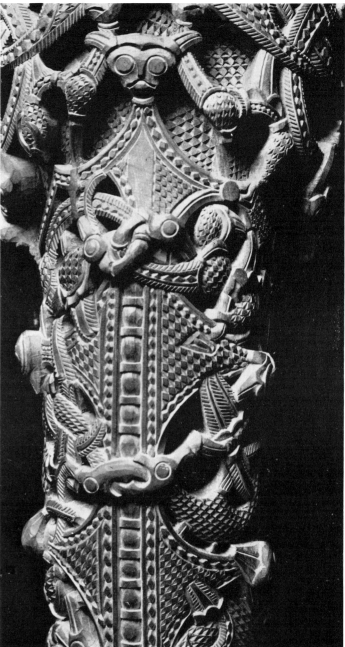

b.

Pl. XIII. (*a*) Detail of 'Carolingian' animal-head post and (*b*) detail of a copy of the 'first baroque' animal-head post from the Oseberg ship-burial.

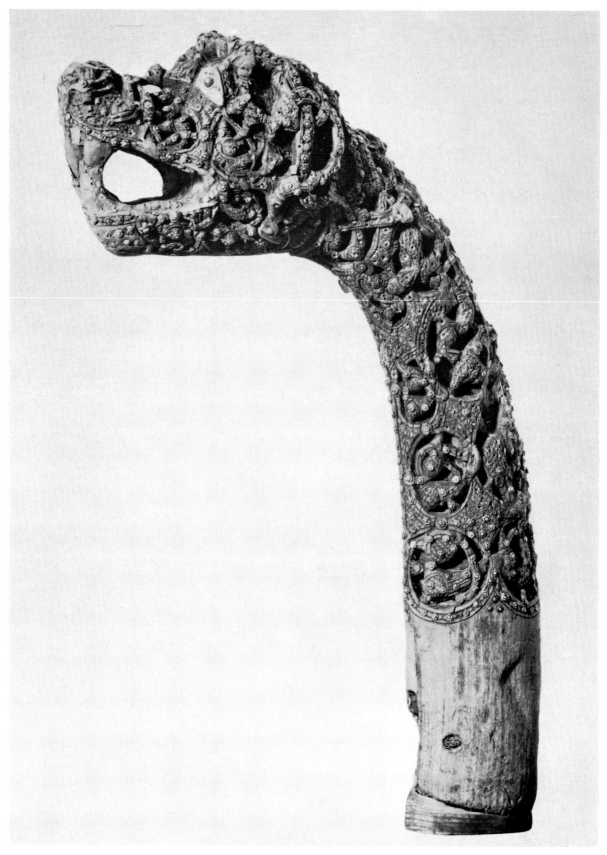

Pl. XIV. The 'first baroque' animal-head post from the Oseberg ship-burial.

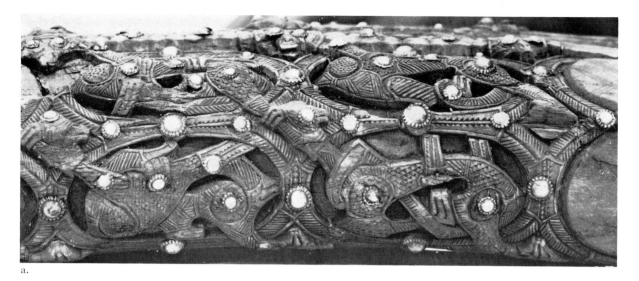

a.

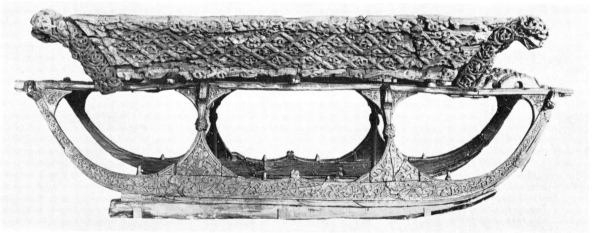

b.

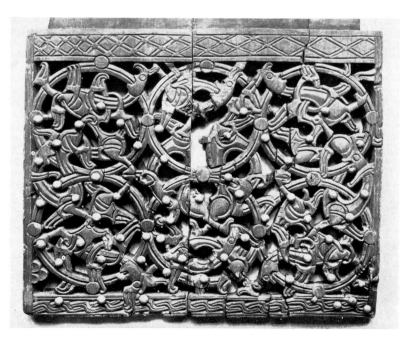

c.

Pl. XV. (*a*) Detail of the complete sledge shaft from the Oseberg ship-burial. (*b*) Fourth sledge from the Oseberg ship-burial. (*c*) Detail of back plate from the fourth sledge from the Oseberg ship-burial.

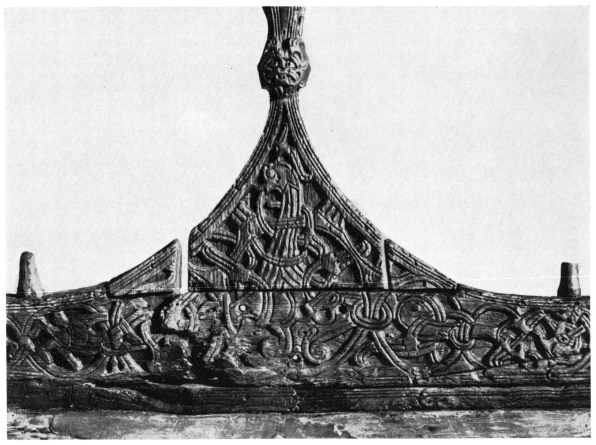

a.

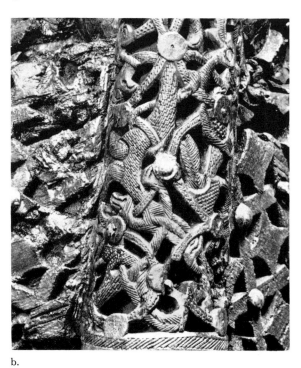

b.

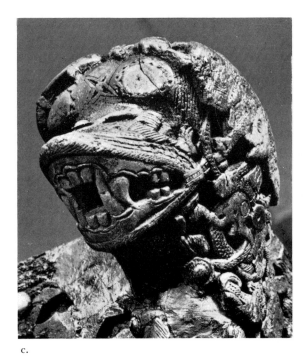

c.

Pl. XVI. (*a*) Detail of the runner of the fourth sledge from the Oseberg ship-burial. (*b–c*) Details of the ornament of Gustafson's sledge from the same.

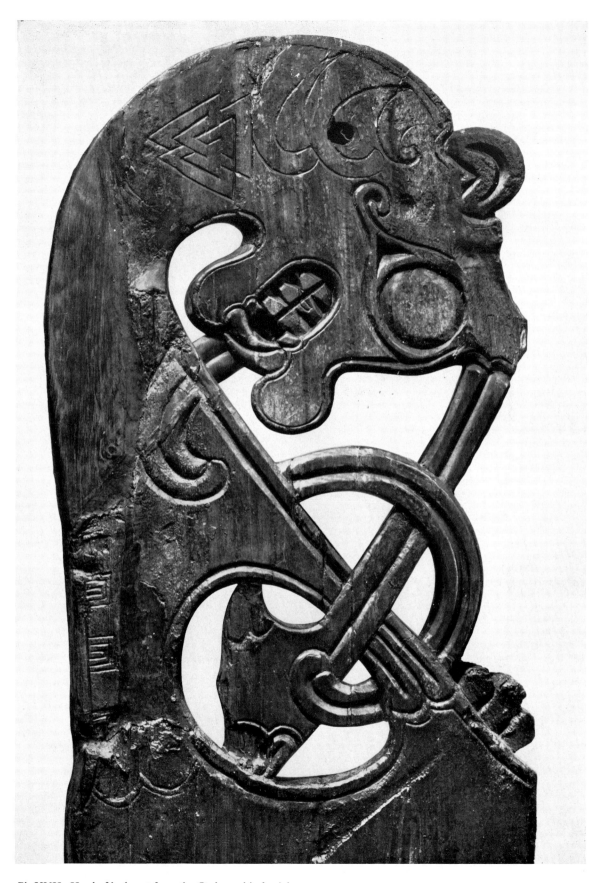

Pl. XVII. Head of bed-post from the Oseberg ship-burial.

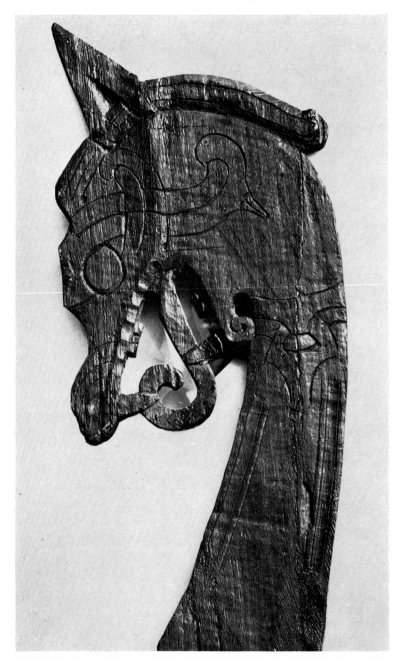

Pl. XVIII. Head of tent-post from the Gokstad ship-burial. *Universitetets Old-saksamling (Viking Ship Hall, Bygdøy), Oslo.*

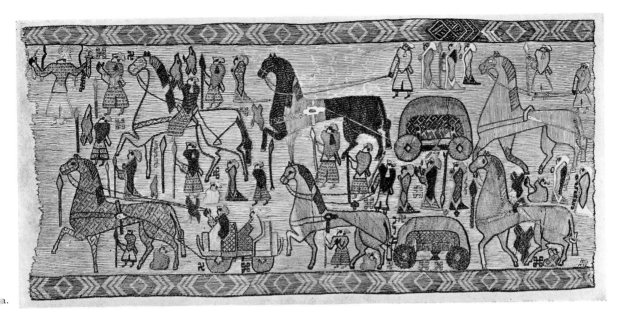

a.

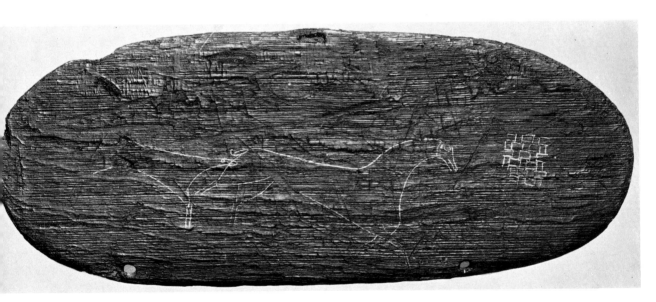

Pl. XIX. (*a*) Reconstruction of a tapestry from the Oseberg ship-burial. (*b*) Lid of a hunting basket from the Gokstad ship-burial. *Universitetets Oldsaksamling* (*Viking Ship Hall, Bygdøy,*) *Oslo.*

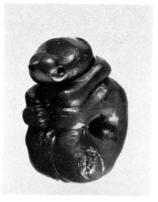

a.

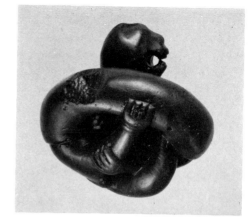

b.

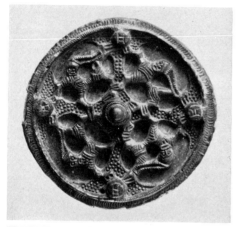

c.

d.

Pl. XX. (*a*) Jet animal figure from Haugsten, Råde, Østfold, Norway. (*b*) Jet animal from Inderøen, N. Trøndelag, Norway. (*a*) and (*b*): *Universitetets Oldsaksamling, Oslo.* (*c*) Two views of a bronze brooch from Alva, Gotland, Sweden. *Statens Historiska Museum, Stockholm.* (*d*) Fragment of a gilt-bronze brooch from Gjønnes, Hedrum, Vestfold, Norway. *Universitetets Odsaksamling, Oslo.* 1:1.

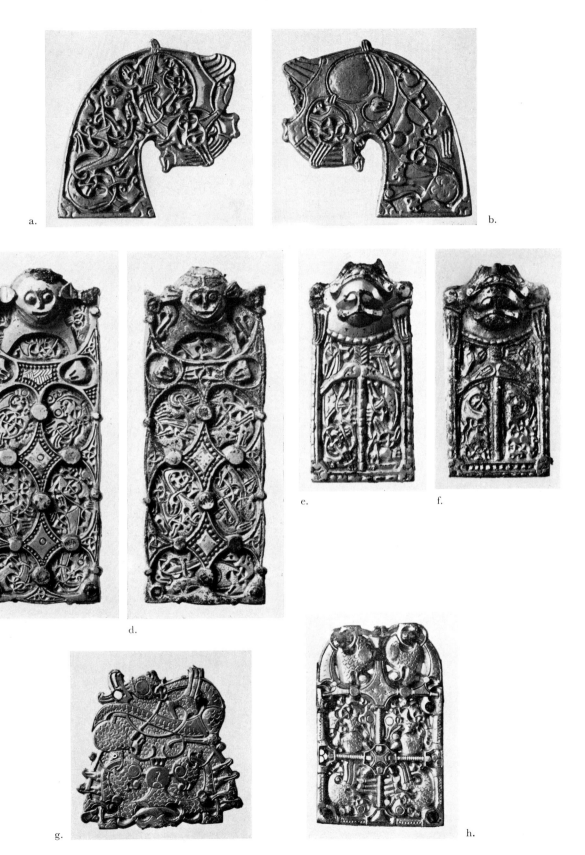

a.

b.

c.

d.

e.

f.

g.

h.

Pl. XXI. Group of gilt-bronze mounts from Broa, Halla, Gotland, Sweden. *Statens Historiska Museum, Stockholm.* 1:1.

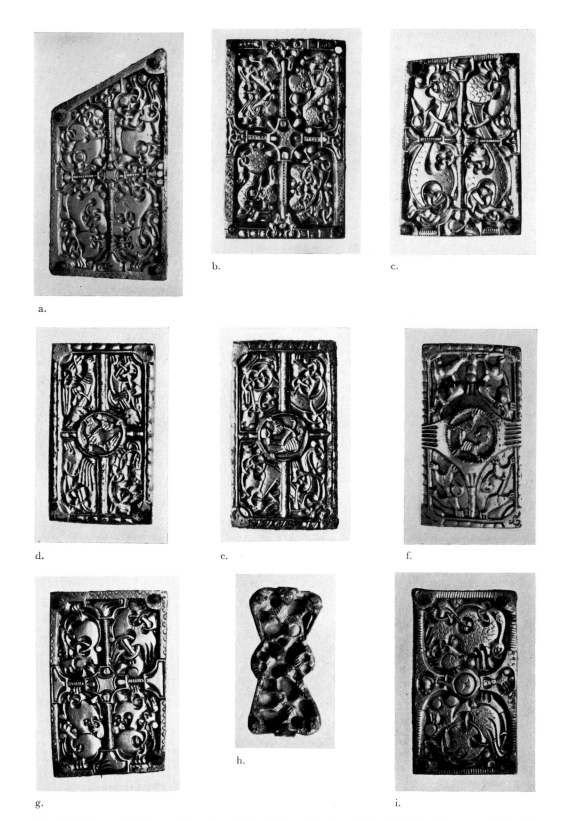

a.

b.

c.

d.

e.

f.

g.

h.

i.

Pl. XXII. Group of gilt-bronze from Broa, Halla, Gotland, Sweden. *Statens Historiska Museum, Stockholm.* 1:1.

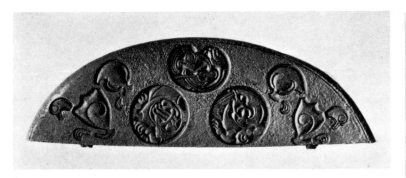

a.

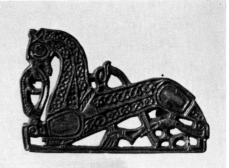

b.

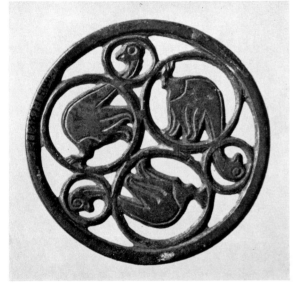

c.

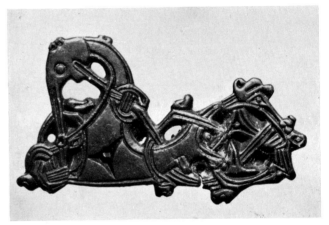

d.

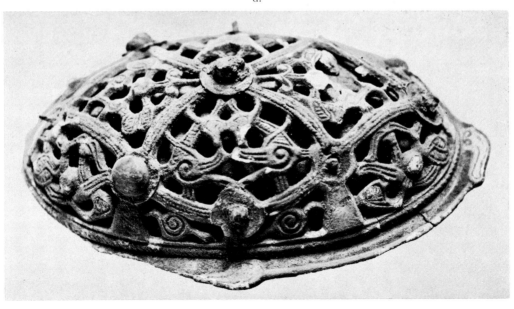

e.

Pl. XXIII. (*a*) Bronze sword-pommel mount from Stora Ihre, Gotland, Sweden. (*b*) Bronze-gilt figure of a horse from Birka, Uppland, Sweden, grave 854. (*c*) Openwork brooch from Othem, Gotland, Sweden. (*a–e*): *Statens Historiska Museum, Stockholm.* (*d*) Gilt-bronze figure from Kaupang, Tjølling, Vestfold, Norway. *Universitetets Oldsaksamling, Oslo.* (*e*) Bronze oval brooch from Ytterdal, Norddal, Sunnmøre, Norway. *Historisk Museum, Bergen.* 1:1.

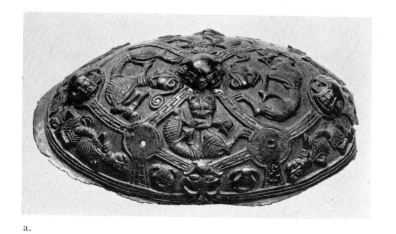

a.

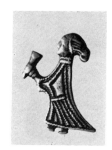

c.

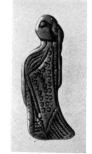

d.

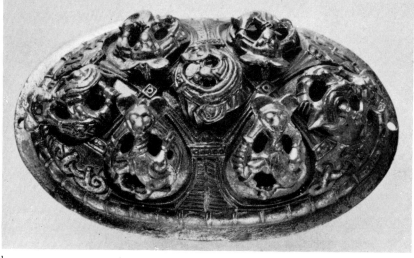

b.

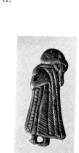

e.

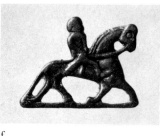

f.

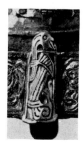

g.

Pl. XXIV. (*a*) Bronze oval brooch from Lisbjerg, Jutland, Denmark. *National Museum, Copenhagen.* (*b*) Bronze oval brooch from Norway (no provenance). *Trondheim Museum.* (*c–e*) Silver-gilt female figures from Sweden— Klinta, Köping, Öland; Birka, Uppland, grave 825; Sibble, Grödinge, Småland. (*f*) Silver figure of a rider from Birka, Uppland, Sweden, grave 825. (*g*) Detail of disc-on-bow brooch from Nygårde, Vesterhejde, Gotland, Sweden. (*c–g*): *Statens Historiska Museum, Stockholm.* 1:1.

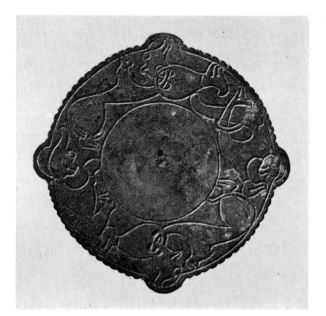

a.

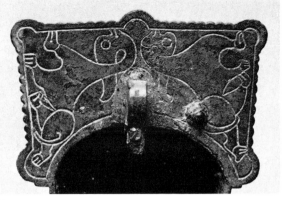

b.

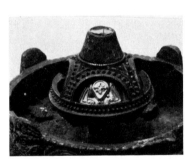

c.

d.

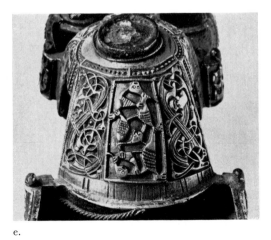

e.

Pl. XXV. *(a–c)* Details of a gilt-bronze disc-on-bow brooch from Broa, Halla, Gotland. *(d)* Silver-gilt strap-end from Stora Ryk, Färgelanda, Sweden. *(e)* Detail of gilt-bronze disc-on-bow brooch from Gumbalda, Stånga, Gotland. *Statens Historiska Museum, Stockholm.* 1:1.

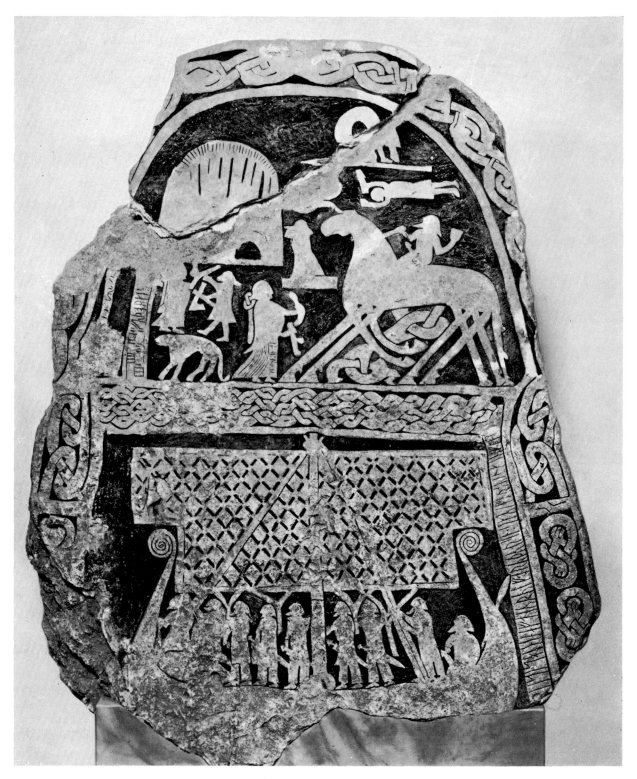

Pl. XXVI. Picture-stone from Tjängvide, Gotland, Sweden.

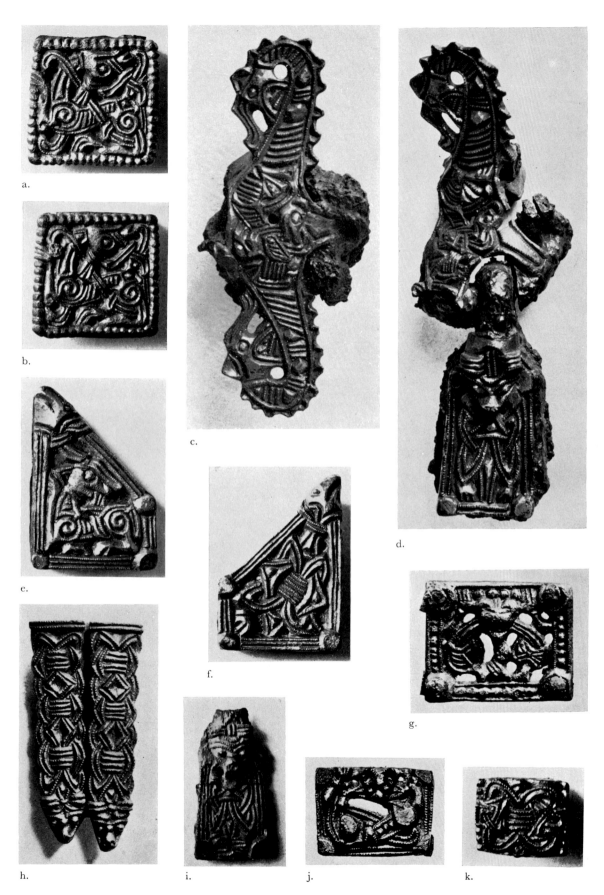

a.

b.

c.

d.

e.

f.

g.

h.

i.

j.

k.

Pl. XXVII. Gilt-bronze mounts from Borre, Vestfold, Norway. *Universitetets Oldsaksamling, Oslo.* 1:1.

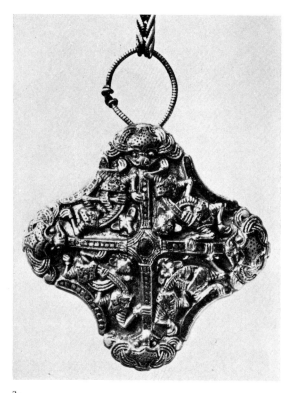

a.

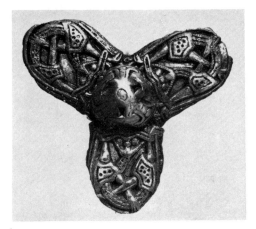

b.

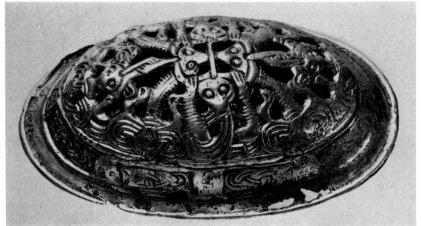

c.

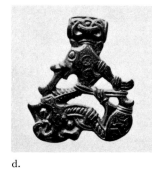

d.

e.

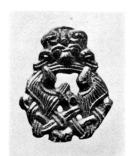

f.

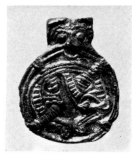

g.

Pl. XXVIII. *(a)* Silvergilt, nielloed brooch from Rinkaby, Skåne, Sweden. *Statens Historiska Museum, Stockholm.* *(b)* Silver, nielloed trefoil brooch from Åserum, Hedrum, Vestfold, Norway. *(c)* Bronze oval brooch from Renålen, Ålen, Norway. *(d–g)* Silver and gilt-bronze *(g)* pendants from Østborg, Frol, Levanger, Norway. *Trondheim Museum.* 1:1.

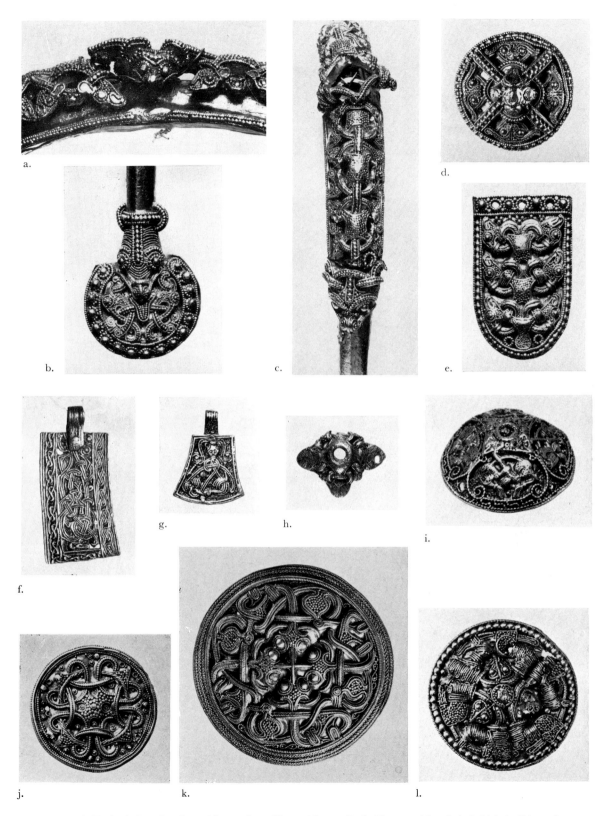

Pl. XXIX. (*a–c*) Details of a gold spur from Værne kloster, Rød, Norway. (*d* and *e*) Gold belt-slide and strap-end from the same find. (*f–i*) Silver-gilt and gold (*g* and *i*) objects from the Hon, Norway, hoard. (*a–i*) *Universitetets Oldsaksamling, Oslo* (*j*) Gold mount from Lackalänge, Skåne, Sweden. (*k*) Silver brooch from Finkarby, Taxinge, Södermanland, Sweden. (*j* and *k*) *Statens Historiska Museum, Stockholm.* (*l*) Gold brooch from Vester Vedsted, Jutland, Denmark. *National Museum, Copenhagen.* 1:1.

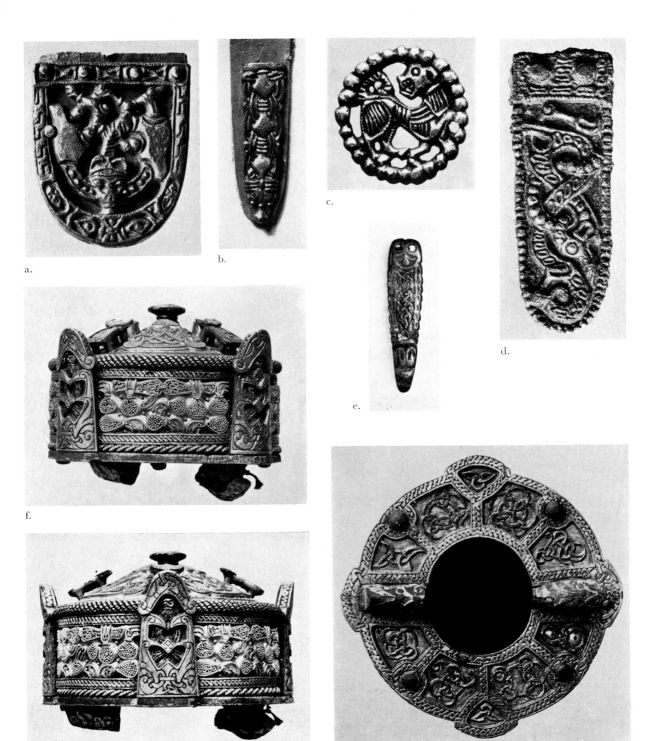

Pl. XXX. (a–d) Mounts from the Gokstad ship-burial. *Universitetets Oldsaksamling (Viking Ship Hall, Bygdøy),* *Oslo,* (e) Bronze, nielloed strap-end from Youlgreave, Derbyshire, England. *British Museum.* (f–h) Drum brooch from Martens, Grötlingbo, Gotland. *Statens Historiska Museum, Stockholm.* 1:1.

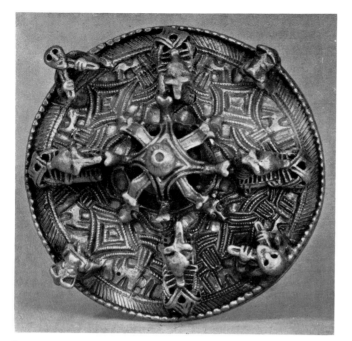

a.

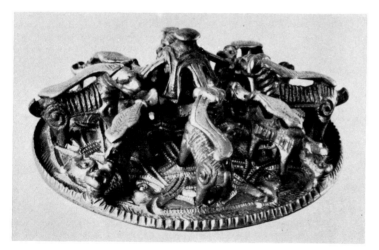

c.

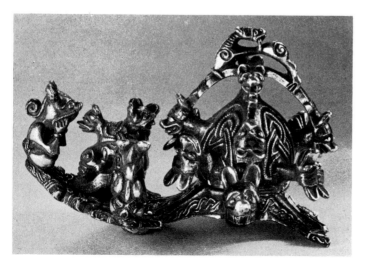

d.

b.

Pl. XXXI. (*a*) Silver brooch, possibly from Gotland, Sweden. *British Museum*. (*b*) Silver and niello ringheaded brooch, from Birka, Uppland, Sweden, grave 561. (*c*) Silver brooch from Torsta, Hälsingtuna, Sweden. (*b* and *c*) *Statens Historiska Museum, Stockholm*. (*d*) Silver brooch from Jelets, Voronez, U.S.S.R. *Hermitage Museum, Leningrad*. 1:1.

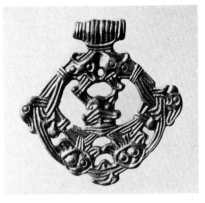

a.

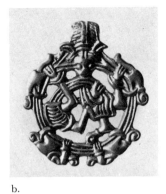

b.

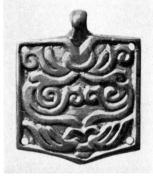

c.

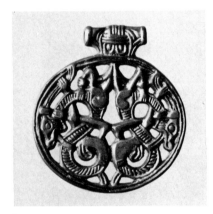

d.

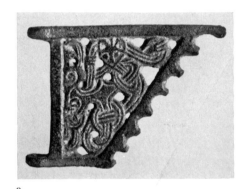

e.

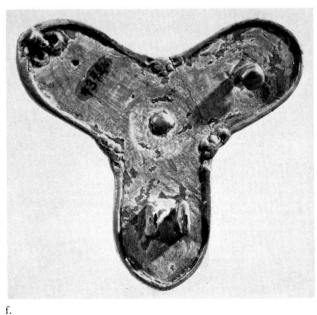

f.

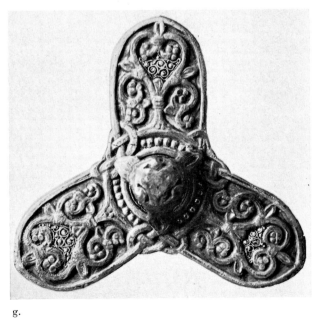

g.

Pl. XXXII. (*a–d*) Gilt-silver pendants from a hoard from Vårby, Huddinge, Södermanland, Sweden. *Statens Historiska Museum, Stockholm.* (*e*) Gilt-bronze mount (perhaps model of weather-vane) from Rangsby, Saltvik, Åland, Finland. *National Museum, Helsinki.* (*f–g*) Silver brooch with inlaid gold plates from Mosnæs, Rogaland, Norway. *Historisk Museum, Bergen.* 1:1.

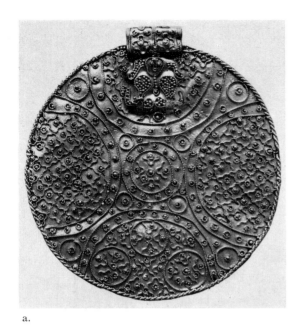

a.

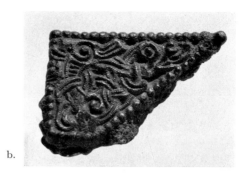

b.

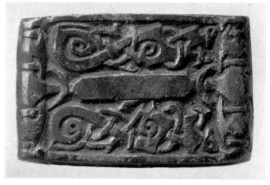

c.

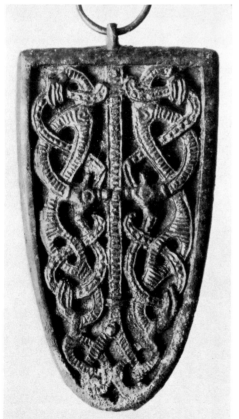

d.

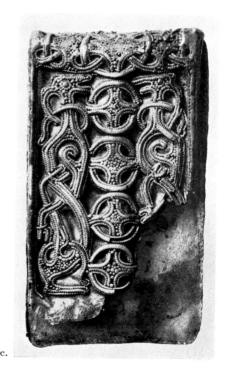

e.

Pl. XXXIII. (*a*) Gold bracteate Ringsome, Alva, Gotland. *Statens Historiska Museum, Stockholm.* (*b*) Bronze mount from Gnezdovo, U.S.S.R. (*c*) Bronze die from Mammen, Jutland, Denmark. *National Museum, Copenhagen.* (*d*) Bronze brooch from Birka, Uppland, Sweden. (*e*) Silver brooch from Ödeshög, Östergötland, Sweden. (*d* and *e*) *Statens Historiska Museum, Stockholm.* 1:1.

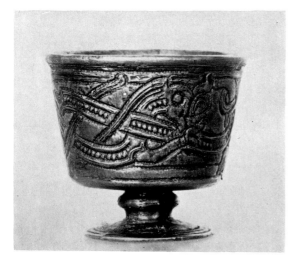

a.

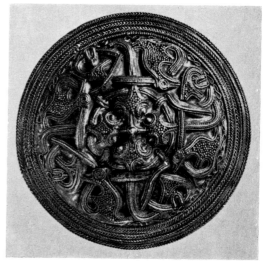

b.

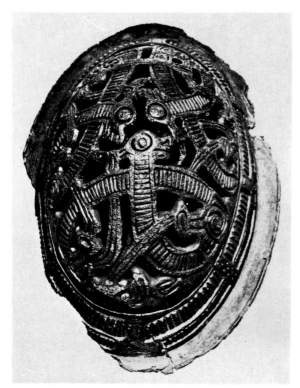

d.

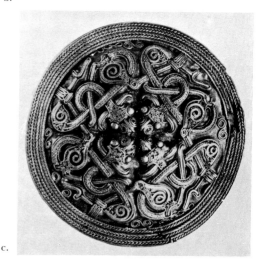

c.

Pl. XXXIV. (*a*) Silver cup from Jelling, Jutland, Denmark. (*b*) Silver brooch from Nonnebakken, Odense, Fyn, Denmark. (*a* and *b*) *National Museum, Copenhagen.* (*c*) Silver brooch from Central Sweden. *Statens Historiska Museum, Stockholm.* (*d*) Bronze oval brooch from Morberg, Røken, Buskerud, Norway. (*e*) Silver brooch from Tråen, Rollag, Buskerud, Norway, hoard. (*d* and *e*) *Universitetets Oldsaksamling, Oslo.* 1:1.

e.

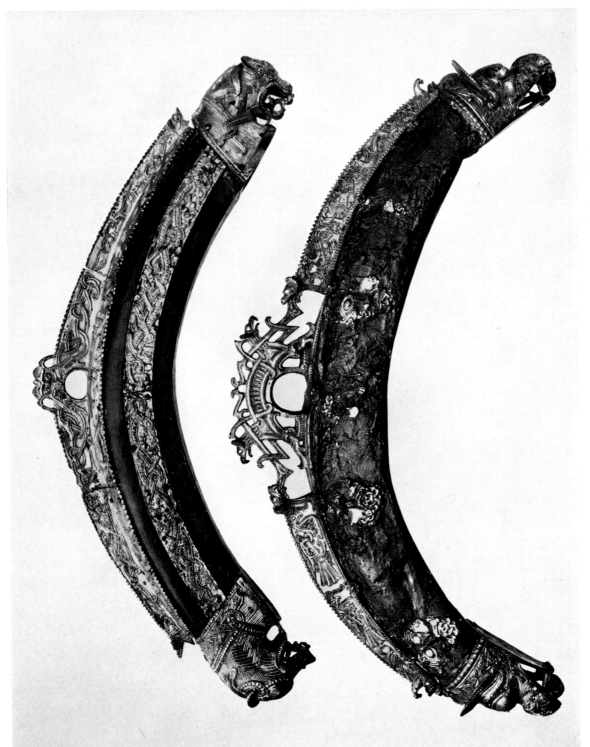

Pl. XXXV. The horse collars from Mammen (*a*) and Sollested, (*b*) Denmark. *National Museum, Copenhagen.*

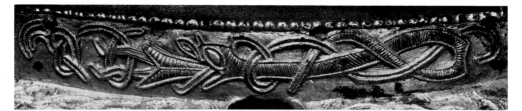

a.

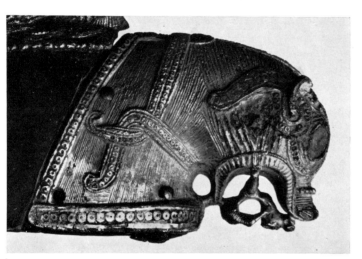

b.

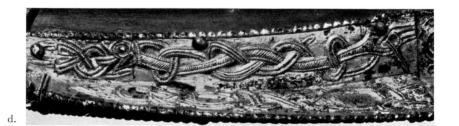

c.

d.

Pl. XXXVI. Details of Mammen horse collar. *National Museum, Copenhagen.*

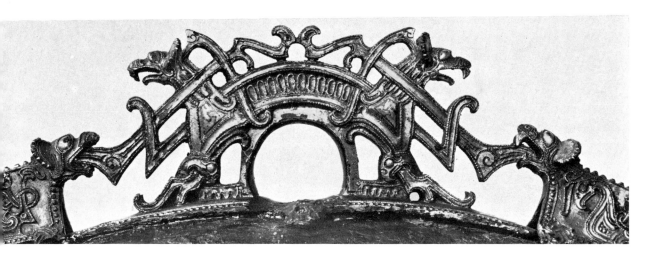

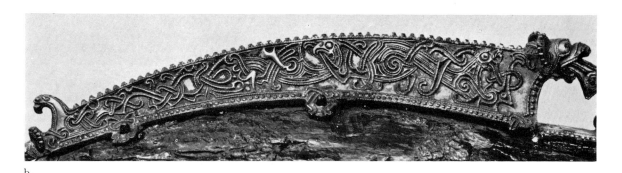

b.

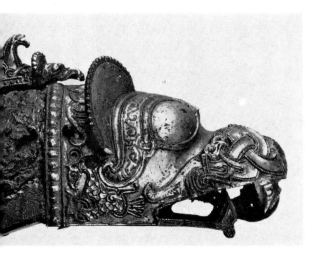

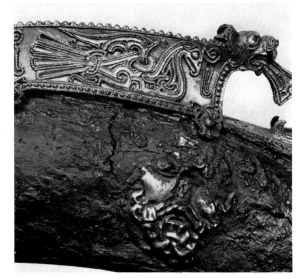

d.

Pl. XXXVII. Details of Søllested horse collar. *National Museum, Copenhagen.*

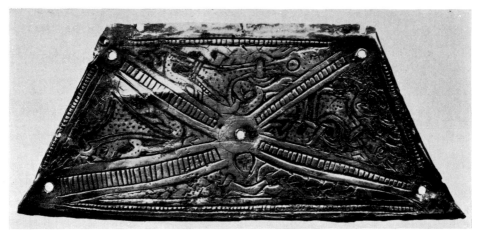

a.

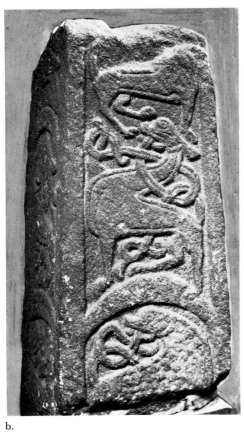

b.

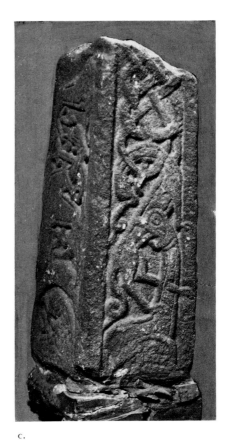

c.

Pl. XXXVIII. (*a*) Silver and niello plate, without provenance. *British Museum*. 1:1. (*b–c*) Fragment of cross-shaft from St Alkmund's church, Derby.

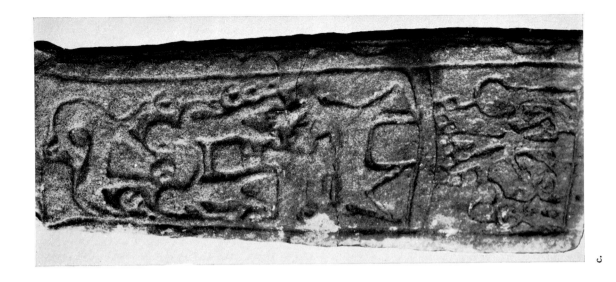

c.

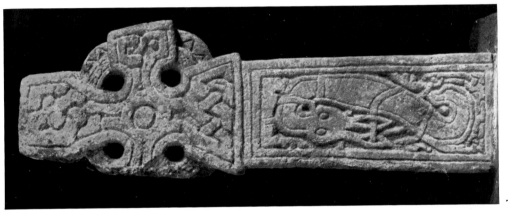

b.

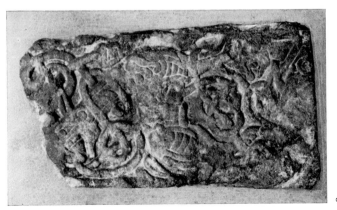

a.

Pl. XXXIX. (a) Fragment of cross-shaft from St Oswald's Priory, Gloucester. *City Museum, Gloucester.* (b) Cross from Middleton, Yorkshire. (c) Fragment of a cross-shaft from Dacre, Cumberland.

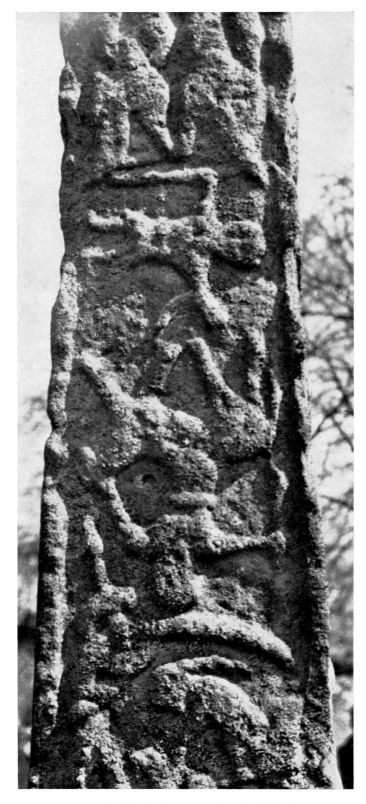

Pl. XL. Detail of shaft of cross from Gosforth, Cumberland.

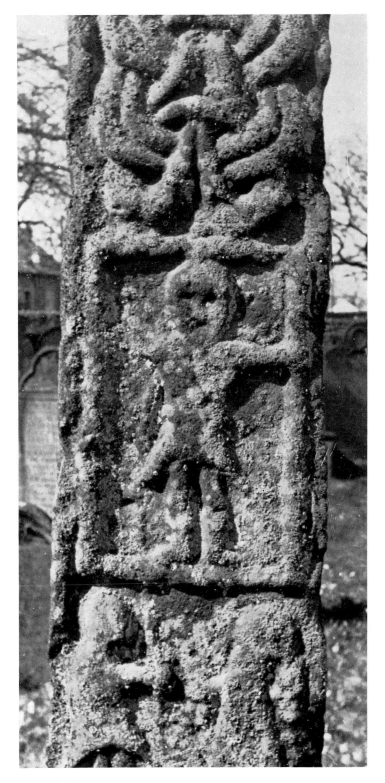

Pl. XLI. Detail of shaft of cross from Gosforth, Cumberland.

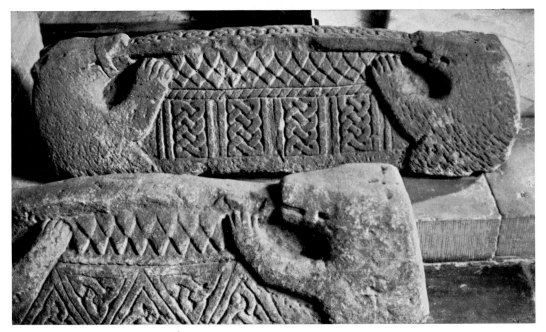

a.

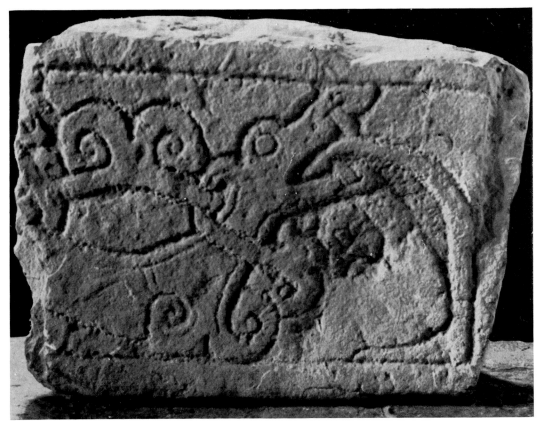

b.

Pl. XLII. (a) Hog-backed tombstones from Brompton, Yorkshire. (b) Fragment of tombstone from Levisham, Yorkshire.

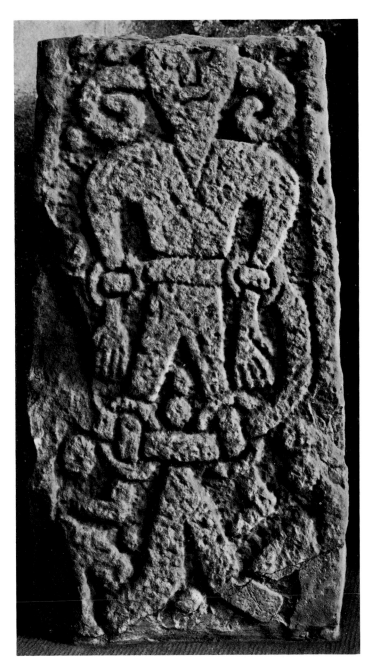

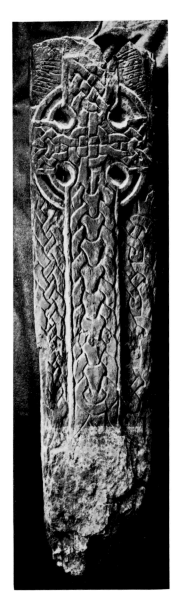

a.

b.

Pl. XLIII. (*a*) Fragment of a cross-shaft from Kirby Stephen, Westmorland. (*b*) Gaut's cross, Kirk Michael, Isle of Man.

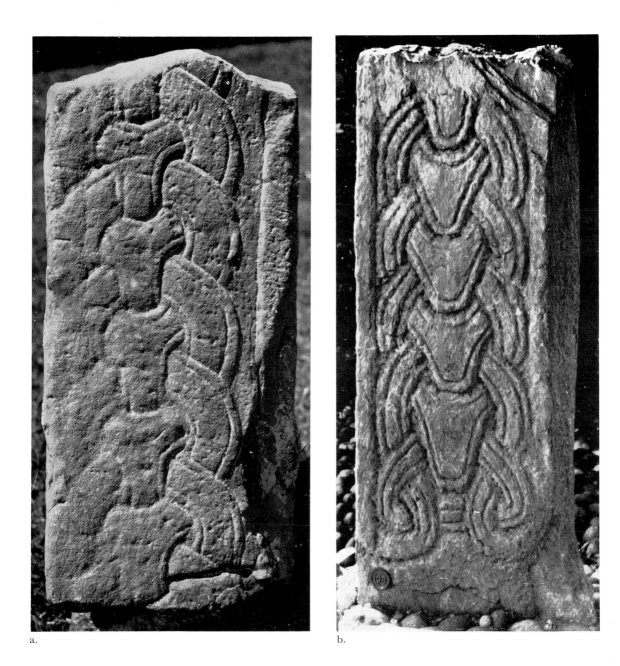

a.   b.

Pl. XLIV. (a) Stone from Väsby, Skåne, Sweden. (b) Stone from Kirk Maughold, Isle of Man.

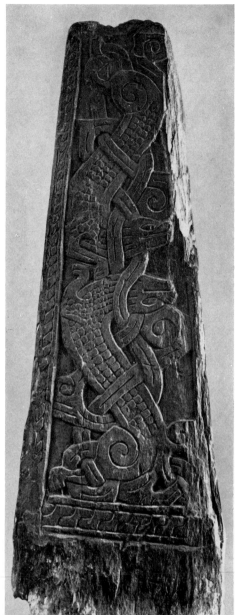

a.

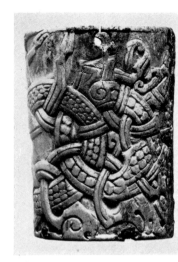

b.

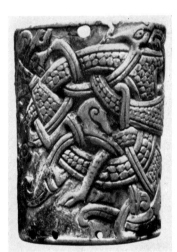

c.

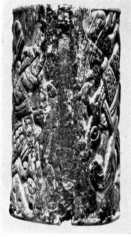

d.

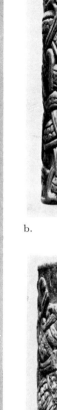

e.

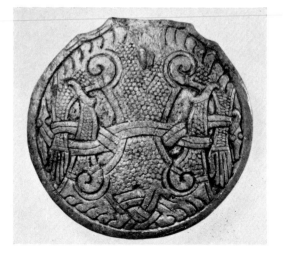

f.

Pl. XLV. (*a*) Fragment of Odd's cross-slab from Kirk Braddan, Isle of Man. (*b–e*) Bone sleeve from Årnes, Stangvik, Nordmøre, Norway. *Trondheim Museum*. 1:1. (*f*) Bone plaque from River Thames, London. *British Museum*. 1:1.

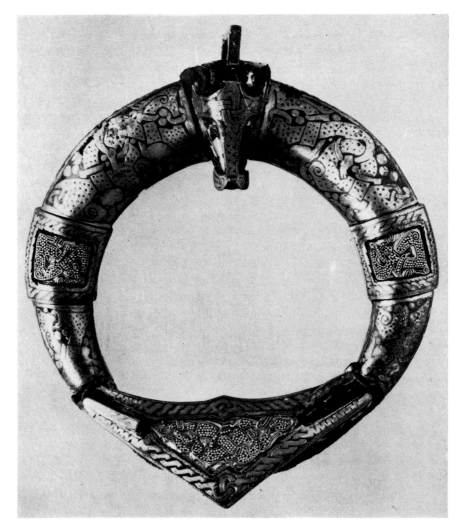

a.

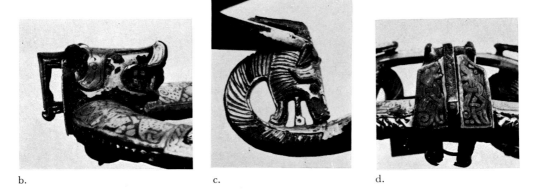

b. c. d.

Pl. XLVI. General view and details of silver, niello and gold brooch from Austris, Tingstäde, Gotland, Sweden. *Statens Historiska Museum, Stockholm.*

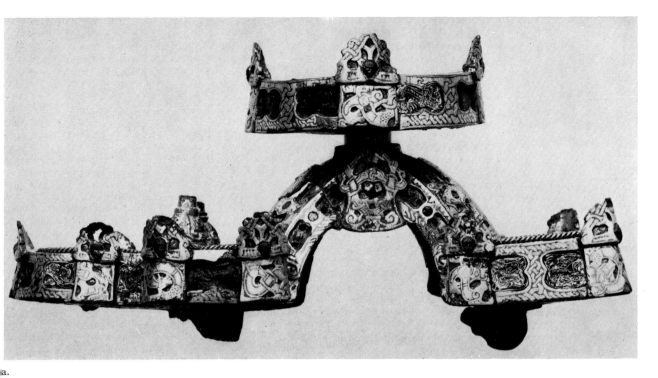

a.

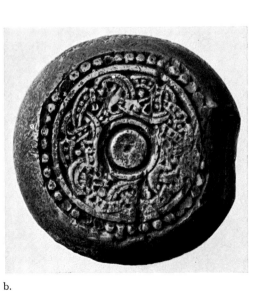

b.

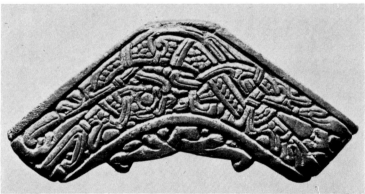

c.

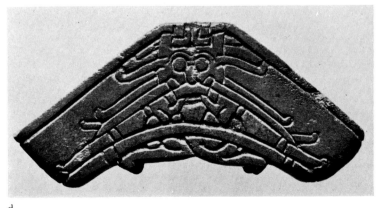

d.

Pl. XLVII. (*a*) Brooch from Valla, Klinte, Sweden. *Statens Historiska Museum, Stockholm.* (*b*) Bone object from Kastager Strand, Utterslev, Denmark. *National Museum, Copenhagen.* (*c–d*) Sword mount from Sigtuna, Sweden. *Statens Historiska Museum, Stockholm.* 1:1.

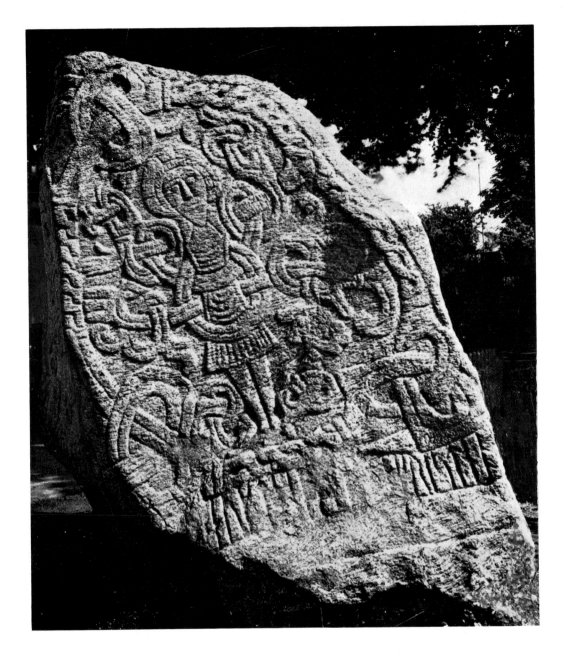

Pl. XLVIII. The Jelling stone, Denmark.

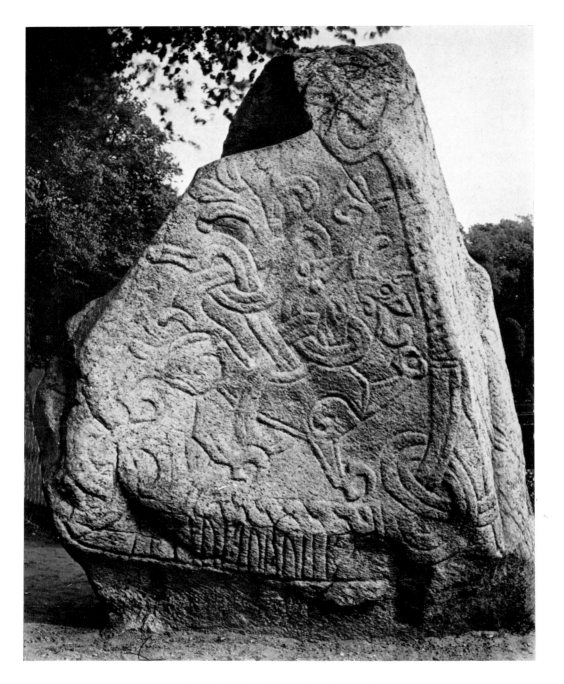

Pl. XLIX. The Jelling stone, Denmark.

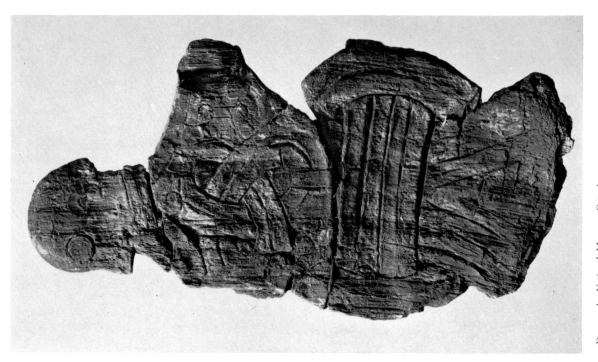

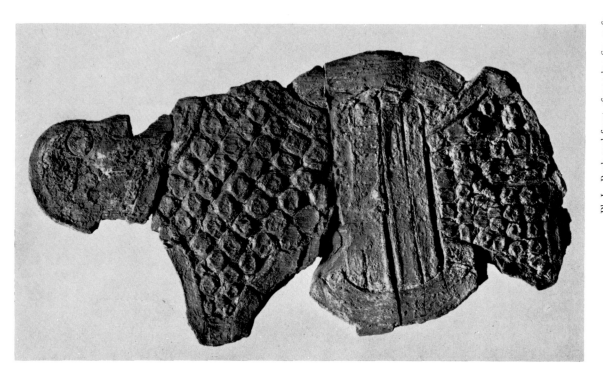

Pl. L. Back and front of wooden figure from Jelling, Denmark. *National Museum, Copenhagen.*

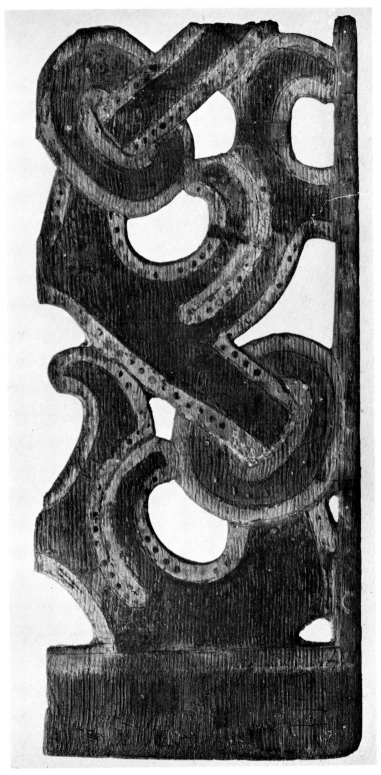

Pl. LI. Painted wooden fragment from Jelling, Denmark.
National Museum, Copenhagen.

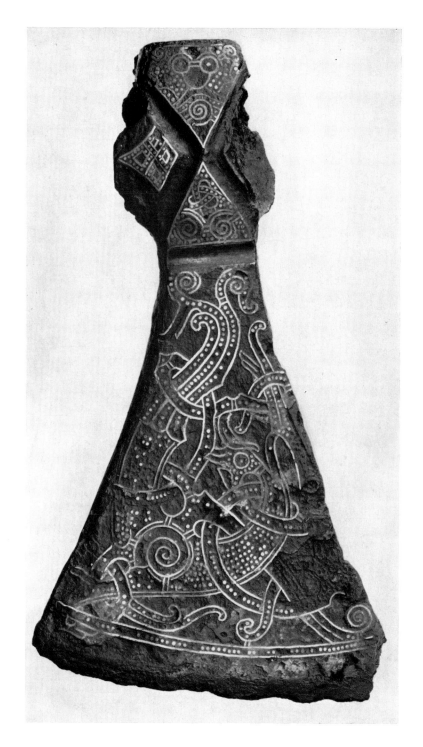

Pl. LII. Inlaid iron axe from Mammen, Jutland, Denmark. *National Museum, Copenhagen.* 1:1.

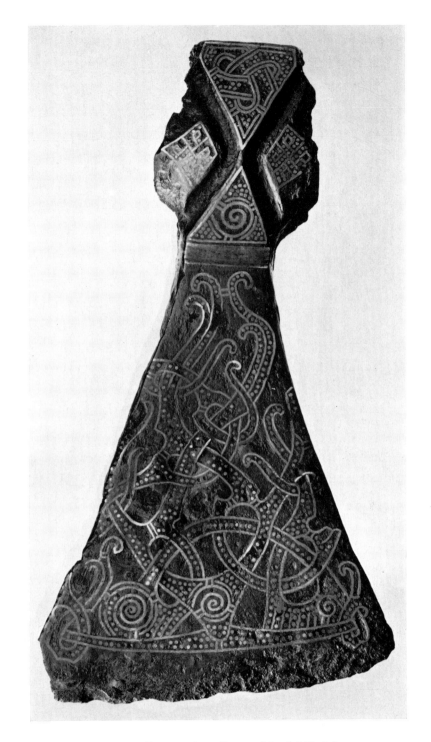

Pl. LIII. Reverse of axe illustrated in pl. LII. 1:1.

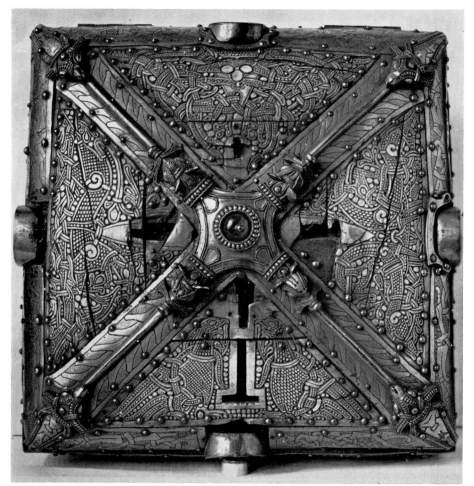

a.

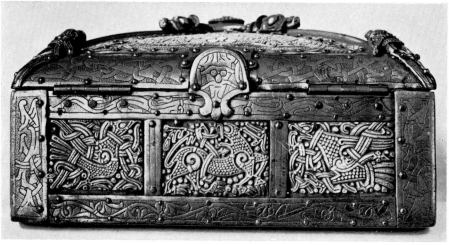

b.

Pl. LIV. The Bamberg casket. *Bayerisches Nationalmuseum, Munich.*

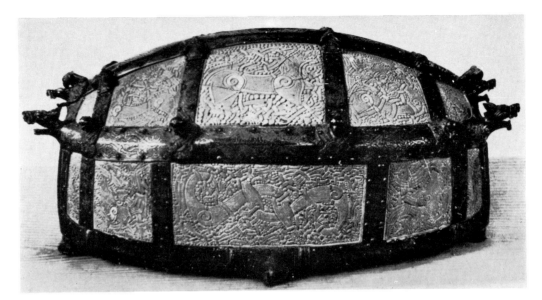

a.

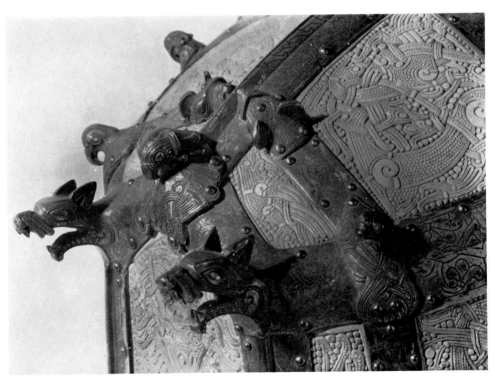

b.

Pl. LV. General view and detail of Cammin casket. *Destroyed*.

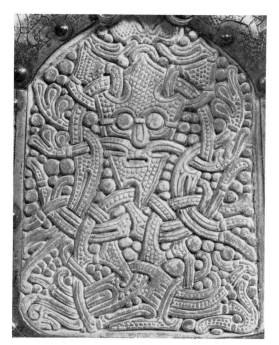

a.

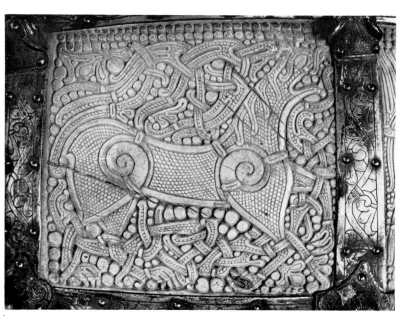

b.

Pl. LVI. Details of Cammin casket. *Destroyed*.

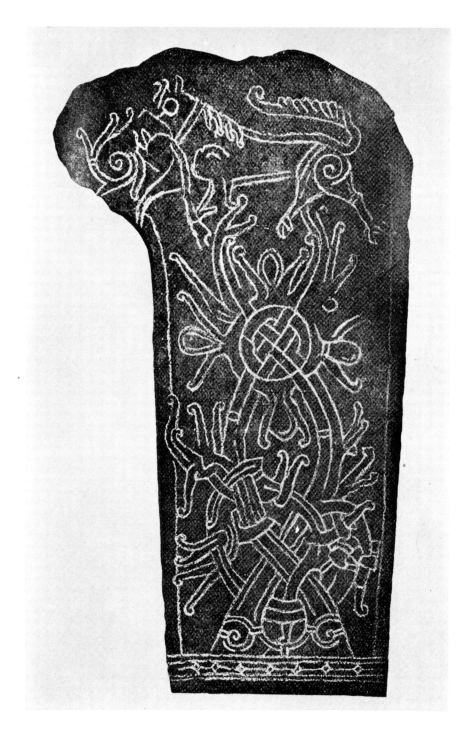

Pl. LVII. Stone from Vang, Valdres, Norway.

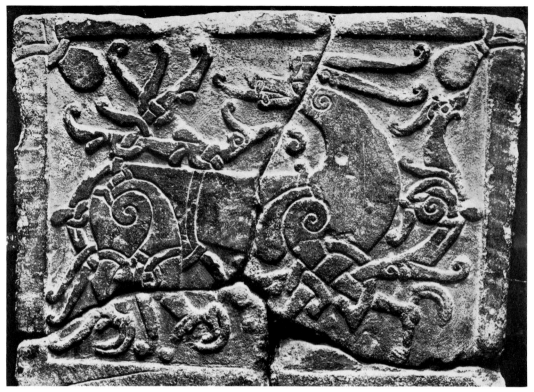

a.

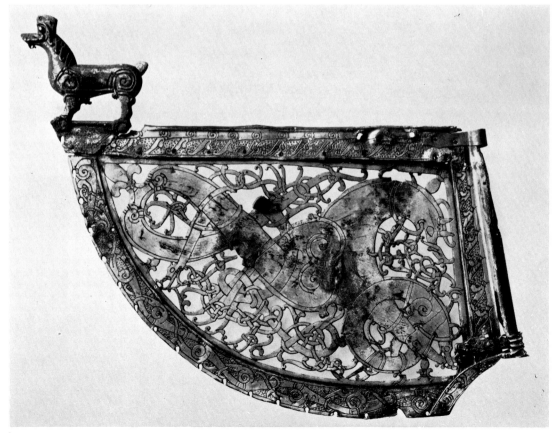

b.

Pl. LVIII. (*a*) Stone from sarcophagus. St Paul's churchyard, London. *Guildhall Museum, London.* (*b*) Gilt-bronze weather vane, Söderala, Hälsingland, Sweden. *Statens Historiska Museum, Stockholm.*

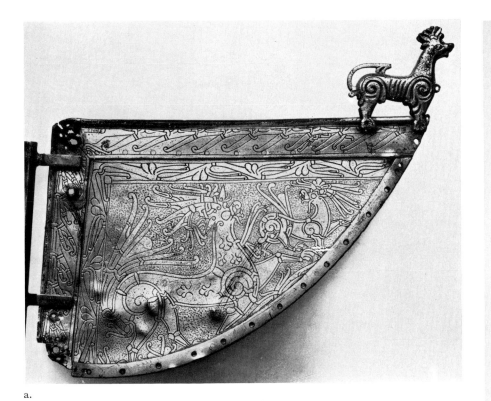

a.

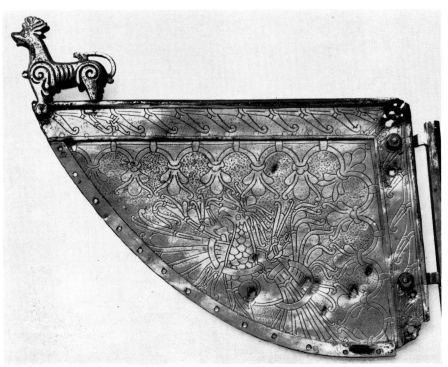

b.

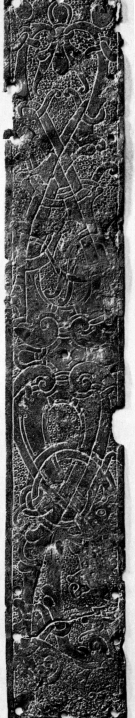

c.

Pl. LIX. (*a–b*) Bronze-gilt weather vane from Heggen, Modum, Norway. *Universitetets Oldsaksamling, Oslo.* (*c*) Gilt bronze plate from Winchester. *Winchester Cathedral Library.*

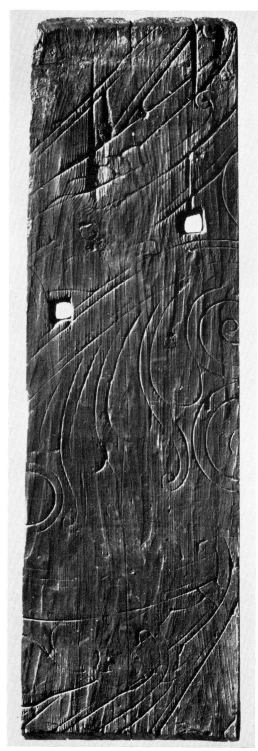 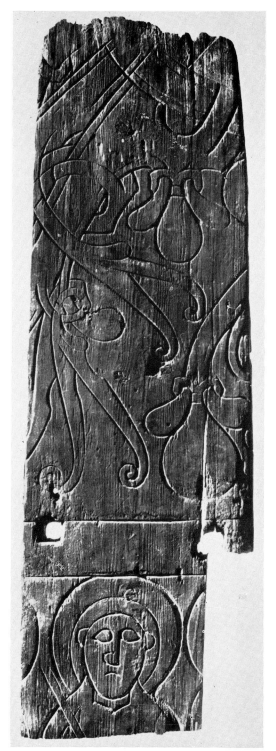

a.   b.

Pl. LX. Two wooden panels from Flatatunga, Iceland. *National Museum, Reykjavik.*

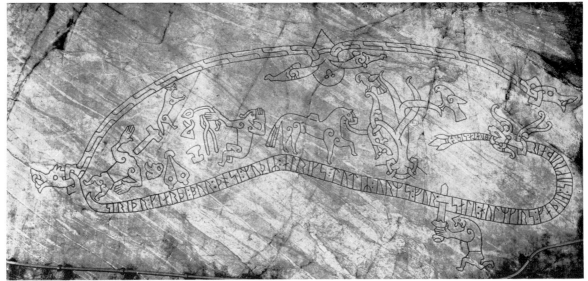

a.

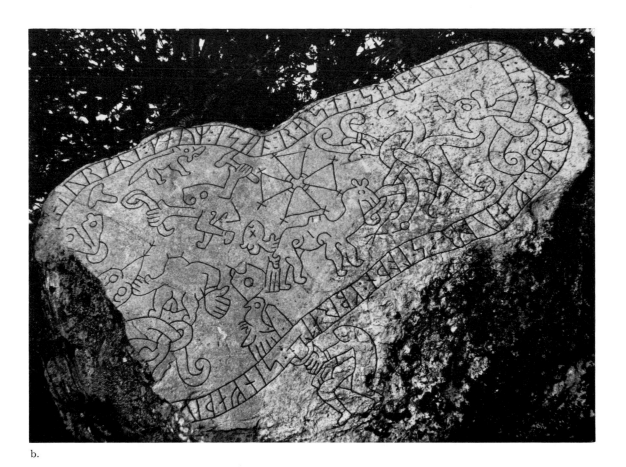

b.

Pl. LXI. (*a*) Rock-engraving from the Rasmus rock, Jäder, Södermanland, Sweden. (*b*) The Gök stone, Härad, Södermanland, Sweden.

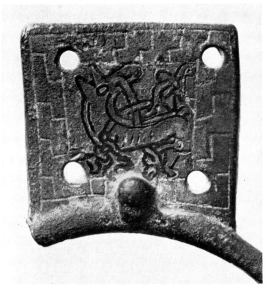

a.

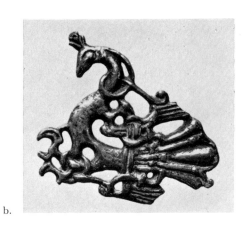

b.

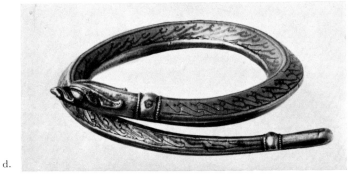

d.

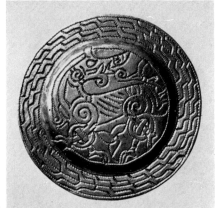

c.

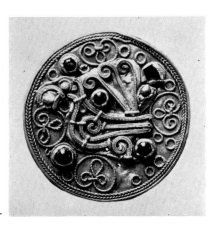

e.

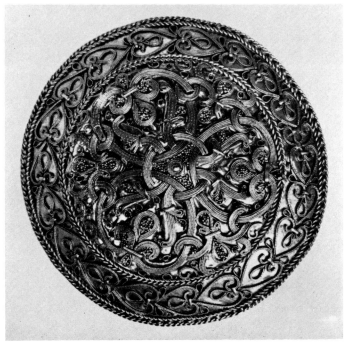

f.

Pl. LXII. (*a*) Detail of the fragment of a bronze stirrup from Stenåsa, Öland, Sweden. *Statens Historiska Museum, Stockholm.* (*b*) Silver-gilt figure of a bird from a hoard found at Græsli, Tydal, Selbu, Sør-Trøndelag, Norway. *Trondheim Museum.* (*c*) Silver brooch from Espinge, Hurva, Skåne, Sweden. (*d*) Silver, nielloed armlet from Undrom, Boteå, Sweden. (*c* and *d*) *Statens Historiska Museum, Stockholm.* (*e*) Gold brooch from Vestvik, Beistad, Nord-Trøndelag, Norway. *Trondheim Museum.* (*f*) Gold brooch from Hornelund, Horne, Øster Horne, Denmark. *National Museum, Copenhagen.*

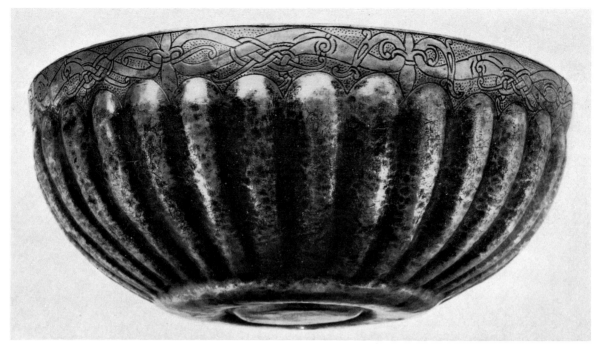

a.

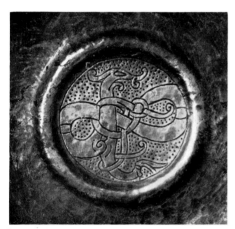

b.

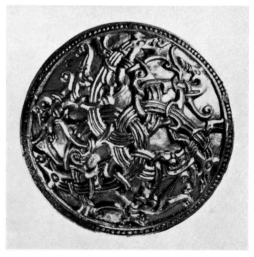

c.

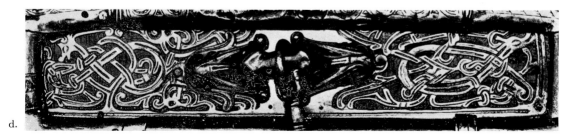

d.

Pl. LXIII. (*a*) Silver bowl from Lilla Valla, Rute, Gotland, Sweden. (*b*) Detail of internal panel of same. (*c*) Silver brooch from Gerete, Gotland, Sweden. (*a–c*) *Statens Historiska Museum, Stockholm.* (*d*) Detail of the 'Misach'. *National Museum, Dublin.*

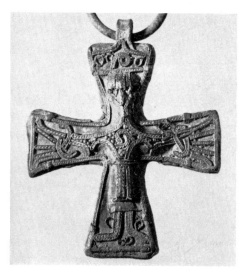
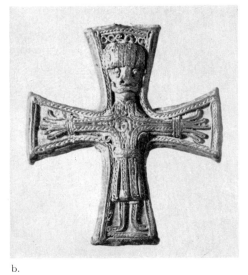

a.

b.

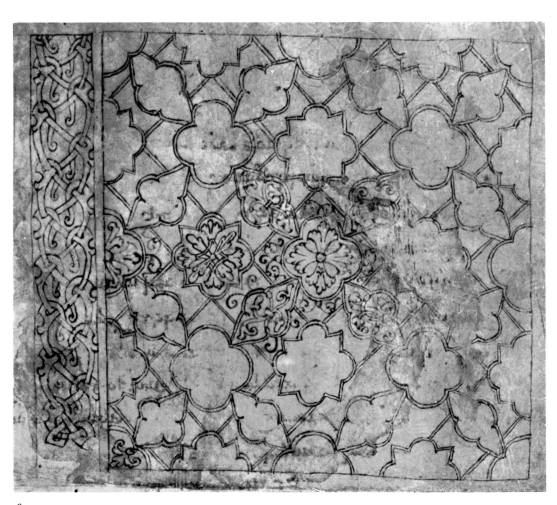

c.

Pl. LXIV. (*a* and *b*) Silver crucifixes from Trondheim, Norway. *Trondheim Museum*. 1:1. (*c*) Detail from Caedmon MS. Junius II. *Bodleian Library, Oxford*.

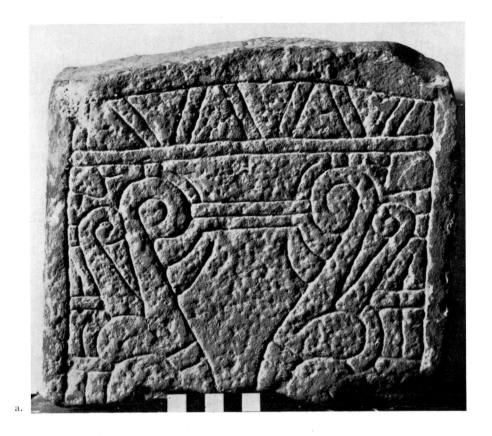

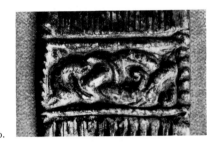

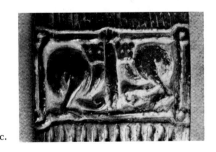

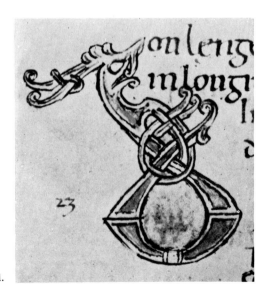

Pl. LXV. (*a*) Fragment of tombstone from Otley, Yorkshire. (*b* and *c*) Detail of ivory comb without provenance. *British Museum.* 1:1. (*d*) Details of MS. Ff.I.23. *University Library, Cambridge.*

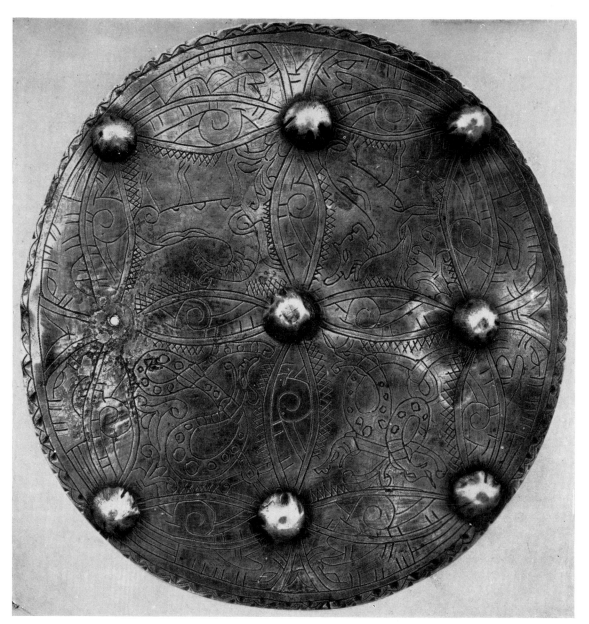

a.

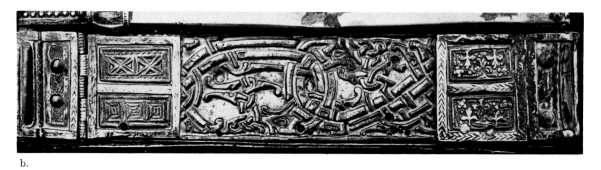

b.

Pl. LXVI. (*a*) Silver disc brooch from a hoard at Sutton, Isle of Ely, *British Museum*. (*b*) Side panel of the 'Cathach'. *National Museum, Dublin*.

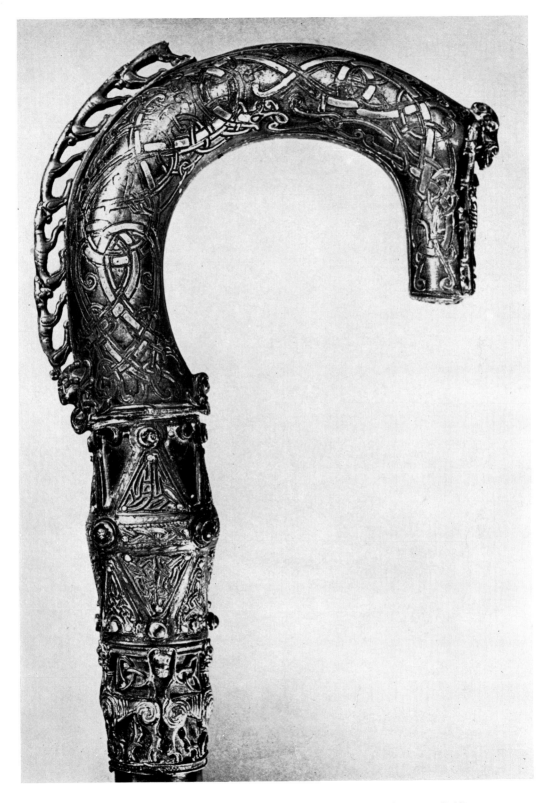

Pl. LXVII. The Crozier of the Abbots of Clonmacnoise. *National Museum, Dublin*.

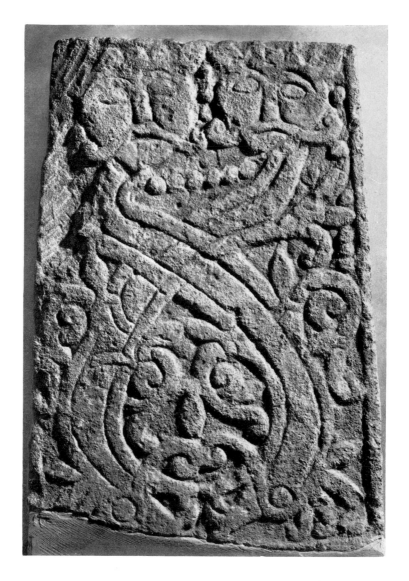

Pl. LXVIII. Cross slab from Bibury, Gloucestershire. *British Museum.*

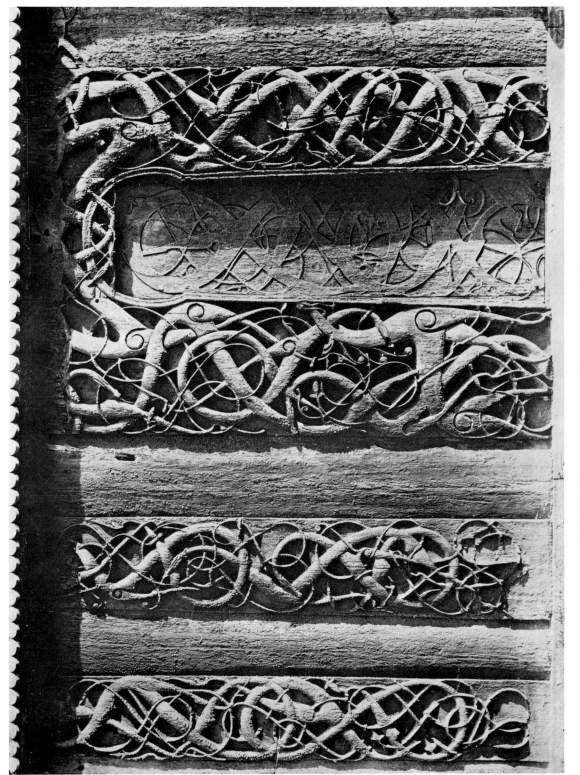

Pl. LXIX. The north portal of the Urnes stave church, Norway.

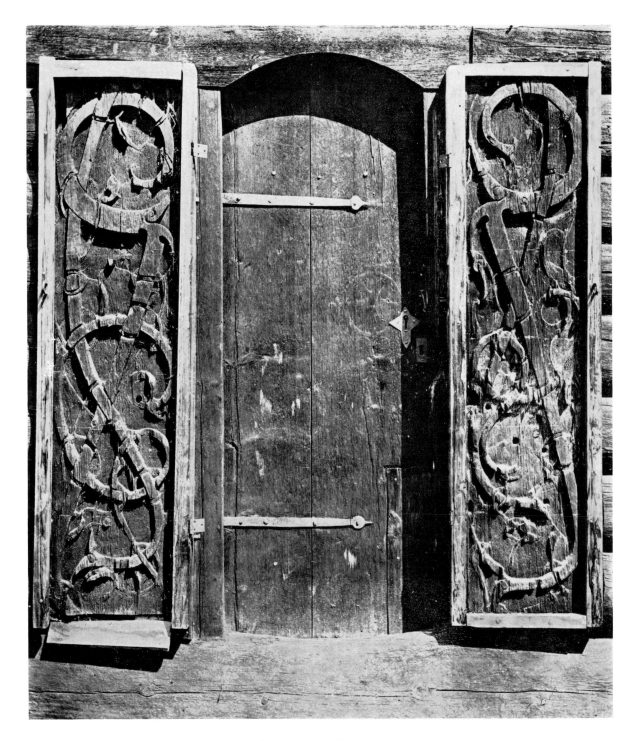

Pl. LXX. Portal of the church at Bjølstad, Heidalen, Norway.

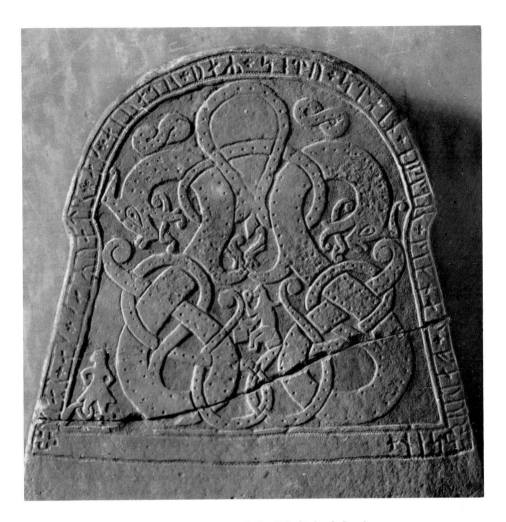

Pl. LXXI. Rune-stone, Ardre III, Gotland, Sweden.

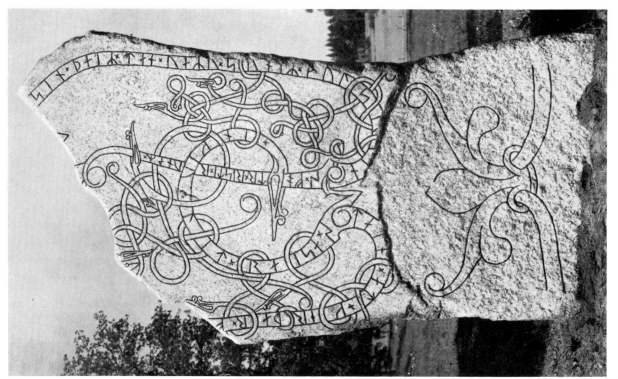

b.

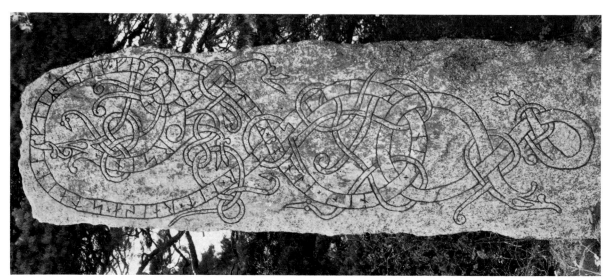

a.

Pl. LXXII. (a) Rune-stone from Skråmsta, Haga, Uppland, Sweden. (b) Rune-stone from Stav, Roslagskulle, Uppland, Sweden.

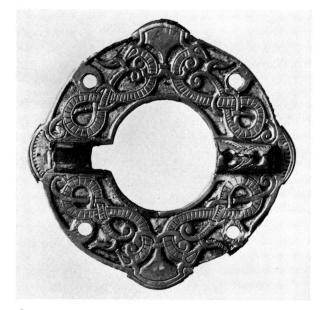

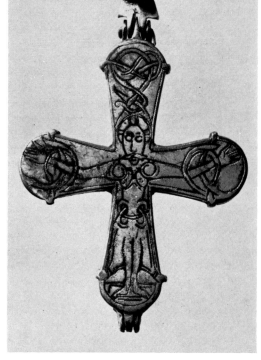

a.

c.

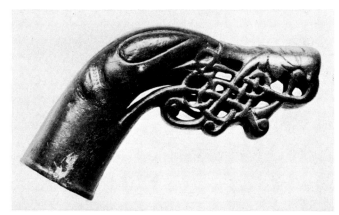

b

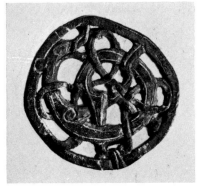

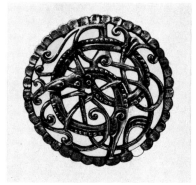

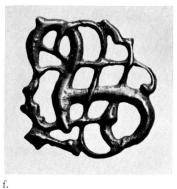

d.

e.

f.

Pl. LXXIII. (*a*) Base-plate of drum brooch from Tåndgarve, Sweden. (*b*) Bronze animal-head probably from Gotland, Sweden. (*c*) Silver and niello crucifix from a hoard from Gåtebo, Öland, Sweden. 1:1. (*a–c*) *Statens Historiska Museum, Stockholm.* (*d*) Bronze mount from Wisbech, Cambridgeshire, *Wisbech Museum.* 1:1. (*e*) Gilt-bronze brooch from Pitney, Somerset. *British Museum.* 1:1. (*f*) Bronze brooch without provenance. *National Museum, Copenhagen.* 1:1.

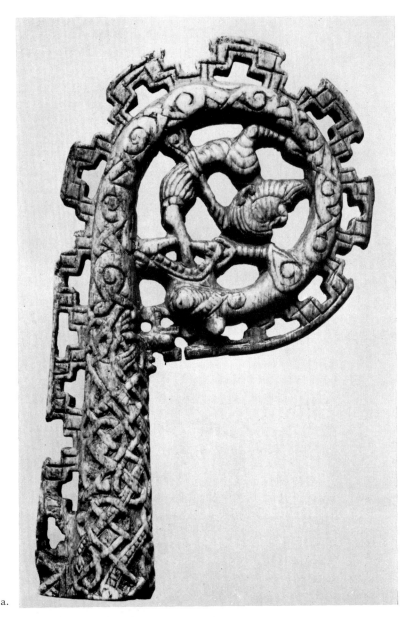

a.

b.

Pl. LXXIV. (a) Morse ivory crozier-head from Aghadoe, Ireland. *Statens Historiska Museum, Stockholm.*
(b) Side of the Cashel sarcophagus.

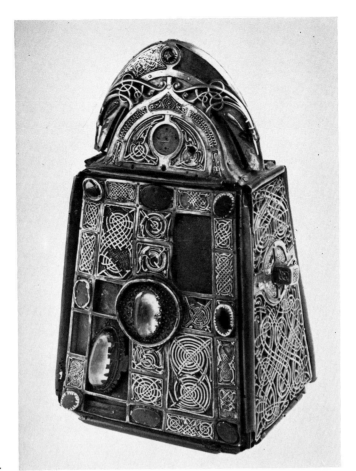

a.

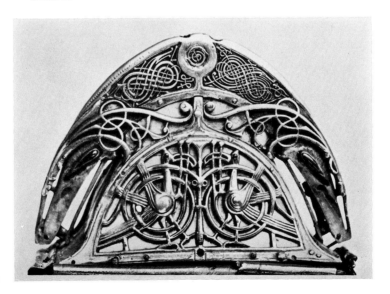

b.

Pl. LXXV. The shrine of the Bell of St Patrick's Will. *National Museum, Dublin.*

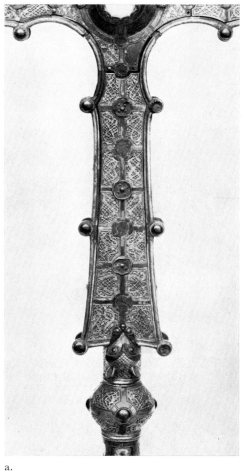

a.

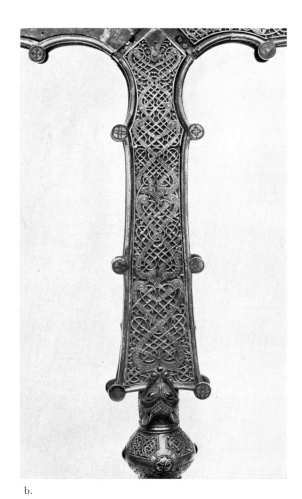

b.

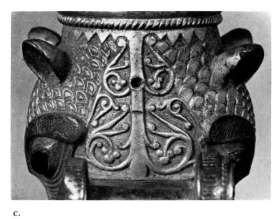

c.

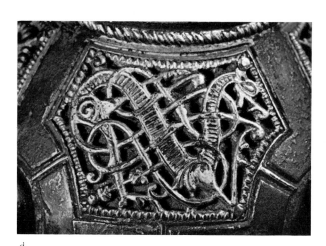

d.

Pl. LXXVI. Details of the Cross of Cong. *National Museum, Dublin.*

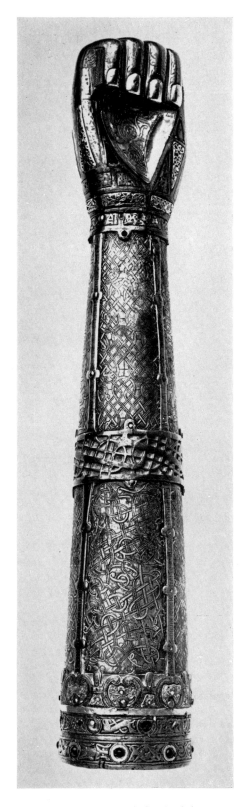

Pl. LXXVII. Shrine of the Lachtin's arm.
National Museum, Dublin.

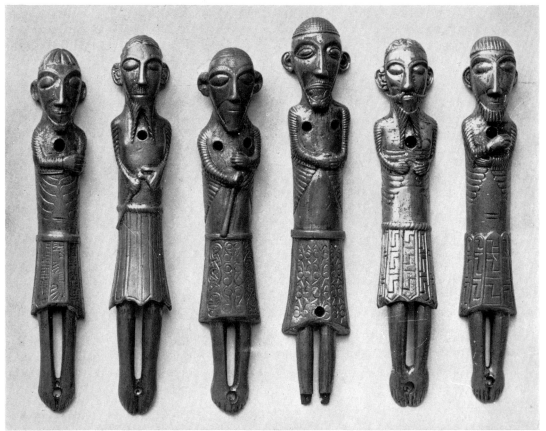

a.

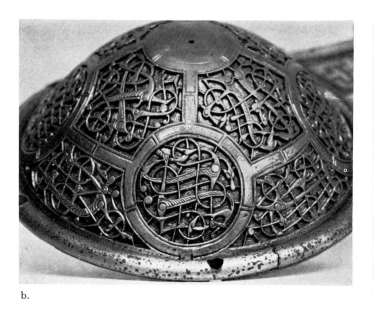

b.

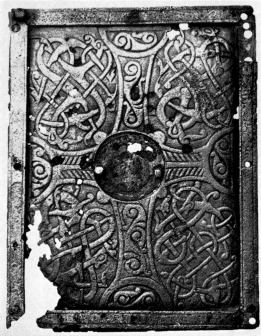

c.

Pl. LXXVIII. (*a* and *b*) Details of the St Manchan's shrine. *Private Possession.* (*c*) Plate from Holy cross. *National Museum, Dublin.*

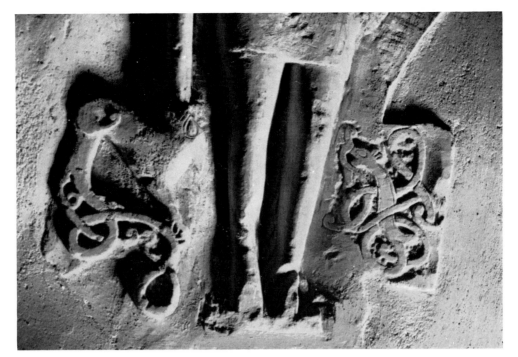

a.

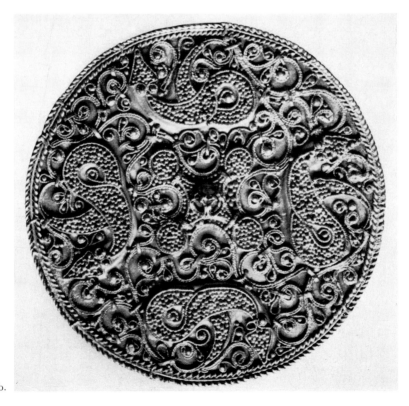

b.

Pl. LXXIX. (*a*) Sculpture from Jevington, Sussex. (*b*) Brooch from Gåtebo, Öland, Sweden (with pl. LXXIIIc). *Statens Historiska Museum, Stockholm.*

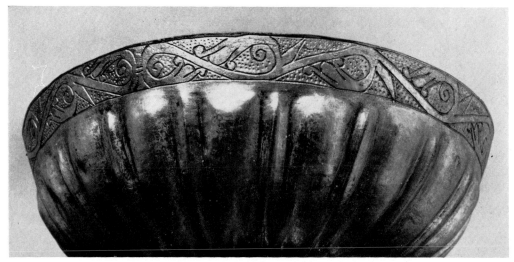

a.

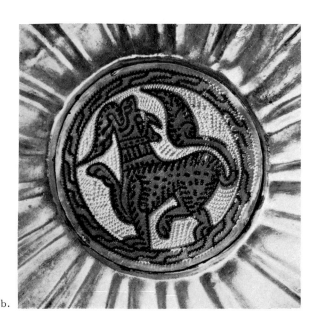

b.

Pl. LXXX. Details of silver bowl from Old Uppsala, Sweden. *Statens Historiska Museum, Stockholm.*

INDEX

INDEX

INDEX